BURKE COUNTY NORTH CAROLINA, RECORDS

1755 - 1821
(Including Wills Index 1784-1900)
Volume IV

Compiled by:
Edith Warren Huggins

Southern Historical Press, Inc.
Greenville, South Carolina

Please direct all correspondence and orders to:

www.southernhistoricalpress.com
or
SOUTHERN HISTORICAL PRESS, Inc.
PO BOX 1267
Greenville, SC   29601
southernhistoricalpress@gmail.com

ISBN #0-89308-621-5

Printed in the United States of America

ACKNOWLEDGEMENTS

To my son, Dewey W. Huggins, Jr., for typing both Volumes III and IV; purchasing a Zenith Computer capable of indexing these volumes; entering them into the computer; printing them; and spending countless hours in the endeavor, my most grateful thanks.

Also, to my grandson, Dewey Wesley Huggins, III, for his unwavering assistance in driving many countless miles from the eastern portion of North Carolina to assist in solving problems with the computerizing of these indices, I offer my thanks.

Finally, and certainly not least, to my other grandson, Lt. James (Jim) Wiley Huggins (currently stationed in Colorado Springs, Colorado) for his expertise and long distance advice to both his father and brother when computer problems arose and a need for additional advice was needed, my thanks.

Both Wesley's wife, Joanna, and Jim's wife, Susan, have been most understanding and supportive in these assistances.

DEDICATION

To my ancestors listed in this volume: William Bost, William Deal,
Michael Houck, John (Devault) Hunsucker and Susannah, Henry Pope,
John Presnell, James Presnell, George Smith and Susannah, John
Smith, John Smyre, Conrad Wagner, Robert Warren, William Warren,

and to my husband's ancestors: Bostian Cline, Simon Haas, George
Haas, Henry Propst,

and to my family, including the unlisted names of ancestors of
our deceased daughter-in-law, Kathryn (Dobbins) Huggins (May 15,
1931 - September 20, 1981).

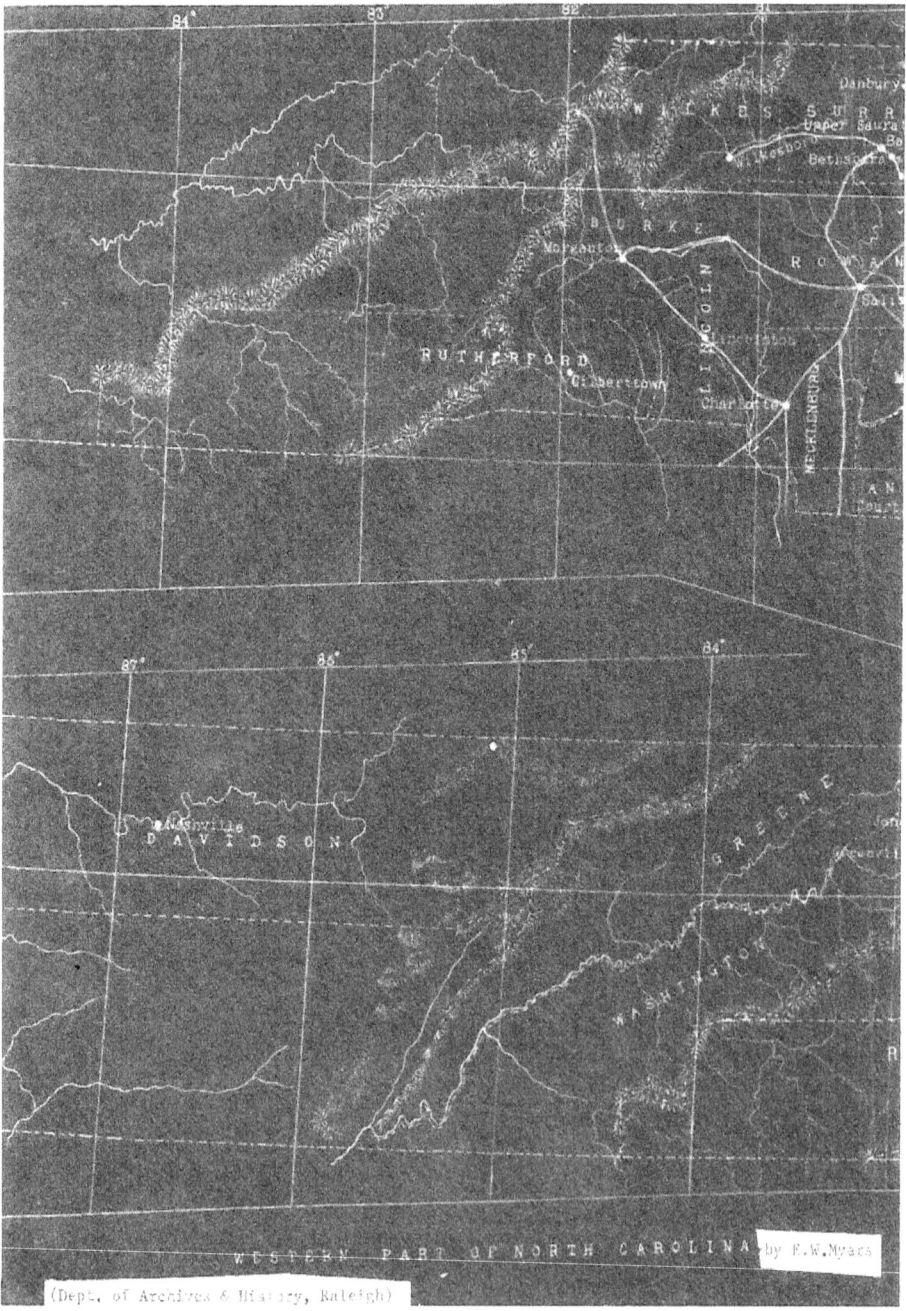

WESTERN PART OF NORTH CAROLINA by E.W.Myers

(Dept. of Archives & History, Raleigh)

TABLE OF CONTENTS

(continued next page-)

LAND ENTRIES 1790

(Unpaginated, Use Numbers)

#163, Matthew Patton, "on Swannano above Aron Patton;"
164 (again) = Aron Patton, Jr., trans, to Geo. Cunningham; 183(is next)
John Sumter, 2,000 a. for iron works; 185 (next) - John Sumter, 500 for
iron works; 185 (again) - Joshua Young, Muddy Cr. inc. Actions old place;
186 - Henry and Jacob Bolinger, Mt. Cr. of Parrots Mt. (Barretts);
removed to Little Bald Mt. Cr, judgment for above in Secretary's Office;
187 - Henry Bollinger; 188 - Mark Ammons; 189-191 - John Hinds; 192 -
Daniel Paine; 193 - Joseph Dobson and Wm. Neil, partnership; 174 -
Phillip Hoodenpyle and George Baker; 175 (again)- Churchwell Jackson;
196 - (is next) - Aron Tredaway, trans. to Bouns; 197- Robert Shearman;
198- David Byler; 199 - Samuel Stout; 200 - Joshua Young, Muddy Cr.
Inc. Henry Young's old imp; 201 - Robert Shearman; 202- William Morris,
Mountford's Cove joining tract purch. of John Grier; 203 - Joseph
Dobson, Jr.; 208 (is next) - Philip Anthony, joining lines of his father
Paul Anthony, Mill Shoal Br; 207 - Alexander Robertson, trans. to
Jospeh Dobson; 208 - John England; 209 - Field Bradshaw; 188 (again)
-John Cooper, Jr.; 211 (is next)-Thomas Smith, trans. to Joseph Dobson,
Sr.; 212 - Thomas Smith, trans. to Joseph Dobson and Gabriel Ceaths;
213 - Benjamin Austin; 214 - WilliamAustin; 215 - Joseph Dobson and Wm.
Neil, partnership; 216 - Jacob Spencer (or Speers(?)), Upper Little R;
217 - Fred. Donathan, trans, to Joseph Dobson; 218 - Abraham Hunsucker,
Middle Little R; 219 - Joseph Dobson; 220 - John Hall, Jr. 221 -
Joseph Dobson; 222 - Thetick Smith; 223 0 Joseph Dobson; 223 (again)
Joseph Dobson; 224 - Casper Weston, trans. to Jos. Dobson, Henry Worley
and Willis Wiggins; no no. 225; 226 Joseph Dobson; 227 - Joseph Dobson,
joining flower garden beginning John McDowell's; 228-Joseph Dobson,
trans, from Wm. Wofford; 229 - Jacob Suttlemire, above wagon ford which
runs through my field near John Gibbs, crossing my R, to my spring; 229 -
Joseph Dobson and James McKay; 230 - Joseph Dobson; 231Jacob Forney;
232 - Joseph Dobson;233 - John Headley; 234 - Jacob Winkler, Foxes waggon
rd; 235 - Benjamin Wallis; 236 - Mark Amons, Catawba R, inc, fishery; a
cav. ent. by Albert Corpenny; 237 - Albert Corpenny; 238 - James Craig;
239 - Isaac Ferrill and Robert Montgomery, near Wm. Moore, Hez. Hyat,
Henry Wakefield and schoolhouse; 240- ReubinEastis, inc. tract purch.
from Isaac Perkins; 241- Isaac Atwater; 242 - Jacob Suttlemire; 243 -
Francis McClure, Catawba R, where he dwells; 244 - Thomas Hemphill and
James McDowell, Moores or Jonathan Cr. of PR near Indian houses; 247(is
next)- same; 248 -Same; 249 - Augustin Gunter; 250Joseph Dobson; 245
(is next) James W. Williams, trans. to Jos. Dobson; 246 - Joseph Dobson;
254 (is next)- James Greenlee, Esq., Catawba R. near John Bowman, Chas.
McDowell and land in contest between George Killian, Thos. Black and
execrs. of John Bowman; 253 - Joseph Dobson, Jr., inc. his fishery on
Catawba R.; 254-257 - Waightstill Avery, Esq; 258 - William Baldwin,
inc. his fishery; 259 - Edward Bowman; 259 - Wm. Baldwin; 260 - Conrod
Winckler, Sen., 10 a. water in Catawba R. inc. his own fishery; 262 (is
next) - Edward Bowman; 263 - Edward Bowman; 263 (again) - James Mackey,
Catawba R., covered with water, inc. his fish basket, 10 a., and mentions
Black and Killianland dispute; 264 - Joseph Dobson, disc; 264 (again) -

1

- William Gudger; 265-267 - Waightstill Avery, Esq; 267 (again) -
Robert Sellers; 268 - Michael Hart; 230 (again) - Adam Suttlemire,
100 a. in Catawba R, covered with water...Bunts line... fishing place;
269 - (is next) Jacob Suttlemire, 20 a. in Catawba R; 270 - Jacob
Suttlemire, trans. to 269; 271 - James Ainsworth; 272 - Wm. Ryen,
E. side FB, where he dwells; 273 - Cornelius De Wee, trans. to Jno.
Lykins; 274 - Cornelius De Wee, trans. to Wm. Tradaway, Jr.; 275-276-
Joseph Dobson, the last one tran. to James Sams; 277-278- Joseph Dobson;
281 - Wm. Murphy; 282 - Thomas Smith, trans. from no. 193 D. Hinton;
283-284 - Alex. Hamilton Kelly; 285 - David Sorrell, joining his
father's old survey; 286 - Joseph Dobson, Paddies Cr, joining Green-
berry Wilsons.. 2 banks iron ore; 287-288 - Hezekiah Oneal; 289 -
George Scott; 290 - James Mackey, near James Locke; 291- Thomas
Gallien; 292 - Joshua Oaks, Second BR. above place where he now dwells,
trans. to Thomas Plemons; 293 - William Murphy; 294 - Cornelius DeWee;
295 - James Lock, two years tax pd, form. surv. by David Vance; 296 -
John Davis; 297 - Joseph Dobson; 298 - William White; 299-300 -
William White, Esq; 301-302 - Reuben White; 303 - John Wilson, W.
side of Thomas Wilson plantation on Crib Cr. inc mill, trans. to no.
262; 304 - John Wilson; 305 - Joseph Dobson; 306 - Isaac Martin;
307- Joshua Young, Muddy Cr. on N side Joshua Young's Mt; 308 - John
Armstrong, trans. to James Lee; 309 - Isaac Anglen; 310 - Henry Baker,
relinquished; 311-312- Jacob Suttlemire; 313-315- Joseph Dobson, inc.
old Indian Camp.   (1790 Ends)

NOTE: Please add to Vol II, p. 83, #35, William Brittain, 50 a, N.
      fork Reams Cr, beg, David Vance's line up both sides, entered
      10 Mar. 1789.
                      Vol II, p. 68; #22 Henry Reed, 100 a. N. fork
                      Middle Little R, beg. upper line James Barnes
                      up both sides, 6 Sept 1786, Warrant Iss'd.
(These were in my files and no further information, therefore, if
neeeded, possible to acquire from Division of Archives and History.
No further research was planned at time of abstraction - EWH.)

LAND ENTRIES AND DEEDS 1789 - 1797

1791 Entries from Entry Takers Book:
    Benjamin Austin, Jr., Jacob Speirs, A. Huntsucker; J. Greenlee,
John Mackey, Wm. Morris.

Bounty Land for Iron Works: No. 215 Clizby Cobb ent. Dec 3, 1792,
High Shoals of Muddy Cr. near Francis Worley's tub mill.   No. 224,
Clizby Cobb and Andrew Baird, 3,000a. ent. Dec. 11, 1792.   Thomas
Smith, E.T.

Warrant for survey 25a. Thomas Williams - entry of July 26, 1793.
Thomas Smith, Entry Ofc.

A small booklet of Young and Tate vs. Ainsworth.
No. 92. Thomas Young and John Tate ent. 50 a. on N. Cove of Catawba R, on
the east side, Aug. 20, 1789.   Joseph Dobson.   Attached to above;
Thomas Young vs. James Ainsworth for "tryal" Dockett April 1794.
"To add John Tate's name."   John Ainsworth, 100 a. E. side of N. Cove
Cr.   Thomas Bouchell on Jan. 18, 1796 attested above two copies were
correct, signed: Stevelie, J. P., J. Glasgow on Dec. 15, 1791, author-
ized suspension of James Ainsworth's grant upon complaint of Tate and
Young.

Bounty lands for Iron Works.   Charles Pierce ent. No 289, 500a. on
Isaac Cr. or Kellers Mill Br. to the Middle R. by Thomas Smith, E.T..,
No. 289 on Jan. 30, 1793.   He ent. No. 234, 1200 a. beg. at Jacob Perrey's,
to John Barnhart's, Alexander Carson's, Charles Pierce's, Silver Creek,
 Rocky Creek and E. side of Gunpowder Cr.   Ent Dec 21, 1792.

Henry Bollinger's entries for Iron Works, Oct. 31, 1793.
    No. 99, 1,000 a beg. John Dudley's old survey, ent Sept 1, 1789.
No. 100, 1,000 a on N. side of Little R. beg. Dudley's line, Sept. 2, 1789.
No 103, 500 a. on lower side of Upper Little R, ent Sept 3, 1789. No 101,
500 a Gunpowder Cr... .. on Spencer's line, ent. Sept 20, 1789.   Smith, E.T.

Jno. Bradburn ent. 5o a. on Barret's Mt, surveyed by Mr. Boyd, works not
returned.   E.T. ordered to grant warrant to Bradburn.   Oct. 2, 1797.
J. Hall, Chm.

CR. 14.087
1795-1830
Abstracted 1791-1797

David Dickey, yeoman, of "Buncome" vs. Philip Hoodenpyle.   William
Sharpe for pltff, J. Hughes, Sher. of Buncome Co.

Clizby Cobb grant No. 215, entered on Dec 3, 1792, by Clizby Cobb
for 3,000a. around High Shoals on Muddy Cr, N. Fork, inc. Shoal where
tub mill now stands; Jurors to view: Capt. John McDowell, Robert
Burlew, George Dodge, John Dugard, Joseph Dobson, Hezekiah Hitt,
Robert Montgomery, William Gardner, John Pague, John Tetum, Charles
Findley, Andrew Hunter, Henry Chamblis, Joseph Cowen, Andrew Woods,
Robert Patton   , Sr., James Morrison, Sr. (crossed out), William
Morrison, Sr.   Executed by J. Bell.

Clizby Cobb and Andrew Beard ent. 3,000a. in Burke on Gunpowder Cr, E.
to Jeremiah Murphy's plantation for Ironworks.   Thomas Smith, E.T.,
Sept 11, 1793.

Oct 1793 term: Jury ordered to view and condemn 3,000a. for Ironworks:
Thomas Scott, Wm. Sherrele, Jacob Winkler, John Hill, Ben Austin,
Isaac Martin, Will Pain, Robt. Pain, Jonathan Fincannon, Will Reed,
Wm. Fullerton, Henry Reed, James Reed, Abraham Hunsucker, Clisby Cobb.
J. E. Erwin, C.C.

Joseph Brown bond Sept 14, 1793 to James Neely of "Bolitote," Va.,
by John Davidson for 200 pounds, if Joseph Brown and John Davidson
make over to Daniel Monrow 100a deed inc. improvements John Adkins
lives on.   Wit: John Hawkins. (On reverse) March 28, 1795, I promise
to pay Joseph Brown 42 pounds 5 shillings.

Sub. to Abraham Erwin as wit. for John McClure vs. Wm. Porter, Sept 4,
1794.

Land grant NO. 1231 to George Sealey, Aug 22, 1795 from Richard Dobbs
Spaight, Gov. of N, C.

Jan 9, 1796: 8 double-pages to Justices of Co. Court of Wilkes. Thomas
Harris of Mecklenburg and Walter Braly of Rowan ent, caveats vs. claim
of William Lenoir, Hillair Roussau, Joseph Herndon, Richard Allen,
Charles Gordon, Jr., Benjamin Jones, George Hulme, Robert Nall, Thomas
Isbell, to 750,000 a. in Wilkes ent. on Jan 2, 1795.   Jury's verdict
favor of William Lenoir at Nov. court 1795.   Spruce Macay, Atty,
desires record certified.   Justices: William Mitchell, Nathaniel
Vannoy, Richard Gwynn, Wilkes court, Aug 3, 1795.

Plan of disputed claim of 240 a. on middle fork of Caney R. in Buncombe
Co, of David Dickey vs. Phillip Hoodenpyle.   Agreeable to order of
Superior Ct. March-August, 1795, William Sharpe, Esq., failed to appear.
Jurors of view: William Morrison, William Moore, Joseph Young, Thomas
Young, John McDowell. (Several papers.)

David Andres to "Enterataker of Burke County." A "transfair" entry
of 150 a. to Alexander West, Oct 14, 1797, wit: Abraham Hunsucker.

Francis McCorkle affidavit on April 20, 1797: On Dec 11, 1778 he ent.
several tracts, paid purchase money to Charles McDowell, E.T., and
has not obtained warrants.   Sig. of McCorkle.   He ent. 500 a on E.
side Mountain Cr. joining Joseph Crounkellon and Benjamin Pirkins on
Dec 11, 1778.   Another 500 a. ent. on same date on E. side of Catawba
R. joining William Pirkins.   Another 400 a. same date on Mountain Cr.
Another 500 a. on Mountain Cr. same date, inc. Henry William's improvements.   No. 104 John McDowell ent. for 640 a. "on South Fork of Cayney
R. where Capt. Winslow light hers camped."   John McDowell ent. 640 a.
on W. fork of Caney R. on Aug 3, 1778.   Sig. of McCorkle.

Gilbert Bowman affidavit on Apr 25, 1797, that he paid Thomas Smith,
E.T. for 200 a, No. 542 on Oct 29, 1793 and has receipt.

Thomas Smith, E.T., on Jan 25, 1797 has receipt that Henry Bullinger
ent 3,000 a. for an Iron Works, No. 3233.

James Ainsworth affidavit: April 27, 1797, he paid Thomas Smith, E.T.,
for two tracts ent. on July 21, 1791, No. 46, and No. 484 on Sept 11
and 26 of 1793 for 200 a.

Hugh Fox affidavit on Oct 25, 1797 for land warrants he ent. for 130 a.
in Charles McDowell's (E.T.) office for David Andrews, paid for it,
and land was surveyed.

Alexander Erwin, Esq., Oct, 1798, made oath he paid purchase money to
Charles McDowell, E.T., for two 600 a. tracts ent. in his office in Burke
Co, now in Buncombe. "I can have no land that the warrants lost on
both tracts..."

State vs. Edward Williams, Oct 15, 1799.

Pet. for jury of view from Richard Henley's to Reedy Br. as Muddy Cr. is
impassable: Wm. Walton, James McEntyre, J. Hall, Benjamin Burgin,
Robert Carithers, Edward Felhson, Benj. Bird, James Murphy, Dav.
Crawford.   W. Avery note of agreement if .... (torn).   No date.

William Sims deposition.   Patent to James Byers on April 13, 1771 of
300 a. near David Byers' corner, conveyed to Michal Muclewrath.

Jos. McDowell vs. John Lowrance, May 6, 1780, whose grant of 640 a. was
suspended by James Glasgow, Sec. of State.

Delaware Commonwealth of Penn.   Daniel Thompson of Chester, Scrivener,
post master, heard and saw Jacob Hinkel in May, 1775 ... given by said
Ja ... to Wm. Reese on April 13, 1795.   Chester Co. formed from Dela-

ware County. Edward Hunter, J. P., Sept. 1776, Wm. Reese of Newtown in Chester, yeoman, signed by Mary Reese. Wit: M....... (mrak) Masters. (Several papers, fragments.)

Mutual Agreement, Frb. 27, 1796: Tench Coxe of Philadelphia, Penn., and Wm. Polk of Charlotte (N.C.) re: lands in Mecklenburg County, of 17 patents, Nos. 1309-1325.

State vs. Jesse Martin, land dispute, undated.

Jno. Blanton vs. James Miller, land dispute; platt; undated.

John Perkins and Frederick Irons, land controversy; Griffith Rutherford, General, summoned. Alex. Erwin, C. C. Undated.

Survey for Benjamin Wilkinson to Elias Morgans. Undated, but John McCurry's deposition on March 3, 1797 petitioned as to a Rutherford County grant.

William Porter vs. John McClure, 18 tracts, Sept. 4, 1794; wit: Alex. Erwin.

Lincoln County Land Dispute: Jan. and Feb. 1798 order for surveys in dispute between William Beatty and Reuben Long, tenant. Signed: Wm. Scott and Lwn. (Lawson) Henderson.

ENTRY TAKERS RETURNS 1793-1799

The following is a continuation from Vol. II, p. 147:

<u>Nov 2, 1793</u>: List of names by Robert Logan, Surveyor: (gives no. of
warrant, date, acreage, quantity, water courses, on original paper,
but due to lack of space impossible to abstract.   If desired, a
Xerox copy may be obtained from the Dept. of Archives and History.)

<u>One double page</u>: (The following on first side.): Daniel Andrews,
Michael Cook, George Cook, Hugh Tate, John Noblet, John Davidson,
Andrew Woods, Benjm. Parks, Thomas Roberts, James Alexander, Robt.
Payne, Hugh Tate, James Ainsworth, Hodge Rayburne, George Damerel,
John Matlock, John Hall, James Oxford,Robt. Boyd, Sen., Jesse Stroud,
Wm. Givens, Wm. England, John Trimble, Joseph Young, Esq., Matthew
Mashburn, Isaac Alewater, John Pittillo.
                    (Second side.): Conrad Helterbrand, George Penland,
David Templeton, John Sheet(?), Joseph Noblet, George Read, Greenberry
Wilson, Willm. Austin, John Connelley, Barnet Payne, William Reed,
James Reed, Adam Fullerton, Willm. Fullerton, James Presley(Presnell),
Robt. Boyd, Sen., Phillip Austin, John Haas, Wm. Roberts, Martin Keller,
Isaac Martin, Jacob Suttlemire, Cornelius Redicks, Thomas Bailey,
Joshua Penley, John Polleet((Poteet ?), Richard Ozgatharp, Samuel
Demire, Henry Justice, John Andrews,

<u>1795, A loose sheet</u>: Adam Cook, Samuel Durmiah, Samuel Auston, Robert
Trosper, Edward Leatherwood, William Roberts, James Armstrong, Lodwick
Blankenship, Samuel Bright, Sen., William Panland, William Penland,
                                        Thomas Smith, E.T.

<u>1795 Large Booklet</u>: (Names, acres, dates for each, some with many
entries.)
"Feb 14, 1795 - Dec.last 1795:" Thomas Smith, E.T.: Samuel Tate,
Benjamin Newland, Conrad Helterbrand, Abraham Plumley, Thomas Plemons,
Pete Plemons, Joseph Berrey, Frances Patton, Joseph Berrey, John Waters,
William Cathcart, William Steedman (Many entries), -- (Each of the
following 640 a.): William Cathcart, William Steedman, William
Cochran , William Tate, Andrew Beard, David Baker, Samuel Meeker and
Alexander Cochran, John Brown, Anderson Hunt, William Tate and John
Tate, William Nail and William Alexander,William Tate and Hugh Tate,
William Tate and RobertTate,Jno. Brown, Hugh Tate and James Greenlee
and William Erwin and James Erwin - (End of 640 a each.) - Archable
Templeton, John Harden, Joseph Deprest, Jacob Beck, Abraham Smith,
Elijah Patton, William Keeton, Ambrose Carlton, John McDowell, Joseph
Nobled, Benjamin Aleson, John McGimpsey, Mark Ammons, Matthew Atkeson,
William Penland, William James, John Erwin, Phillip Antoney, John
McKinney, Charles McKinney, William Devenport, Thomas Burlson, Nathaniel
Armstrong, Richatd Medlock, Pumeter Morgan, Paul Cochran, John Murray,
William Reed, Richard Brown, Frances Asbury, Robert Trosper , Moses
Templeton,James Murphy, Joseph England, Thomas Morrison, Samuel
Hollingsworth, Richard Pruit, John Hall,John Mundgumry, Joseph Burton,

David Russ, Elijah Trosper.

1796 Booklet, torn, attached to 1795 Booklet: Thomas Smith, E.T.:
John Jones, Charles McKinney, Paul Antony, John Hughes, Benjamin Coffee,
John Clarke, William James, Abraham Wagler, Permenter Morgan, John
Spencer, John Jones, Eafrom Eaven, John Craig, J___(torn) Bellew,
Peter Mull, John McGimpsey, John McGalliart, Samuel Garish, Thomas
Gallion, William Penland, John Mullens, William Hill, Lauzrus Tilley,
Swinfield Hill, Bowas Mamin(?), Booker Mullens, Archible Cathey,
Samuel Bright, Charles Hopper, John Mullens, Able Simkens, Mathias
Hips, Benjamin Aleson,, Daniel Andrews, Matthias Winkler, Mark Ammons,
King(no given name), James Greenlee & William & James Erwin, John
Dellinger, Andrew Beard,Henry Wood, John Bradburn, Stephen Ballew,
John Harden, Samuel Wilson, William Walton, Nancy Erwin, Thomas Largent,
Thomas White, William Tate, William Tate & Hugh Tate, John Brown, John
McDowell, Joseph McDowell, James Mashburn, William James, Robert
Coruthers, Edward Teague, Thomas Fullerton, Waightstill Avery, George
Hartley, David Baker, Reuben White, Elizabeth Burchfield, Joseph Dobson,
Lazarus Phillips, Peter Angle, Hugh Tate.
Thomas Smith, E.T.

1797 Double Page, by Thomas Smith, E.T.
George Sealey, Joseph Scoles, William McKinney, Daniel Toge(?), James
Buchan, John Green, Joseph Buchanan, Richard Fortain, John Deal, William
Porter, Richard Jacks, Henry Bullenger, Jonathan Fairs, John Smith,
William Jones, Thomas Moody, Asay Ogylbee, David Baker, Benjamin Burgain,
John Rutherford, William Davis, Andrew Hunter, Joseph Dobson & Lewis
Beard, Calep Barr, Sherwood Bowman, David Mashburn, John Aldredge, James
Hemphill, John Clarke, Mary Adams, Thomas McClarken, Patrick Onail,
William Conley, John Jones, Andrew Polsor, Adam Fullerton, George Tomson,
Elizabeth Burchfield, John Berrey, John McGimpsey, David Spradling,
Thomas Curtes, Samuel Wilson, Peter Rust, Abraham Husher, John Hall,
Waightstill Avery , Walles Alexander, Blaker Siles, George Brooks,
Mereman Megee, Simon S. Huff, Jacob Winkler, Lot Berrey, Richard Gibbs,
William McKinney, Joseph Dobson, Charles McKinney, Robert Belew,
Charles Baker, Jessey More, Phillip Martain, Abraham Wagler , Joseph
Berrey, Micaigah Allen, Thomas Bird, Hugh Fox,Henry Baker, William
Rippetoe,Nicholus Jones, Conrad Winkler, Sen., Luke White, Nathan Delton,
John Hood, Waightstill · Avery,Alexander Glass, John Younge, James
Edmiston, Benjamin White, Thomas Parkes, Waightstill Avery, James
Edmiston, John McGimpsey, Nicholas Keller, James Fox, Alan Fox, Titus
Fox, John Fox.
Thomas Smith, E.T.

1798 Double Page, Thomas Smith, E.T.
William Murphy, James Lock, John McGimpsey, Samuel Pruit, William Moor,
Andrew Smalley, William Reed, Nathaniel Armstrong, William Reay, Henry
Inmand, John Weakfield, Charles Weakfield, Benjamin Moor, Thomas Weakfield,
Nathan Smith, Harmon Cox, Thomas Highdon, Richard Roads, William White,
Jules Nukem, Joseph Alexander, Henry Justes, Jacob Winkler, Jessy Moor,

Jessey Burkins, Thomas Macky, John Brown, Archable Carmon, John Walton,
William Scott,Richard Green, William Perriman, Thomas James, James
Collear, Lewis Coffee, Andrew Gwin, Benjamin Austen, Jesse Spradling,
Jacob Yount, James Moor, William Bradshaw, Zachariah Enness, William
Bradshaw, Sen., Joseph Winkler, Charles Finly, Thomas King, Peter Mull,
James Alexander, Charles McKinney, Waightstile Avery, Bernard Baker,
Thomas McGimpsey, Lewis Powell, Benjamin White, John Stepp, Eli Littlejohn
William Ray, Rice Mederis, Reuben Fletcher, John Murray, John Fincannon,
John Haus, David Sprodling, Corban Tompson, Samuel Clark, John
McGimpsey, Mager Gipson, John Reed, Thomas & Abner Pain, John Hughs,
John Wilbrooke, William Wiseman, William Reed, James Steele, James
Medley, John Loven, John Green, John Harper, William Husbands,
Richard Emmet, James Moody, John Bradford, Joseph Green, William Roberts,
Thomas Green, Daniel Farmer, James Oxford, Jessey Briner, Thomas Walkens,
Reuben White, John Perkens, Jacob Miles, Anguish Camble, Christyan &
Daniel Renhart, Gray Buth, John Miller, Nichlas Day, John Blair, James
Day, Solomon Smith, Peter Holt, Thomas Wiseman, Elias Powell, Reuben
Coffey, Jun., Jeremiah Green, Archable Tempelton, Joseph McClure, ·
Phillip Gier, William Steevens, Posey Allison, Arthur Buchannon, Aron
Burleson, James Buchhannon, John McGimpsey, Samuel Steel, Hezekiah
Innman, William Tate, Robert Mungumrey, John Martain, Solomon Stansberrey,
& Abraham Plumly, John Browning, Jr., John Browning, Sr., Christian
Rinehart, Jr., John Armstrong, James Greenbe, George Parkes, David Lyn,
David Crafford, John Groves,Reuben Odle, Thomas McClurken, William
Culthbaertsyon (Cuthbertson ?)

Thomas Smith, E.T.

1799 Large Booklet:
P.1: John Erwin, Jr, Charles McDowell, Lewis Beard, Abner Henly, John
Trammel & William Alexander,Archable Cathey, Thomas Moody, Jr., Jacob
Beck, Daniel Beck, David Tate, John Carson, Jonston King.
P.2: Henry Stoner(?), Jessey Pool, Thomas McEntire, Sr. & William
Walton, Jun. & Brice Collens, Thomas McEntire, Sen,(many), James Smith,
Eaphrom Jones.
P.3: Thomas Watkins, Thomas McGimpsey, John Young, James Alexander,
Reuben White, George Reed, Jacob Beck, David Baker, Thomas McKinney &
John Green, David Baker, Alexander Erwin, William McDowell, William
Gragg, James Blair, Reed Hight, Jessey Moore,Jun., Reuben Stallings,
Jacob Antoney, John Hughs, Joseph Gelbert.
P.4: Allen Fox, William Moor, James Panland, William Panland, Patrick
Florerady, William Allison, Drury Mashburn, David Lin, Thomas Curtes,
Charles Wakefield, Jun., William Moffett, John Maloney, John Fox, John
Moor, Josheway Curtis, Joseph Young,Abner Chaffin, Bartlet Henson,
David Tate, Aron Britten, Hugh Tate, James Tomson, Peter West, Samuel
Barr, John McGimpsey, John Mull.
P.5: John McGimpsey, John Hall, William Penland, Daniel Poge(?), John
Goage, Josyh Dobson, Jacob Bowman, David Bowman, Joseph Dobson, Noble
Alexander, John Perkens, Jun., John McGimpsey, John Groves, David Tate,
Peter Holt, Jun., John McGimpsey, Blake Percy, John Allon, John Dowell,
Henry Barlow Baker, Jacob Rose, EdmonMorres, James Sellers, Jun.,

John Clark,John Forsyth, William Sherrell, William Tate, John McGimpsey,
John Burchfield, Hugh Tate.

P.6: Nicolus Day, Arter Erwin, William Adams, John Browning, Sen., Field
Bratcher, John Burgan, Charles McDowell, Edward Jackson, Tobias
Peterson, Frances McClure, Benjamin Nulan, John Boyd, Daniel Sullivant,
FerdenandFlechman, William Tucker, William Colverd, Waightstile Avery,
Alexander Long, W.A., William McDowell, Alexander Andrews, Perminter
Morgan, William Dyson, Eaphrom Greay, William Lee, Tillman Walton,
Tillman Walton, Charles McDowell, Thomas Brevard, Tobias Peterson,
Michal Peterson, Michal Pinkly, Joseph Justes, Sen., Patrick Fluraday,
John McGimpsey, James Edmonson, David Beadle, James Oxford, James
Critchlow, William Rey, Thomas White, Benjamin Nullan, James Mashburn,
Sen., William Deupese , Christian Shiffler, Christian Rinehart, James
Tomson, John Sellers, William Adams, Conrad Helterbrand, Robert Hodge,
James Ainsworth, Gilbert Bowman, James Maloney, Lanard Highdon,
Alexander Glass, Simeon Perkins, James Hogan.

S.S. 553, Entry Takers Returns
1778-1799, 1778-1905
Loose Papers, Boxed.

DEES RECORDED IN COURT MINUTES
1791 - 1796

Due to the destruction of Burke County Deeds by Union soldiers in
1865, the following may prove of interest and some value, although
deeds in court minutes rarely mention a residence prior to Burke.

Oct., 1791: p. 10, Commsrs. of Town of Morganton to James McEntire
for part of lot inc. the late temporary Court House, July 20, 1791.
No. 11, 12 poles square.
                    ½ lot, 6p.x12, No. 12, Oct 20, 1791 from John
Hughes to James McEntire, pr: Alex Erwin.

Jan. 1792: p. 14, Lot #2 from Commsrs. to Wm. Erwin, ¼ full lot,
April 9, 1791, pr: Jno. Sellars.
                    Abr. Fleming to Fredk. Beall, a Negro girl,
Liza, July 1, 1791, pr: Reuben Estes.
                    Also assignment on sd. B. S. from Fredk. Beall
to Wm. Erwin, Dec. 10, 1791, pr: James Erwin.
                    Peter Moll, H. Sher., to Wm. Erwin, lot #3,
form. prop. of George Wolpe(?), June 2, 1791, pr: Thos. McCantire.
                    Daniel Beale for 2 bay horses, Sept. 1, 1791,
pr: James Erwin, Jr.

April, 1792: p. 22, James Stringfield to John Henry Stevelie, 560
(or 568 ?) a. on Mill Fork of Hunting Cr. & Catawba R., pr: Wm. Erwin,
Mar. 4, 1792.
                    D.G.: John Pattolo to John Pittello, Jr., Negro
boy Adam, also 100 a on Crooked Cr., pr. by Sam'l. Adkins. Feb 18,1792.
          p. 25, Wm. Sharpe, Esq. to Wm. Erwin for 873 a.Cany R.,
Feb. 3, 1792, pr: by Thos. Sharpe.
                    Jacob Killen (Killian) to Robert Wier, 182 a. on
S. fork Muddy Cr, April 20, 1792, pr: Thos. McIntire.
          p. 26, Jacob Settlemire to Wm. James 150 a., Catawba R.,
Oct. 28,1782, pr: Jno. Connolly, Esq.
          p. 28, Bill of Sale, Thos. Bell, Const. to Wm. Erwin, Negro
wench, March 24, 1792, pr: Robt. Montgomery.
          p. 29, House on lot #11 in Morganton from Sher. to Wm.
Lewis, Apr. 21, 1799, pr: Alex. Erwin.

July, 1792, p. 38, Wm. Brandon to Wm. Thomson 640 a. ack.
                    Thos. Patton to John McGahey 100 a., pr: Joseph
McDowell.
          p. 39, Thos. Patton to John McGahey 100 a, pr: Jos. McDowell.
          p. 41, James McDowell to Jno. Carzon, 87 a., ack.
          p. 42, Robert Weer to Thomas McIntire 25 a., July 2, 1792,
pr: Wm. N. Foster.
          P. 46, Jacob Gyer to Charles Wakefield, 50 a., Nov. 16, 1791,
pr: William White.
                    Jacob Gyer to Charles Wakefield 300 a., Nov. 16,
1791, pr: William White.
                    Same as above, 100 a.

11

Oct. 1792, p. 47, Joseph Wolford (Wofford ?) to John Rutherford, Negro wench, Nance, also child, Bets, Undated, pr: (X leg.)

    p. 48, William Hamilton to James Hughey, various articles, pr: Wm. Welsh.

    p. 56, Joseph Prewit to Waighstill Avery, Negro slave child, Jack, "or sometimes Jonathan," pr: Joseph Prewet.

January 1793, p. 62, James Miller to Waightstill Avery, Esq., 348 a, pr: William Erwin.

    James Miller to Waightstill Avery, Esq., 320 a, pr: William Erwin.

    Robert Hodge to Robert Billew, 200 a, ack.

    Jno. Davidson to Zebulon Brevard 118 a, S. Catawba R., pr: Jos. McDowell.

    Joseph Dobson to Ambros Carlton 100 a, pr: Thomas Bell.

    John H. Steveley to Jacob Wiles (?), 200 a, pr: Thos. Walker.

    John Springfield to Wm. West, 100 a, ack.

    p. 63, William Brandon to William Thomas 64 a, ack.

    p. 71, John Jones to Thomas Welch 100 a, dated Sept. 14, 1791, pr: Col. Jos, (McDowell)

    Matthew Sharpe to Isaac Maxwell 103 a, July 14, 1789, pr: Conrad Winkler.

    Joseph White to John Hall, 200 a, Aug, 25, 1793, pr: Moses Wilkinson.

    Bryon O. Connelly to Hugh F. Connelly, 100 a, July 2, 1788, pr: Jean Connelly.

    Hugh Connelly to John Connely, 100 a , Jan, 6, 1793, ack.

    Jonathan McPeters to William Dever, 200 a, Feb, 26, 1788, pr: Andrew McClewer.

    p.72, William Rutherford to James Rutherford, a Negro girl, Lusa, no date, pr: Robert Montgomery.

    Richard Morrow to William Wofford, 160 a, Apr. 5, 1787: ack.

    John Walker to William Probet, 150 a, pr: Mumford Wilson.

    D.G.: William Rutherford to David Rutherford, Negro man, Jim, pr: Robert Montgomery.

    Jesse Coffee to Alan McKinsey, 146 a, Jacobs Fork, Town Cr, Oct. 22, 1790, pr: Joel Coffee.

    John Brown and David Nesbit, Exrs. of Hugh Montgomery est, 640 a, to David Bullinger on White's Mill Cr., ack.

    Samuel Snody to Samuel Alexander, 350 a Sept. 16, 1792, pr: Isaac Martin.

    William Wofford to Wm. Cathey, 240 a. July 5, 1788, pr: James Dever.

    p. 73, Alexander McKenzie to Keneth McKenzie, 46 a, Jan, 29, 1793, pr: Joel Coffey.

Aaron Freeman to Thomas Bradburn, 50 a , Aug.
10, 1789, pr: John Bradburn.

John Bunt to Isaac Martin, 250 a, pr.: John
Shell.

Charles McDaniel to Robert Montgomery, 150 a,
Catawba R., Jan. 5, 1793, pr: William Fauster.

Peter Mull, Esq. to Thomas McEntire, 150 a,
Gunpowder Cr., Feb. 1, 1793, ack.

Joseph Dobson to James Murphy, Esq., 200 a, Feb.
1, 1793, ack.

Peter Mull to William Lewis, house in Morgan(ton)
formerly prop. of Alex. Cummens, Apr. 2, 1792, pr: Alexander Erwin.

James Montgomery to Robert McGomery, for Negro
man "York," Negro boy, Ben, 15, Jack, 13, Feb. 28, 1793, pr: Ambrose Carlton.

P. 74, Erasmus Mays to William Hawkins, 100½ a , Mar. 20,
1789, pr: Augustin Hawkins.

John Nesbit to Solomon Smith, 220 a, May 24,
1792, pr: George Seman(?)

George Davidson to Benjamin Bergin, 6 1/4 a,
Sept. 4, 1792, pr: Samuel Hollinsworth.

William Hawkins to Joseph Hawkins, 140 a, June
20, 1790, ack.

Daniel Workman to Christopher Seeman, 100 a,
Oct. 5, 1791, pr: Samuel Brown.

William Brandon to William Thompson, 640 a,
undated, ack.

P. 75: James Stringfield to John H. Stevilie, 568 a, S.
Catawba R, Mar. 14, 1792, pr: Wm. Erwin.

Thomas Wilson to Barret(Barnet) Pain, 100 a,
S. fork Little R, Nov. 3, 1789, Pr: John Bradburn.

Samuel Swaringan to Rich'd. Cheek Swarengan,100 a.
Zack's fork, Feb. 1, 1791, pr: Jno. Bailey.

Nicholas Day to John Blair, 112 a , Town Cr.,
Apr. 20, 1790, pr: Wm. White.

John Blanton to Ab. Fleming in 1 part 300 a. &
ref. 2 other tracts in orig. deed, pr: Alex. Erwin.

Abraham Fleming to John Fleming, 300 a. Catawba
R., also refer. to orig. deed for 2 other tracts., April 10, 1792, pr:
Alex. Erwin.

William McDowell to Isom Shook, 333 a, Silver
Cr., Nov. 12, 1791, pr: Wm. Probet.

P. 76, Wm. Probet to Wm. McDowell, 347 a, E. of Muddy Cr,
1790, pr: James Dysard.

Thomas Rayburn to Hodge Rayburn, 300 a, Humphries
Cr., Oct. 20, 1785, pr: Ben Adams.

Abraham Fleming to John Fleming, 125 a, April
10, 1792, Alex. Erwin.

Jacob Suttlemire to Wm. James, 150 a, 1790, pr:
Jno. Connelly.

Thomas Bell to Wm. Erwin, Negro girl Jude, dated
Mar. 24, 1792, pr: Robt. McGomery.

Jacob Keller To Robert Wer(?), 182 a, Muddy Cr., Apr. 20, 1792, pr: Thomas McEntire.

Ben Wallace to Joseph Scales (Scaler ?), 100 a. Humphries Cr., Sept. 13, 1791, ack.

P. 77, James Naile to John Townson, 250 a , 1791, pr: Abraham Sudderth.

John Wilson to Isaac Cox, 250 a, North Cove, Oct.17, 1791, pr: Thomas McKinsey.

Joseph White to John Hall (or Hale ?), 640 a. Mar. 10, 1791, pr: John Hall (or Hale ?), Jr.

Samuel Woods to Andrew Elder, 74 a, Muddy Cr, Feb. 19, 1791, pr: James Dysard.

John Barber to Wm. Gardner, 280 a, Muddy Cr., July 13, 1790, pr: T. Norrison.

D.G., Thomas Rayburn to Sarah, a Negro boy, Sawney, July 8, 1788, pr: Hodge Rayburn.

James McGomery to Solomon Good, 122 a , Hunting Cr., Oct. 11, 1783, pr: Robt. McGomery.

Daniel Morrow to George Sealey, 100 a, Whitener Cr., July 16, 1791, pr: Jno. Orr (?).

P. 78: Wendell Wyant to Andrew Holshouser, 320 a.or ½ survey granted Conrad Mull by deed from Earl Granville Nov. 3, 1753, N. Catawba and Upper Cr. "Proved."

Commsrs. of Morganton to Jno. Spears, house and lott, July 22, 1791, pr: James Greenlee, Esq.

Joseph Morgan to John Dellinger, 100 a, Hunting Cr., Nov. 23, 1789. Ack.

Joseph Harth to Abraham Pinington, 100 a, N. Catawba R., Aug.17, 1789 pr: John Perkins.

James Patterson to John Barber, 280 a, Muddy Cr., Nov. 1, 1788, pr: William Gardner.

Richard Simmcons (Simpson ?) to Daniel Sullivan 580 a.Catawba R, March 18 1791, pr: Joseph Dobson.

Daniel Beale to Reuben Estes for various particulars, Feb.21, 1791, pr: Len Estes.

P. 79: Samuel Bright to John Browning(?), 200 a, Oct. 1, 1791, pr: Wm. Wiseman.

John McDowell, Sen. to William Whitson, land on Swannanoa, Jan. 24, 1791., Ack.

Charles McDowell to John Stillwell, 140 a, S. Fork Catawba R, Oct. 18, 1791, ack.

John Stillwell to Henry Miller, 140 a.No fork Catawba R., Oct. 21, 1791, Ack.

Arthur Erwin to John Patton, 200 a, Swannanoa,Ack.

Phillip Stephens to Jery Thomson for a horse, Sept. 2, 1791, pr: Henry McKinney.

Ambrose Coffey to Daniel Moore, 100 a , Oct. 11, 1791, pr: Jesse Moore.

David Witherspoon to Albert Colpinney for Negro girl, Hannah, Feb. 21, 1791, pr: Alex. Erwin.

John Patton to Arthur Erwin, 300 a, Muddy Cr., Oct, 20, 1791, ack.

P. 80: William James to Mason French, 360 a, May 23, 1791, pr: William Crye.

William Sumpter to William Sumpter. Jr., 400 a, Oct· 23, 1790, ack.

Richard Gibbs and Wife to George Sealey, 100 a, Jacobs R., Oct· 15, 1791, pr: John Gibbs.

Thomas Polk to John Martin, 300 a. Apr. 5, 179X, pr: John Wilson.

Daniel Beal to James Murphy, Negro boy, Antony, Mar. 13, 1790, pr: Wm. Erwin.

James Verrell to Daniel Beal , Negro boy, Antony, Feb. 15, 1790, ack.

William McCormack Sparks to James McEntire for Negro Cuffy, alias Quash, June 14, 1790, pr: Joseph McDowell.

Jesse Walker to Phillip Brittan, 273 a, Jan; 14, 1792, pr: John Walker.

James Jernison to Joseph McKinsey, 200 a, Canoe Cr., Nov, 7, 1791, pr: James Penland.

Samuel Woods to Andrew Elder, 100 a. Muddy Cr., Feb. 19, 1791, pr: James Dysard.

P. 81: John Hughes to John Spears, house and lot in Morganton, 1791.

John Hodge to Christo. Nations, 100 a., Crooked Cr., Apr, 10, 1792, pr: Alex. Hodge.

Allen Alexander to William Alexander, 250 a, Little R., May 7, 1791, pr: James Alexander.

Moses Wilkeson & John Hall to John Macky, 4 Negro women (names illegible), Sept. 8, 1790, ack.

Joseph Dobson to Henry Props (Propst ?), 220 a Nov. 14, 1791, ack.

David Beek to Jacob Beek for love, 275 a, on Upper Cr., Nov· 26, 1791, pr: Reuben White.

Jno. McGomery to James Murphy, Negro, Jean, Oct· 25, 1787, pr: Ham. McGomery.

Thomas Woodliff to James Murphy, Negro, Charles, Mar. 16, 1791, pr: Henry McKiney.

P.82: Alexander McGinty and Hannah (?) his wife to James Murphy, 551 a, Canoe Cr., Oct· 20, 1791, ack.

Hezekiah Hoyett to James McGomery, 100 a., Shadraks, Jan. 17, 1792, pr: Robt. McGomery.

Richard Ozgatharp to Erasmus Mays, 300 a. Hunting Cr. Apr. 10, 1790, ack.

John Greer to William Morris, 75 a., Mar, 27, 1789, pr: Benja. Davis.

Thomas Raburn to John Greer, 75 a., Oct· 8, 1788, pr: Mark Hailey.

April, 1793, p. 98: Robet Wear to Thomas McEntire, 250 a., pr: William Foster.

      Thomas Patton to John McGahey, 100 a., July 17, 1791, pr: John McDowell.

      Charles Baker, John & James & David to Phillip Giger (?), 140 a., Sept. 23, 1791, pr: William White.

      David Baker to Joseph Pruet, 150 a., Sept. 5, 1792, pr: James Erwin.

      Roland Alexander to Luke White, 325 a., Aug. 17, 1789, pr: Joseph Mahaffey.

      Alexander McGinty to William Murphy for sorrel horse & saddle, Feb. 17, 1792, pr: John Tipton.

      P. 99: William Lewis to James McEntire, house in Morganton, July 26, 1790, pr: William Foster.

      James Forgay to William England, 150 a., Feb. 9, 1786, pr: Thomas Day.

      Edward Wilson to George Hartley, 190 a., July 20, 1792, pr: William White.

      John Davidson to Thomas Davis, 100 a., Apr. 15, 1792, pr: William England.

      Peter Moll to John Hinds, 100 a., July 27, 1792, pr: William Sumpter.

      Joseph Prewit to William Sherrill, 150 a., Oct. 22, 1792, pr: William White.

      Will Moore to William Davidson, 100 a., Oct 21 1786, ack.

      P. 100: William Roberts to Matthew Cocks, 300 a., Aug. 3, 1792, ack.

      Thomas Devinport to William Sherrell, 100 a., Oct. 15, 1792, pr: William White.

      Peter Moll, H. Sher., to Robert Wier, 250 a., July 27, 1792, pr: William Foster.

      John Stillwell to Shedrich Stillwell, 100 a., July 16, 1792, pr: Alexander Erwin.

      James Sherrill to Joseph Prewit for Negro boy, Jonathan, Negro Woman (Name illegible), Mar. 14, 1793, pr: William White.

      P. 101: John Dysard to Thomas Roberts, 365 a., Mar. 16, 1793, pr: Robt. Craig.

      Peter Mull to Michael Caller, 346 a., May 31, 1793, pr: Jno. Dellinger.

      John Hunsucker and wife Susannah to Jacob Winkler, 200 a., Feb. 19, 1793, pr. John Hedlee.

      Wm. Avery to Wm. McKiney, 100 a., July 24, 1793, ack.

      John Eger to John Gibson, 40 a., Sept. 15, 1788, pr: Stephen Gibson.

      P. 102: Benjamin Davidson to Thomas McEntire, 200 a., July 23, 1793, pr: William Erwin.

      John White to Elisha Hedlen, 100 a., July 24, 1792, pr: Joshua Hedlen.

James Davidsonto John Carson, 153 a., July 23, 1793, pr: Reuben Wood.

John Edger to Stephen Gibson, 200 a., Aug. 26, 1788, pr: Major Gibson.

Jonathan Allen to Geo. Dowell, 200 a., Feb. 8, 1793, pr: Simon Ramsey.

Ann Dobson Exrs. to William Tate, 200 a., July 25, 1793, ack.

Thomas Smith to William Tate, 200 a., July 25, 1793, ack.

Charles McDowell, John Blanton, Alex. Erwin, Commsrs. to Arthur Graham, a lot, July 24, 1793, pr: William Foster.

P. 103: Jeremiah Murry to William Tucker, 164 a., Gun-powder Cr., Apr. 20, 1793, pr: Frederick Grider.

John S(mith)to William Gibson, 40 a., pr: William Smith.

Reuben White to Bartlett Henson, 310 a., ack.

William James to Abraham Fleming, 70 a., pr: Jesse Moore.

Martha Morgan to William Scott, 75 a., pr: Reuben Coffey, Sr.

William Brittain to Thomas Kell, 200 a., pr: Robert Penland.

John Bradburn to Edward Barnes, 250 a., pr: Thomas Bradburn.

Thomas Worley to Jo. Dobson for Articles 1793, ack.

Christian Isom to Joseph McDowell, 150 a., Apr. 24, 1793, ack.

John McDowell & Joseph, Exrs. to Jonathan Fear, 200 a., Apr. 25, 1793, Ack.

Thomas McEntire, H. Sher., to Jesse Moore, 300 a., on Globe, Apr. 25, 1793, ack.

P. 105: Samuel Lusk to Henry McKinney for bay horse, Mar. 28, 1793, pr: John Spears.

Waightstill Avery to Elias Ledford, 100 a., Apr. 25, 1793, pr: John Hardin.

Jacob Tennison to Christian Isom, Articles, Apr. 8, 1793, pr: John Page.

July, 1793: No deeds recorded.

October, 1793, p 133: Thomas Patton to William Robertson, 130 a., ack.

William Sherrill to Philip Solomon, 250 a., Clarks R., pr: Jacob Winkler.

Henry Reed to Elisha Austin, 150 a., pr: Benj.Austin.

Aaron French to William Fowler , 100 a., June 20, 1793, pr: William Cry.

James Duglen to William Austin, 200 a., Nov. 8, 1792, pr: Phillip Austin.

P. 134: John Speer to Peter Mull, 376 a., June 21, 1793,ack.
Charles Dement to Richard Brown, 123 a., Oct.
22,1793, pr: Robert Hodge.
Thomas Brown to Richard Brown, Articles,pr:
Jospeh Spencer.
John Allen to Frederick Shull, 250 a., Octo.
31, 1793, pr: Joseph Spencer.
John Allen to Frederick Shull, 250 a., Octo.
31, 1793, also, 150 a., ack.
Henry Reed to John Jehu Barns, 150 a., Octe.
29, 1793, pr: Will Reed.
Robert Kirkpatrick, P.A., to William White, Debt
Collection, Sept 27, 1793, pr: Waightstill Avery.

January, 1794, P. 155, Joseph Dobson to James Greenlee for land, Jan.
30, 1794, ack.
James McGomery to Robert, 100 a., Jan 1, 1793,
pr: William Fauster.
Thomas Young to Robert McGomery, 100 a., Jan.
30, 1793, pr: William Foster.
Mortgage from John Hughes to Joseph Spencer,
630 a. and mills, Dec,13, 1793, pr: John H. Stevelie.
Covenant of Warranty, Hance Hamilton, Robert
Hannah & Daniel Gill as pay to Waightstill Avery, Negro slaves, Dec.
26, 1793, pr: Alexander Erwin.
P. 156: Joseph Brown and Thomas to James Neely, 231 a.,
Sept. 14, 1793, pr: John Davidson.
Thomas Young to John Duncan, 150 a.,Jan.7,
1793, pr: John Penland.
Thomas Young to Joseph Payatte(?), 100 a., pr:
John Penland.
P.A.: Ann Dobson to Joseph, Dec. 29, 1793, pr:
Abraham Plumly.
Receipt from Joseph McDowell of Ann Dobson by
Thomas Smith, 723 lb.15 sh.
James McDowell to John Carson, Negro woman, Sall,
and child, Rose, Apr. 9, 1793, ack.
P. 157: Jacob Anthony to Paul, 200 a., Jan.6, 1794, pr:
Felix Wiles.
John Taber to John Clark, 200 a., Nov. 8, 1793,
pr: William James.
Alexander Harbeson to Joseph Scott, 640 a., Dec.
27, 1793, ack.
David Barnett to Reuben Coffee, 75 a., Sept. 10,
1793, pr: Felix Walker.
Jacob Anthony to Felix Wilds, 100 a., Jan, 1794,
pr: Paul Anthony.
D. G.: Nicholas Trosper to Elijah , Mar.10, 1793,
pr: Geo. Culberson.

P.A.:Robert Donaldson & A. Ferguson to William Erwin, Jr., Jan.11,1794,, pr: Waightstill Avery.

P. 158: Armon Gibson to Richard Davis, 100 a., Aug. 6, 1791, pr: Thomas White.

George Walker to Conrad Heltebrand, 29 a., Jan. 23, 1794, pr: Geo,Walker.

Daniel McConnel to Andrew Given, 257 a., Sept. 4, 1793, pr: John Spea.

Jo McCrary to Pete Thompson, horses, May 13, 1790, pr: Geo. Simral. Bond: Michael Grindstaff to Joshua Perkins for title, land on Catawba R., Jan 14, 1785, pr: Henry Holman.

P. 159: Hance Hamilton of Guilford to Waightstill Avery, (many slaves), Dec. 26, 1793,Wit: Ad. Osborn, J. McDowell, Alex. Erwin.

January, 1794, P. 159: Hance Hamilton, Robert Hannah & Daniel Gillaspie of Guilford Co., bound to Waightstill Avery of Burke, (slaves).

P. 165: Michael Grindstaff of Burke bound to Joshua Perkins of Lincoln, Jan. 14, 1785, Wit: Nathan Armitage, Henry Holman (mark of :M".)

April, 1794, p. 188: Alexander Erwin, Esq. & Brig. Gen. McDowell to Joseph Hughes, lot on E. Green St., May 2, 1794, pr: John Tate.

William Grayson from John Bailey, 100 a., May 1, 1794, ack. by John Bailey.

Boling Branttell to Joseph White for 7 years servitude, Mar. 10, 1794, pr: Wm. White.

Mason French to James Connelly, 260 a., Mar. 10, 1794, pr: Hugh Connely,

William Moore to William Davidson, 90 a., Oct. 10, 1785, pr: John Davidson.

William Morrison to John McDowell, 96 a., Apr. 29, ____(no Date), ack.

Lazarous Phillips to James Barns, 150 a., Feb. 15, 1794, pr: John Penland.

P. 189: Thomas White, Sen. to Reuben, 520 a., May 7, 1793, pr: William White.

Mary Wagner from John Shell, 50 a., Mar. 19, 1794, ack.

Veze Husbandto Thomas Crawford, 114 a., July 15, 1793, pr: William White.

John Blanton to Abr, Fleming, 200 a, Apr. 30, 1794, pr: Alex. Erwin.

John Bradburn to John Shell, 150 a., Jan. 29, 1794, pr: Isaac Martin.

Nicholas Trosper to John Carson, 100 a., Apr. 4, 1793,

P. 190: Thomas Brandon to Nicholas Trosper, 100 a.,, July 21, 1792, pr: Joseph McDowell.

William Hamilton and Elizabeth to Joseph Hughey for love, May 1, 1794; pr: William Panland.

Daniel Bullinger to William Pain, 100 a., May 1, 1794, ack.

Thomas McEntire to Daniel Bullinger, 300 a., May 1, 1794, ack.

James McDowell to Thos. McEntire, Mar.17, 1794, for "un", half of 600 a., Buncombe Co., ack.

Edward Willson to John McGimpsey, 250 a., Apr. 22, 1794, pr: William White.

Reuben Estes to Laben, 140 a., Feb 18, 1787, pr: William White.

P. 191: Andrew Wood to Richard Price, 150 a., Feb.5, 1794, pr: Andrew Wood.

Thomas Bradburn to Joseph Jones, 50 a., Dec. 25, 1793, ack.

Ann Dobson to Joseph, 400 a., Dec.10, 1791, pr: Thomas Smith.

James Davidson to Joseph McDowell, "28th 1794", 66 a., pr: John Davidson, Sr.

Eli Littlejohn to Thomas Moody, 200 a., N.O., ack.

Charles Dement to David, 120 a., June 18, 1793, pr: Robt. Logan.

Andrew Miller to Paul Anthony, a lot, Apr.23, 1794, pr: Geo. Penland.

P. 192: Reuben Estes to Reuben Fletcher, 237 a., Apr. 4, 1794; also,60 a., Feb 16, 1787, pr: Wm. White.

Samuel Owens to William Sumpter, 87 a., Dec.14, 1793, "pro. by oath."

Robert Kirkpatrick to William Sumpter, 200 a., Sept.1, 1793, pr: Samuel Ownes.

Ambrous Parks to Martin Calter, 200 a., Apr. 23, 1794, pr: William Sumpter.

Ann Dobson to Joseph, 70 a., Dec.10, 1791, pr: Thos. Smith.

Thomas McEntire, Sher., to Daniel Bullinger, 300 a., May 1, 1794, ack.

P. 193: Charles McDowell, Gen., & Alex Erwin, Esq. to John Tate, a lot, May 2, 1794, pr: Jos. Hughey.

Charles McDowell & Alex. Erwin, Commsrs, to Waightstill Avery, lot #1, Mar. 8, 1794, pr: Bruce Collins.

John McDowell, Sr. of the P. Gardens & Joseph McDowell of same, 1,050 a., Oct.24, 1793, ack.

July, 1794, p. 216: George Penland to John Erwin, 200 a., Mar. 5, 1794, pr: John Parks.

John Griffeth to Stephen Fuller, 300 a., Dec. 2, 1786, pr: Anthony Dukey.

Richard Singleton to Robert Sellars, Jr., 100 a., Dec.27(?), 1793, pr John Hall, Jr.

20

William James to Paul Cochron, 300 a., May 17, 1794, also for 150 a., May 6, 1794, ack.

Deed Mtg.: Isaac Martin to John Smaires (Smyre) 500 a., Jan.15, 1793, ack.

P. 217: Willaim Cathey to Daniel Brown, 250 a., May 17, 1793, pr: Joseph Young.

William Baldwin to Jacob Yunt, 350 a., Mar. 11, 1794, pr: Phillip Killian.

Jacob Absher to Jessee Coffee, 146 a., Dec. 24, 1784, pr: Wm. White.

Wm. Davidson to Jesse Stroud, 171 a., Mar,10, 1794, pr: James Hughey.

James Prichard to Olive Branch, 50 a., Aug. 2, 1794, ack.

October, 1794, p 240: James Pain, Geo., & Robert Pain, a Negro, Grace, & Children, Oct.20, 1794, pr: J. McDowell & Thos. McEntire.

William Hicks to John McGimpsey, 200 a., Sept. 24, 1794, pr: William White, Esq.

Isaac Ferrell to James Greenlee, Articles, July 2, 1794, pr: William Welsh.

William Welsh to John England, 257 a., undated, ack.

Deed Mtg.: Joseph Hughey to James Greenlee, Esq., a lot, May 3, 1794, pr: John Tate.

Commsrs. to John Tate, May 2, _____(undated) pr: Joseph Hughey.

P. 241: Cleveland Coffee to Joshua Penly, 100 a., May 16, 1793, pr: Rd. Osgatharpe.

Benj. Powell to Thomas Powell, 250 a., Apr,23, 1793, pr: Wm. White.

Charles McDowell & John Davidson to Michael Penley, 150 A., Aug.20, 1794, pr: John McGimsey.

Charles McDowell & Alex. Erwin, Commsrs., to John McGimsey, lot #20, Sept 10, 1792, pr: James Erwin.

William Fullerton to Adam, 100 a., Oct.22, 1794, pr: William Reed.

P. 242: Hugh Reed to Wm. Boyd, 300 a., Oct.22, 1794,pr: William Reed.

David Baker to Bruce Collins, 476 a., Oct.29, 1794, ack.

John Armstrong Erwin to Albert Corpening, 200 a., Aug.20, 1794, pr: Wm. Erwin, Esq.
Stephen Fuller to Francis Wooldly, 300 a., Jan.11, 1790, pr: Robert Johnson Dukie.

John & Joseph McDowell to John Armstrong Erwin, 185 a., Oct.21, 1794, ack.

George Hartley to John McGimsey, 96 a., Oct.29, 1794, ack.

January, 1795: p. 259: William Davis to Christian Absher, 25 a., July 20, 1795,(1794 ?); pr: Reuben Bray.

John McDowell, Sr. to Jacob Holensworth, 320 a., Dec. 23, 1794, pr: James Ainsworth.

John George Hipps to Geo., 150 a.,, Apr. 29, 1794, pr. Samueal McMurry.

James Morris to Joseph Goodbread, 120 a., Oct. 28, 1793, pr: William Morris.

P. 260: Reuben Estes to Wm. Loving, 150 a., Jan. 17, 1795, ack.

Mtg. Bond: Francis McClewer to Paul Atoney, 225 a., Apr. 17, 1794, pr: Joseph Anthony.

Robert Sloan to John Barns, 240 a., , 1 part in Wilson, Jan. 3, 1795, pr: Brinsley Barns.

William Erwin & Robert Craig to John Barns, 400 a., Nov. 26, 1794, pr: Benj. Austin.

P. 261: Commsrs. of Morganton, Alex. Erwin & Charles Mc-Dowell to James McEntire, 3 lots, Nov. 1, 1794, pr: Bruce Collins.

P.262: John Bunt to James Folkner, 300 a.,Mar. 6, 1795, ack.

David Baker, John, James, & Charles, 1794, 130 a to Bruce Collins, pr: Wm. White.

Enoch Berry to Robert Mcgomery, 381 a., Dec. 10, 1 794, pr: John McGomery.

Fredrick Shell to Frederick Rider, 116 a., Sept. 20, 1793, pr: Wm. White.

Frederick Shull to George Sigmon, 259 a., Sept. 20, 1793, pr: Wm. White.

Abraham Hunsucker to Bejamin Austin, 100 a., Octo. 4, 1794, pr: Nathan Austin.

James Powell to Thomas Prowell(Powell(?), 30 a., Sept. 24, 1794, pr: Wm. White.

Jean Logan to John Petillo, Sr., 100 a., July 12, 1793,pr: John Petillo.

Samuel Giles to Wm. Clark, Mar, 10, 1794, pr: Wm. Cry.

P. 264, Thomas Reybourn, Sr. to Wm. Green, 125 a., Aug. 15, 1787, pr: Wm. Morris.

David Sorrill to Joseph Dobson, 100 a.,Jan. 26, 1795, pr: David Causby.

Patrick Davis to James Oxford, 200 a., Jan. 27, 1793, ack.

P. 265: George Mosley to John Jones, 180 a., Nov.24, 1794, pr: Alex. Wakefield.

Eras(mus) May & Robert Kell to Martin Maney, 200 a., Sept. 12, 1794, pr: Thos. Kell.

Reuben White To Jeremiah Austin, 100 a., Feb.
10, 1794, pr: Thos. White, Sr.

P. 266: Morris Rone to Patrick Davis, 200 a., Oct. 23,
1789, pr: John Woodside.

Hugh McCory to John Franklin, "articles,"
Jan. 4, 1795.

APRIL, 1795: p. 284: Zachariah Downs to Henry Garrison, 183 a., Oct.
3, 1794, pr Robert Kell.

John Carson to William Sherrill, 500 a., June
3, 1787, pr: Joshua Sherrill.

John Fleming to Abraham, 125 a., May 16, 1794,
d. 300 a.,._____ 1794, pr: Jas Wood.

John Simpson to James, 150 a., Apr. 9, 1795,
pr: Jas. Washam (?) or Washbon.

John Baker to Benj. White, 202 a., Feb. 8, 1792,
pr: Reuben White.

Zaheriah Downs to Peter Stalcap, 133 a., Oct.
30, 1794, pr: Robt. Kell.

P. 285: David Vance to Edward Jackson, 186 a., pr: Robt.
Carrethen (Carruthers?)

David Vance to Robert Coruthers, 100 a., Mar, 9,
1795, pr: "Petillo."

John Doty to Joseph Chaffin, 92 a., Aug 1,
1794, pr: Amos Chaffin.

Abner England to Robert Bellew, 200 a., Jan.
27, 1794, pr: John Andrews.

Henry McKimsey to Wm. Erwin, 1227 a., Feb. 27,
1794, pr: James Erwin.

William Green to John McElroy, 200 a., Aug. 13,
1792, pr: Peter Thomson.

(End of Book, Part I), CR.14.036.1, 1791-1796.)

(BEGINNING PART II):

JULY, 1795, p. 302: Reason Howard to William West, 100 a., Oct. 20,
1795, pr: Peter West.

John McGarghey to Waightstill Avery, 100 a.,
Feb. 4, 1795, pr: James Greenlee.

Benja. Adkinsto Labon Estes, 200 a., Oct. 24,
1795, pr: Thomas Coleman.

Daniel England to William Hughes, Negro man,
Simon, Sept. 7, 1795., pr: John Hughes.

Robert McGomery to James Ainsworth, 381 a.,
Jan 28, 1795., ack.

John Hughes to Thomas McEntire, ½ lot in Morganton, 72 sq. p, Sept. 10, 1795, pr:William Wofford.

John Carson to Elijah Trosper, 100 a., Oct. 17, 1794, pr: Robert Trosper.

Mary Crawford to William Lowrance, 285 a., Oct. 8, 1793, pr: John Harper.

P. 304:Edward Poteet to Richard Osgathorpe, 200 a., Sept. 16, 1794, pr: West Walker.

John Waters to Hanry Holselaw, 50 a., July 7,, 1795, pr: Thomas Coleman.

Charles Coker to Jesse Moore & Jesse Moore, Jr., 300 a., Oct.15, 1795(?), pr: Daniel Moore.

Reuben White to William Tucker, Negro girl, Hannah, Feb 3, 1795, ack.

P. 305: John Durham to Samuel Love, 100 a., Oct. 25, 1795, pr. William Durham.

Joshua Penley to John Durham, 100 a., June 19, 1793, pr: William Durham.

John Wood to James Collier, 400 a., Aug. 26, 1794, pr: John McGimsey.

Samuel Swaringim to John Durham, 100 a., Oct. 1, 1790, pr: Samuel Swaringen, Sr.

Adam Lord to William Perriman, 200 a., Dec. 3, 1793, pr: William White.

P. 306: Joseph Chaffen to William Walton, 115 a., Feb. 20, 1795, pr: John Walton.

Daniel Andrews, Sr. to Daniel Andrews, Jr.,140 a., Nov. 10, 1794, pr: John Andrews.

William Gardner to David Andrews, 280 a., Apr. 26, 1794, pr: Robt. Bellew.

Richard Hailey to Thomas Plemons, 125 a., June 18, 1792, ack.

John Waters to John Beard, 150 a., Jan. 23, 1793, pr: Eilijah Hammond.

P. 307: Joseph Steel to Phillip Anthony, 132 a., Mar. 5, 1795, pr: Albert Corpenny.

George McDonald to John Andrews, 100 a., Sept. 11, 1794, pr: William Morrison.

Charles McDowell to John M. Willson, 424 a., July 28, 1795, ack.

Joseph Chaffon to John Gilliland, 115 a., Feb. 20, 1795, pr: John Walton.

P. A. Martha White & John Sawyers, to John Hall, Jr.,Sept.16, 1795, pr. Joseph White.

Joshua Hall to James Sellers, 222 a., Aug. 3, 1795., Ack.

P. 308: Abraham Hunsucker to Peter Hunsucker, 100 a., Feb. 13, 1795, pr: Benj. Austin.

William Austin to Elijah Austin, 200 a., June 30, 1795, pr: Phillip Austin.

Phillip Martin to Thomas Winkler, Esq., 96 a., June 5, 1783, pr: Abraham Winkler.

Benjamin Bird to Thomas Bird, 100 a., July 25, 1795, pr: Robert Logan.

Joseph Spencer to Joseph Chaffen, 230 a., Aug· 16, 1793, ack.

P. 208: William Ussery to Thomas Winkler, 300 a., Sept· 12, _____(?), pr: Will Wofford.

P. 309: Waighstill Avery to John Robinson, 100 a., org. deed, Feb 9, 1795, ack.

Charles Dement to Joseph Brandon, 100 a., Jan, 11, 1794, pr: Richard Brown·

William Dever to Lewis McCartney, 200 a., Catawba R., Jan 19, 1795, pr: William Dever, Jr.

James Dever to Lewis McCartney, 200 a., Catawba R., Jan, 13, 1795, pr: William Dever, Jr.

Robert Sellers to James Sellers, 50 a., Oct. 12, 1794, ack.

Erasmus May and Elizabeth May to John Kell(?) 150 a., Dec. 22, 1792, ack.

P. 310: Robert Sellers to William Spencer Dorcey, 200 a., Mar. 14, 1795, ack.

John Tate to Sturyar(?) Bouchell, Sr., Morganton, lot, 72 sq, p#9, May 1 1795; pr: William White.

OCTOBER, 1795: (unpaginated): John Hughes to John H. Stevelie, #21, Mar. 11, 1795, pr: James McEntire.

Benj. Wallace to Pat·Sloan, 143 a., July 31, 1795, pr: Benj. Wallace.

Hodge Reyburn to Benj. Adams, 150 a., July 30, 1795, ack.

William Austin to Nathan, 300 a., June 7, 1795, pr: Phillip Austin.

Alex, Erwin to Benj. Clark, 195 a., Oct. 26, 1794, ack.

James Willson to Benj. ... "Articles," Oct. 22 1795, pr: Wm. Wofford.

Francis Patton to Saml. Tate and Hughes Tate, 200 a., May 23, 1791, pr: Wm. Erwin.

Chas. McDowell to Alex. Erwin, #24 & #33 lots, May 30, 1795, pr: James McEntire.

Wm. Morrison to John McDowell, 400 a., Apr, 20, 1795, pr: Wm. Morrison.

Joseph Bellew to Joshua, 250 a., Oct, 24, 1795, pr: Geo. Bellew.

Joseph Bellew to Geo, 90 a., July 16, 1795, pr: Joshua Bellew.

Wm. Bright to Wm. Mays, 50 a., "28th, 1795," pr: Wm. Wiseman.

James McEntire & Ben Hall to Wm. Walton, 29, 640 a., Bunc. Co., Oct, 1, 1795; ack.

Corn. Reddick "from to", "from" Joseph Spencer, tract, Dec.7, 1792, ack. by J.S.

John Barnhart, 100 a., to Jacob Derebery, May 9, 1791, ack.

Wm. Bailey to John McGimsey, 569 a., Sept. 10, pr: John H. Stevelie, 1795.

Sol. Right to Saml. Brown, 50 a., Jan. 27, 1796, pr: James Roper.

Alex. Thomson to Thos. Young, 150 a.,, Jan. 1, 1786, pr: Robt. Patton.

James Faulconer to John McGimsey, 200 a., Dec. 9, 1794, pr: Alex. Erwin.

Nathl. Hughes to Joseph Scales(?) 100 a., Aug, 24, 1795, pr: William Walton.

John Hughes to Danl. England, 1 a., July 16, 1787, pr: Chas. McDowell.

Wm. Neil and uxor to James McEntire, 300 a., Jan. 6, 1796, pr: Wm. Wofford.

Daniel Brown to Hiram Wms., 100 a., Dec. 29, 1795, pr. Wm. Cry.

Robert Bellew to John Tips, 200 a., 150 a.,, 67 a., Jan. 29, 1796,1st pr: Robt. Bellew, last two ack.

Daniel Brown & Ezekiel Murrow, Wit. by John Bradburn, Josh. Bellew, Jas. Berry, Shepperd Bowman, Wilson Jenkins, Saml. Giles, Dec. 3, 1795 (for "lye bell.")

Robt. Bellew To Stephen, 83 a., Jan. 29, 1796, ack.

Stephen Piercy to John Miller, 50 a., Apr. 9, 1794, pr: Wm. White.

John McGomery to Hugh Connelly, 361 a., Jan., 28, 1796, ack.

John Perkins to Joseph, 300 a., Jan. 4, 1796, pr: Robt. J. Miller.

James Connelly to Wm, 89 a., and 100 a., Jan. 12, 1796. , ack.

David Baker to Thos. White, 200 a., and 112 q., Jan. 28, 1796., ack.

Wm. Morrison to David McCracken, 250 a,, pr: John Chandler.   (Sher.)

B.S.: Hugh Reed to Lewis Maberry, Nov. 25, 1790, Pr. Wm. Reed.

Jones Bedford to John Higdon, 100 a., Jan. 13, 1795, pr: Thos. Higdon.

Alex. Thomson to Thos. Young, 150 a., Jan. 21, 1786, pr: Robt. Patton.

Alex Carson to Thos. Young, 150 a., Jan. 21, 1786 , pr: Robt. Patton.

John Connelly, James & Hugh, Eliz. Bellew & Rebekah Gibb to Wm. Connely, 117 a., Jan. 1, 1796, pr: Wm.Connely, Jr.

Greenberry Wilson to Saml. Macky, 300 a., Oct. 28, 1795, ack.

"Baker" to Wm. Fullwood, 100 a., Dec. .20, 1795, pr: Wm Devenport.

Jonas Taylor to John Mullins, 100 a., Sept, 16, 1795, pr: James Mullins.

Geo. Davidson to Benj. Bird, 300 a., May 10, 1791, pr: Robt. Logan.

Abr. Sudderth & Thos. to John Townson, 370 a., Jan. 23, 1796, pr: Peter Thomson.

John Davidson to Benj. Bird, 82 a., Aug. 20, 1794, pr: Thos. Bird.

Wm. Kill to Benj. Brittain, 100 a., Jan. 5, 1796, pr: Saml.Brittain.

Benj. Jones to Thoms. Roberts, 500 a., Jan. 23, 1795, pr: Wm. Morrison, Jr.

Benj. White to Stephen Piercy, 100 a., Jan. 19, 1796, pr: Thos. White.

James Carson to Jon. Knight, 300 a., Aug. 21, 1795, pr: Sol. Knight.

Thos. Patten to John Robinett, 213 a., Dec. 22, 1795, pr: Michael Keller.

Charles Baker to Stephen Piercy, 200 a., June 20, 1795, pr: Thos. White.

Benj. Adams to Joseph Kearly, 150 a., Nov, 26, 1794, pr: Hodge Rayborn.

Wm. White to A_____(Illiegible)., 100 a, Aug, 25, 1794., pr: Reuben White.

APRIL, 1796 - Vacant - (Next begins July, 1796, not abstracted)

C R. 14.036.1, I & II, 1791-1798.

A continuation of surveys from Volume III, pages 9-17:

a: Henry Propest(t) (Propst): entered Aug. 1, 1778, surveyed June
    19, 1779, #554.

b: Samuel Mitchel(l): entered Dec. 11, 1778, surveyed Aug. 6, 1779,
    issued Oct. 28, 1782, #1149.

c: Richard Price: entered July 5, 1779, notice to Surveyor by Chas.
    McDowell on Dec, 10, 1780, surveyed Oct. 10, 1788, #1764.

d: Philip Price: incomplete; surveyed Aug. 10, 1779, #432.

Note: Some of these copies were xeroxed imperfectly at the Land
Grant Office many years ago.

STATE of NORTH-CAROLINA.

No. 554

CHARLES M^cDOWAL,
Entry Officer of Claims for Lands in the County of *Burke.*

To the SURVEYOR of the said County, Greeting.

YOU are hereby required, as soon as may be, to lay off and survey, for *Henry Propest* a Tract or Parcel of Land, containing *One hundred* Acres, lying in the County aforesaid, *Lying on the Waters of Clarks Creek Branding on Said Propests Deaded Land and Joining John Wilsons Lines for Complement*

Observing the Directions of the Act of Assembly in such Case made and provided for running out Lands. Two just and fair Plans of such Survey, with a proper Certificate annexed to each, you are to transmit, with this Warrant, to the Secretary's Office without Delay.

GIVEN under my Hand at *Three* the *Third* Day of *October* Anno

(This was entered Aug. 1, 1778 -- see Vol. I p. 52 of Burke County, North Carolina Land Records 1778, by Huggins)

29

Said by a scale of Twenty Chain to the Inch ——

State of North Carolina
Burke County ——

This plan Represents a Tract or parcel of Land Containing Fifty Acres, Surveyed for Henry Propest, Lying on the waters of Clarks Creek and Bounded by the Lines of John Cline, Bostion Cline, Andrew Killian, John Killian James

and his own, Begining at a post Oak in John Cline, Bostian Clines Corner, Running thence West with Clines Line, Thirtyfour Chain to a post oak in Andrew Killian line, thence North with said Killians Line three Chain ... to a Small Black oak Sapling and Stake in John Line, thence North Eightynine degrees East with said Line ... Chain Fifty Links to a Black Oak Said Killians Corner, North three degrees East with Said John Killians Line Forty Twentyfive Links to a post oak, and Stake, Thence East Chain with Kennens Line to a Black oak Kennens — Thence South with Kennens Line Eighteen Chain fifty Links ... ck oak in Henry Propest Line, Thence West Eight Chain ... Line to a post oak Sapling his Corner, Thence South ... Propests Line and John Clines Line, Twentyfive ... the Begining. Surveyed 19th June 1779 ——

william
... Bork }
Cline } Ch. Ca ...
John

C.W. Beekman to Survr

Samuel Mitchell

STATE of NORTH-CAROLINA. No. *1149*

CHARLES McDOWELL,
Entry Officer of Claims for Lands in the County of *Burke*.

To the S U R V E Y O R of the said County, Greeting.

Y O U are hereby required, as soon as may be, to lay off and survey, for *Samuel Mitchell* a Tract or Parcel of Land, containing *Four Hundred and fifty* Acres, lying in the County aforesaid, *lying on the North side of the Catawba river Between Lower and Sandid little river Joining James Mefioy at the lower End and running upwards for Complement including his own Improvement Entd December 11th 1778*

75 acres later sold to Robert
Warren, a neighbor, who was a
chainbearer.

Observing the Directions of the Act of Assembly in such Case made and provided for running out Lands. Two just and fair Plans of such Survey, with a proper Certificate annexed to each, you are to transmit, with this Warrant, to the Secretary's Office without Delay.

Note: Xerox was incomplete, but which
should read: GIVEN under my Hand at Office
(plus date).

31

Samuel Mitchel

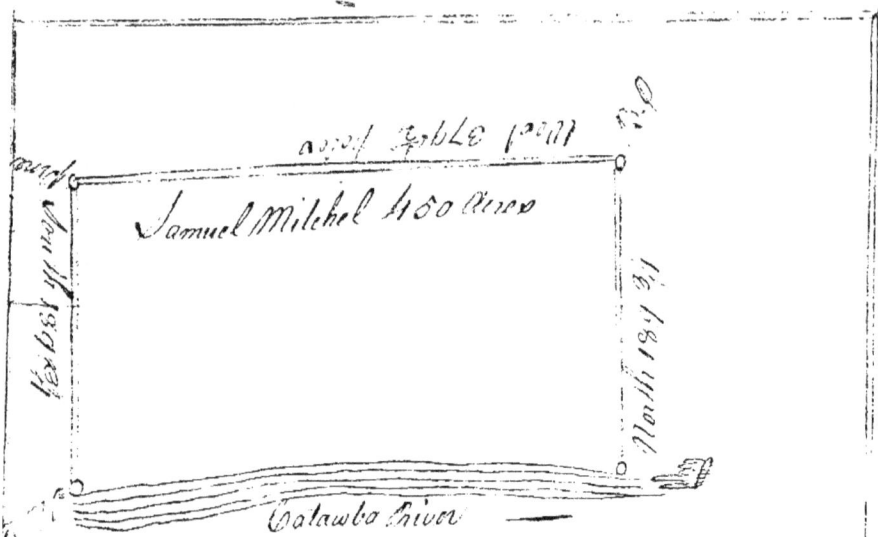

Samuel Mitchel 450 acres

West 379 1/2 poles

North 189 3/4

South 189 3/4

Catawba River

The plan of a tract or parcel of land Surveyed for Samuel
Mitchel Containing Four hundred and fifty acres. Lying
on the North side of the Catawba River. Beginning at a White
White Oak on the Bank of the River and runs North One hundred
and Eighty nine poles and three quarters of a pole, to a Black
Oak along James Beasleys line. thence West three hundred
and Seventy nine poles and a half to a pine. thence South One
hundred and Eighty nine poles and three quarters of a pole, to
a stake on the bank of the river along his own line. thence down
down the various Courses of the River to the Beginning——

Robert Warren
Alexander Grahams } C.C

Surveyed August 6th 1779.

North Carolina Burk County Surveyed for
Richard Price one hundred acres of land —
Lying in the County aforesaid Joining
Faines Presley line Beginning at a Pine
Running South twenty five Chains to a
Stake Thence west forty Chains to a Pine
thence North Twenty Chains to a Stake thence
East to the Beginning Surveyed the tenth
Day of october 1783

Phillip Crice
James Parsley   } CC

R. M. White

for David Vance

State of North Carolina — No 1764

Charles McDowell Entry Officer of Claimer for
Lands in the County of Burke —

To the Surveyor of said County Greeting —

You are hereby Required as soon as may be to lay off
and Survey for Richard Price a Tract or Parcell of Land
lying in the County aforesaid Containing two hundred acres lying on a branch of
mountain Creek between the Line of James Presley and
his own Lines Running so as to Include his Improvements
for Complement Entred the 5th Day of July 1779 —

Observing the Direction of the Act of Assembly in
such Case made and Provided for Runing out Lands
Two Just and fair Plans of such Survey with a
Proper Certificate annexed to Each you are to Return
with this Warrant to the Secretarys Office without
Delay Given under my hand at Office the 10th day
of December AD: 1780

Chas McDowell E. O.

Philip Price

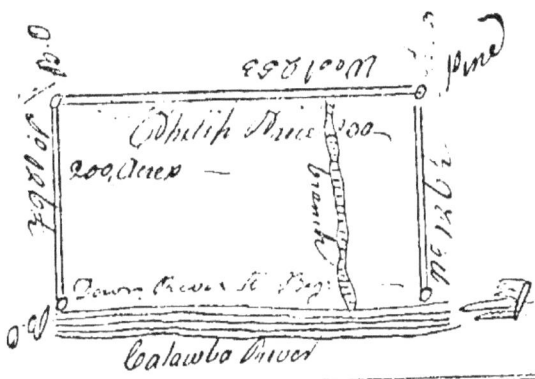

The plan of a tract or parcel of Land Surveyed for Philip Price containing Two hundred acres Lying on the North side of the Catawba River at the Mouth of a branch Beginning at a Black oak Philip Price and Samuel Mitchels Corner and Runs with his line One hundred and twenty six poles and a half to a pine, thence West sixty one poles to a branch Crossing the same Course One hundred and Ninety two poles to a Black Oak, Con ... Robert feels line thence South with his line One hundred and twenty six poles and a half to a ... oak on the Bank of the River between the Island and the River thence down the Several Courses of the River to the Beginning

Robert Warren   } C.C.
Alexander Grahams }

Surveyed August 10th 1779

#432
Surveyed Aug. 10, 1779

35

TAX LIST APRIL 5, 1787

Capt. Wm. Neill's old Company:

(William)....... Wofford
(James) .... Ainsworth
John Sisco Sr. and Jr., and Jacob
(John) . . . . . Vann
.... ha Oakley
.... Crowell
.... Wilson
.... Wilson
(Rd.) .... Medlock
.... Wilson
Thos. Young
Wm. Phillips
Delilah McFalls
Frederick Miller
James Lee
Wm. Moodie
.......es Bennett
.... Hensley (3)
(Thos. Beck) .. instaff
....
....taker
(Thom) as.... Bright
.... Hensley
.... Pickeral
.....e Raddock
(Rob)ert Turner
Samuel Gray
Jonas Griffith
George Holbrok
David McCracken
Thomas Baker
John Armstrong
Henry Gillespie
Rd. Jacks
Tho(mas) (B) arnard
........(Mon) tgomery
....ling
....way
(Samuel) Bright

(G.O. 130)

(Note: Vol. II has early tax lists, but none for 1787)
——— Some are "guessed at" by 1790 Census.

36

COURT MINUTES 1804-1810 OF WILLS, ESTATES, ORPHANS

This chapter is a continuation of the same title found in Volume III
of abstracts of proven wills, executors, inventories and sales of estates, family records (including bastardy), deeds of gift, and many
interesting and valuable information found nowhere else. No earlier
court minutes are preserved (beginning Volume III), however they do
extend to 1868. Naturally these ledgers are handwritten and sometimes very difficult to read, however any page may be xeroxed at the
Division of Archives and History, The Search Room, 109 Jones Street,
Raleigh, North Carolina, 27602.

JANUARY 1804, p. 449: Slaves of Wm. McEntire to Clarissa, James and
Alfred Walton.
                    P. 452: Martha Rhodes "bass born" child.
                    P. 453: Thomas Winklar will proved.
                    P. 453: George Tucker will proved.
                    P. 454-455: James Shanks, dec'd., wid. Fenwell
granted Adm. and year's allowance.
                    P. 458: Leaner Amburn ordered bring children
to next court.
                    P. 464: Moses Whitley's Execr. Thos. Bags.
                    P. 465: Deed of 400 a. to Brice Collins, pr.
by Thomas Baker.

APRIL 1804, P. 468: John Burgess will proved.
                    P. 469: James Going, a 5 to 6 years foundling,
bound to Joseph Dobson for trade of a shoemaker.
                    P. 472: John Moore, dec'd., widow Sarah granted
Administration of estate.
                    P. 476: Gen. Joseph McDowell, dec'd., with his
estate to be settled.
                    P. 476: Abraham Fleming, dec'd., his real es-
tate to be divided.
                    P. 480: Fenwell Shanks' dower, but is now the
wife of John Hall.
                    P. 482: Legatees of James Shanks, dec'd., with
legatees named as Fenevill Shanks, John McCullock, Wm. Black,
Thomas Gribble, James Wylie, Andrew Miller, Andrew Sprot, to Jesse
Martin, 50 acres dated Feb. 20, 1804, proved by John Hall.

(Note: Court Minutes must of necessity be abbreviated where possible.)

37

P. 484: P.A., Geo. & ElizabethDerreberry, P.A. Apr, 25, 1804, to Jonathan Hinds, pr. by John McDowell.

P. 484: York Co. (S.C.) June 10, 1803, Joseph, John, MosesMatthew Corrill & James Clinton, Samuel& Elizabeth Crofts, John M. & Jane Gollogher, Children of Thomas Carrell & Wife Easther (formerly, dau. of Matthew Armstrong, dec'd. of N.C.) for 15 sh, to John Armstrong, our legacy left our deceased mother by her father, Matthew Armstrong, as assigned by our father Thomas Carroll to sd. John Armstrong.

JULY, 1804, p. 488: John Moore, dec'd., year's allowance to widow.

P. 488: Caleb Barr insolvent, over 50 years, exempted from pole tax 1803.

P. 488: John Moore, dec'd. Adm. Sarah Moore.

P. 489: John Franklin, Sr., over age in 1803, overcharged for "pole" tax.

P. 489: Sarah Kinlaw, about 12, bound to Thomas Smith till 18, to be taught reading (etc) & at freedom a suit or 3 lbs. cash.

P. 490: Jean Bradburn, dec'd., estate to be settled by Adm.

P. 490: Solomon Smith, dec'd, estate to be settled by Adm. or Exrs.

P. 496: Paul Prock, dec'd., son John, age 10, bound to Henry Baker to become a blacksmith.

P. 501: Clarke orphans: Nancy, John, James, Mahala, next court.

P. 504: Deed of John, David, Moses & James Edmiston & John Dickson & Wife, George & Samuel Edmiston, to Thomas McEntire, 46 a., Sept 1, 1803, pr. by John Burgin.

P. 506: Six Edmiston deeds. John Dickson & Wife, is Mary.

OCTOBER, 1804, p. 510: John Green, dec'd. will proved.

P. 510: John Hight, dec'd. will proved.

P. 510: Wm. Whitson ordered Gdn. to children, Wm. Joseph, Polly.

P. 510-511: John Shell sales of est; est.of-be settled.   P. 511: Hezekiah Gibson, 16 yrs. 5 mos; son of Wilburn Gibson, bound to James Reed due to abandonment & to be taught trade of husbandry.

P. 513: Adam Overwinterwill proved.

JANUARY, 1805, p. 524: James Walters, orphan, 12 yrs 3 mos., bound to Jonathan Hargis as a shoemaker trade.

P. 525: Justin Branchwell moved.

P. 525: John Shell estate to be settled, will proved.

P. 526: Milly Robison, 9 yrs, deserted by Risbon Robison & wife, bound to Enoch Rust til 18 yrs old.

P. 528: David Ferrell, 17 yrs, Orphan, bound to David Tate to 21, trade of tanner.

P. 528: John Hall & Wife petition for dower to Fenwall Hall, wid. of James Shank, dec'd.

P. 530: Abraham Fleming dec'd., estate to be settled.

P. 532: Ledbetter orphans, Washington, Rebecka, Nancy, chose, Walton Ledbetter as guardian.

P. 535: Abraham Fleming estate division between Betsey (62a), Abraham(105a), David(67a), Frances(67a), Tarlton(87a), John(176a), Rebacka(?).

P. 535: Solomon Good's wife Frances, dower.

APRIL, 1805, p. 548: Wm. McEfee, dec'd. will proved.

P. 549: Thomas Higdon, dec'd., Adm, Gr. Jean Higdon.

P. 550: AnnaBrooks, 12, orphan, bound to Thos. Capehart to 18.

P. 550: Robert Netherly, dec'd., adm. granted, Wm. & Samuel; year's allowance to widow.

P. 550: Grief Lindsey, minor orphan, has Labon Estes as Gdn.

P. 551: Wm. White, Guardian & Grandfather of Kesiah Thomas & Elizabeth Hickman. Thomas, 16 years 4 mos bound to Thomas Hickman "to receive at freedom a set of blacksmith tools."

P. 551: Henry Garrison estate to be settled with Adm.

P. 554: P.A., June 16, 1803, Robert, Wm., John, James Adamsto James Erwin, sons of Wm. Adams, dec'd of county, proven Livingston, Co. Ky.

P. 557: Conrad Winkler, son of Joseph, lost part of left ear from horse bite.

P. 569: Wm. McEffee m. Kerren Happuck Chandler, accordg.to marriage contract of Dec 23, 1801.

JULY, 1805, p. 572: George Deal will proved.

P. 572: Thomas Higdon sales of estate by Jean,Adm.

P. 573: Jacob Loudermilk will pr. by Elizabeth Loudermilk.

P. 575: David Ballew, orphan, 6 yrs, bound to John McGalliard for house carpenter.

P. 577: Nancy Holderfield, 15, bound to Thos. McEntire to 18.

P. 577: Lourance Arney estate to be settled Adm.

P. 577: Elias Stallions, orphan, 13, bound to Abraham Stallion to 21.

P. 580: Paul Antony will proved.

P. 589: Gabriel Loving to son Wiseman, D.G.

P. 590: Ephriam Perkins to Robert Johnson Miller, Thomas Snoddy, John Perkins, Eli Perkins, Alexander Perkins, 44 a., July 23, 1805.

P. 590: David, George & Samuel Edmeston, deed of 50 a., to Thomas McEntire, Sept. 18, 1804, pr. John Burgin.

P. 591: Deeds of Gift, John Carson to Jason, John, Jr., & Joseph Carson, 1805.

P. 591: Deeds of Henry Holman, John Shell, Samuel McCall, Daniel Shell, Isaac Martin, Samuel Shell, Catherine Winkler, to Jacob Sherrill, 250 a., Mar 2, 1805, pr. by Abner Payne.

P. 591: Above to Babel Sherrill, 300 a.,.

P. 594: Deed of Gift Peggy McKenny to Edwin Fielding , July 15, 1805, for articles.

OCTOBER, 1805, p. 595:   Robert Payne will proved.

P. 596: James C. Webb will proved.

P. 596: Peter Mull, dec'd., Adm.John Peter Mull.

P. 596: David McElrath, dec'd., Adm. Robert McElrath.

P. 598: James Reed, dec'd., Admr. gr. Jean, wid., year's allowance.

P. 601: John Brown, dec'd., Adm. Gr. Ailcy, Wid., year's allowance.

P. 607: Leanner Amburn, Wid., children next court.

P. 607: Thos. Higdon, dec'd., year allow.to wid.

P. 613: Deed of Ann Morgan, Daniel Morgan, Joseph Burton,& Martha Burton, John Hicks & Susanna Hicks, to Job Morgan, 74 a., Dec.19, 1805, pr: John H. Stevilie.

P. 613: Same as above, 34 a., same date.

JANUARY, 1806, p. 616: Wm. McEfee, will with James McEfee, Exec.

P. 616: Phillip Martin, dec'd., est. to settle.

P. 617: Thos. Winkler, dec'd., sales returned.

P. 618: James Moore will proved.

P. 619: Wilie Pierce, orphan 13, bound to John Littler-to be blacksmith.

P. 621: Elizabeth Briant's "bass born", reputed father Eli Powell.

P. 621: Thos. Winkler est. to be settled.

P. 621: James Shanks est. to be settled.

P. 623: Will of Samuel McDaniel proved.

P. 624: John Moore, dec'd., est. to be settled.

P. 624: James Edmeston est. to be settled.

P. 626: Wm. Carter will proved.

P. 628: Tisdel Spencer's Gdn, his mother Sarah Spencer, wid. of Joseph Spencer. She appt. gdn. to Lemwl , Samuel, Joseph & Edwin ..

P. 629: Joseph Spencer, dec'd., wid Sarah gr. adm., year's allowance.

P. 630: Tarleton Fleming est., Adm.gr. Abraham
Fleming.

P. 631: David McElrath dec'd., dower to wid.
Christina & land.

P. 636: Elizabeth Cook's children deserted by
father, and she to bring them to next court.

P. 639: John Brown dec'd., year's allowance to wid.

P. 646: Deed of Joseph Allen & wife, Jenny,
John Allen & wife, Elizabeth, Wm. Murphy & wife, Jean, heirs of Hugh
Allen of Rockbridge Co., Va., to Thomas Bags, 173 a., Burke Co.

P. 647: Deeds of Thomas Baggs, Ann Baggs, Samuel
Whitly & wife, Sarah, to James Murphy, 173 a. & 144 poles.

APRIL, 1806, p. 650: Sarah Elledge, 12, orphan, bound to Sherwood
Bowman until 18.

P. 651: John Forbush, 11 yrs 6 mos, orphan,
bound to Wm. Penland to 21, to learn trade of wheelright & chairmaker.

P. 654: Abram Fleming est. to be settled.

P. 658: Joseph Spencer land to be divided.

P. 659: Jenny Brook, 11, orphan, bound to Milly
Walton to 18.

P. 659: Clara Elrod, 14, orphan, bound to
Barbara Moll to 18.

P. 661: Wm. Walton est., Adm. granted Milly
Walton & John Petillo, year's allowance for widow.

P. 678: Abraham Horshaw will pr.

P. 678: Henry Baker will pr.

P. 679: George Johnson, 15 yrs. 9 mos. apprent-
iced formerly to Thomas White, now to Edwin Sharpe till of age.

P. 682: Abraham Horshaw will annexed, Adm.
granted David Repitto & Ann Horshaw.

P. 683: Robert Netherly estate to be settled.

P. 685: John Pierson's widow, Hannah, relinq-
uished administration to John & Isaac Pierson, son's of dec'd. Year's
allowance to widow.

P. 685: Wm. Walton inventory returned.

P. 686: David Hall's estate Adm. by Bartlet
Hinson & Moses Wilkinson.

P. 686: Heirs of Joseph Spencer, dec'd., &
Samuel Church in right of his wife as to land division.

P. 688: John Moore, 16 yrs 10½ mos, orphan,
bound to John McGuire to 21, to learn "art of hatting."

P. 690: Charity Pierson's "bass born" child
by Alexander Penland.

P. 692: Andrew Donaldson & wife vs. Wm. Thompson.
Names: Andrew Russell & wife, Mary, Andrew Morrison & w. Mary,
Andrew Donaldson & w. Elizabeth, Wm. Brandon.

P. 699: Jan. 1, 1805, deed of Rachel, Wm, John,
Henry, James & Edmond Young to Miles Higgins, 200 a. Proved by
John Higgins.

Pp. 703-704: Deeds as follows, re: distributive shares of land of David McElrath, dec'd. John, 215 a; Peter, 200 a; Catherine, 200 a; Robert, 181 a; Sarah, 200 a; Nancy, 147 a; David, 147 a; Dower of relict, Christen, of David, dec'd., 142 a.

OCTOBER, 1806, p. 707: John Brock, orphan, apprenticed to Henry Baker who relinquishes.

P. 709: Joseph Crunkleton, dec'd., heir of land is John (or Joseph ?).

P. 710: John Hughes, dec'd., Adm. to Thomas England & John Hughes.

P. 711: John Pierson, dec'd., petition for 640 a & 600 a., among heirs, Michael, John, Wm., James Pierson; Antony Street & wife; Sarah Revis; Arthur Shoat & wife;Henry Pierson; Mary Pierson; John Pierson, son of Robert, dec'd.

P. 712: Christopher Amburns, dec'd., orphans to be at next court.

P. 714: Matthew Hips, dec'd., Adms.: Wm. McEntire, George Walton & George Hips.

P. 722: John & Henry Whittenburg, Andrew, Daniel & Mary Killian, deed of 200 a. to Peter Cannon on January 4, 1806, pr. by Robert Williamson. (Also 200 a.)

JANUARY, 1807, p. 725: John Wakefield, dec'd., Mary, widow, relinquished to Brittain Yarboro & John Wakefield. Year's allowance to widow.

P. 726: Christopher Amburn, dec'd., Children: Mary Ann, 14 & 10mos. bound to Hugh Tate; John(no age) bound to same.

P. 727: Benj. McGaughay, 15 yrs 9 mos. bound to Caleb Poor, trade of tanning and currying leather.

P. 729: Wm. Cosby will proved.

P. 730: Thomas Wiseman estate, adms. being Benj. White & John Wiseman. Year's allowance to widow.

P. 733: Colbert Blair's will proved.

P. 733: Sarah Grastys two illegitimate children to next court.

P. 734: George Derreberry, dec'd., adm. to Nancy O'Kelly, widow & Elijah Largent. Year's allowance to widow.

P. 734: Charity Piercy vs. Alexander Penland, bastardy child born Mar. 1805, nearly 8 mos. at death.

P. 737: Edward Teague will proved.

P. 737: Wm. Grasty, 15 yrs. 7 mos. & John Grasty 12 yrs. & 10 mos. bound to Wm. Tate to learn trade of husbandry.

P. 738: Mathias Hips, sales of estate returned by Admrs.

P. 739: Christpher Amburn's children to be brought to court.

P. 747: Mat Hips widow, Delilah Hips.

P. 748: John Pierson's heirs division: Wid. Hannah, Henry, Michael, Wm., Isaac Pierson, Arthur Choat, Mary Pierson, Sarah Revis; John Pierson, Jr., Anthony Street.

P. 751: Deed of Job Morgan, Joseph Burton, & Wife, Martha, John Hicks & Wife, Susannah, Daniel Morgan, to John McTaggart, 100 a., Nov. 19, 1804, pr. by George Walton.

APRIL, 1807, p. 758: John Wakefield inv. returned by Admrs.

P. 758: James Moore estate to be settled.

P. 761: James Scott, 5 yrs. 10 mos., bound to John Erwin , trade of tailoring.

P. 761: Thos. Wiseman, Admrs. returned sales.

P. 762: James C. Webb will mentioned.

P. 762: Wm. Payne will proved.

P. 770: John Hughes, dec'd., wid., Ann Hughes, year's allowance.

end of
(C.R. 14.036.2)

C.R.C.R.14.037 , July, 1807- October, 1810.

JULY, 1807, p. 2: John Dockry estate, Wm. Webster granted Admr.

P. 2: Wm. Connelly will proved.

P. 2: George Deal, dec'd., inventory returned.

(C.R.14.036.2)   P. 2a: Wm. Causby will; Nancy Causby qualified.

P. 3: Patrick Obrion's wid. year's allowance.

P. 3: James C. Webb sales of estate.

P. 4a: Patrick Obrion's wid. Martha Obrion granted Admr.

P. 7: Thomas Winkler's estate to be settled.

P. 10: George Deal, dec'd., widow, Edy Deal now wife of Joseph Griffy, ordered to sell personal estate.

P. 10: John Hughes, inv. and sales.

P. 10: George Deal's minor orphan, John, chose Gdn. Michael Keller.

P. 10: George Deal's minor orphans Alexander, Henry, Ebby , Mary, Matilda, with Gdn. Elisha Dossey.

P. 11: John Hughes, dec'd., Lewis, John, Wm., Betsy, Joseph, Frederch Capehart vs, heirs & James Hughes (heir?).

P. 129: Heirs of John Hughes, dec'd., Jno. Hughes, Fred Caphart by his wife, Wm., Betsy & Jo Hughes.

OCTOBER, 1807, p. 20: Jenny Brooks, orphan, formerly bound to Mildred Walton who is about to take her out of the state.

P. 20: Lemuel Durham, 15 yrs 3 mos, bound to Ferdinand Flashman to be bound to Wm. Connelly, blacksmith.

P. 21: John Poteet's exr., Elizabeth Poteet.

P. 21: Wm. Morrison will proved.

P. 21a: John Dockry inventory.

P. 21a: John Brown estate adm. to Thomas Brown. Year's allowance to widow.

P. 22a: George Deal estate to be settled.

P. 24: (Unclear) inv. of property (of Peter Moll) by Mary Brittain....marriage.

P. 26: Jack Owen, about 4 yrs, bound to James Greenlee.

P. 26: Joseph Wakefield bond for maintenance of "bassborn" child.

P. 26a: Joseph Spencer children: Tisdel, Lemuel, Samuel, Joseph, Edwin, Polly Jackson Spencer. Sarah Spencer, Gdn.

P. 27: Sarah Davidson's heirs: Matthew Oliphant & w. Nancy, Robert Mordock & wife Jean, Alexander Young & wife Sarah, Wm. Hall & wife Rachael, James Young & wife Elizabeth, to James Murphy, Claimant under Alexander Davidson from purchase.

P. 30: 3 deeds of Thomas Knight from Jonathan, Mary, & Jonathan.

JANUARY, 1808, p. 32: Jenny Brooks, age 14,6 mos. bound to John Gibbs.

P. 32: John Gribble, dec'd.,; widow Margaret granted Admr. with Thos. Gribble; year's allowance.

P. 35: Mary Bradly estate granted John H. Stevelee; Will.

P. 36: Constable Mark Brittain.

P. 37: Peter Moll estate to be settled.

P. 37: Thomas Davis estate to be settled.

P. 38: Vicy Ballew's two illegitimate orphans, 9 yrs, 2-3 yrs, to be brought to next court.

P. 39: Wm. Walton estate to be settled.

P. 40a: Mary Elrod's male child(illegitimate) to next court.

P. 40a: Nancy Ballew, "baseborn" David Ballew, to next court.

P. 41a: Deed of Gift Jo. Alexander to Polly, Rachel & Nancy, pr: Joseph, Sr.

P. 42: Deed of Joseph Alexander to John Piper Alexander Tate Alexander, 376 a., Oct.12, 1807, proved by Joseph Alexander, Sr.

APRIL, 1808, p. 44a: John Dellinger, dec'd., widow, Barbara, relinq. Admr., which is granted to John H. Stevelee & John Dellinger. Year's allowance to widow, who is appt'd. Gdn. of their children: Betsy, Peggy, Barbara, Polly, Susannah.

P. 47: Samuel McDaniel estate to be settled.

P. 47: Betsy Burton, age 9, bound to Charles McDowell.

P. 48a: Delpha Burton, 11 yrs 6 mos, dau. of Joseph out of the county, bound to Wm. Tate.

P. 50: Henry Smith & John Kerby & wife vs. Heirs of Sol. Smith, dec'd., Samuel Smith & John McCrary in right of wife, who are defendants & out of state. Notice to James Penley & wife, Jacob Smith, Barnet Decker in right of his wife, Ala Smith as Gdn. of Solomon, Augustin & Antoneey Smith.

P. 51: Joseph Spencer, dec'd., dower of Sarah, wid.

P. 53: Vicy Ballew's two "bass borns", one 9 one 2 or 3 years, Nancy Ballews "Bass born" David Ballew to be brought in next court.

JULY, 1808, P. 55: Lewis Terrell, dec'd., wid., Susannah, granted Adm., also Frederick Stevelee., Year's allowance.

P. 56: Elijah Browning estate with Adm. gr. Rachel Browning & John Duckworth; years' allowance to widow.

P. 57: Thomas Largent will proved; Exrs., Elijah & Thos. Elijah Browning, inventory by Admrs.

P. 57: Solomon Smith, dec'd., Gabriel as Gdn. of minor's, Solomon, Augustin, Anthony. Suit of John Kirby & wife, & Henry Smith.

P. 57a: David Hall estate to be settled.

P. 57a: Vice Ballew, illegitimate son, Wilson, 8 yrs., bound to Mary Laughhorn, trade of "saddleary."

P. 58a: James Willis, 11, bound to Isaac Cox, trade of weaving.

P. 61: Laurence Arney's minors: George, David, Lourence bound to Robert Johnson, Nailler, as Gdn.

P. 61a: Mary Elrod's illegitimate child, 5 years, bound to Charles McDowell, Jr., named Wm.

P. 62a: John McGuire's surrender of indentures of John Moore, bound to him.

P. 62a: John Dellinger, dec'd., year's allowance to widow.

P. 65: Heirs of Solomon Smith: Henry Smith, John Curby & Wife vs. James Penly & Wife & Others, heirs.

P. 72: Barbara Moll, Mark Brittain, Phillip Pitts, Jacob Moll, deed to John Moll & Peter Moll, May 23, 1808.

OCTOBER, 1808, p. 73a: George Deal, dec'd., children: John, Alexander, Mary, Henry, Ebby, Matilda, to be brought to court.

P. 74: Thomas Wisemen estate to be settled.

P. 74a: Joseph Patton as gdn. of Brooks Smallwood.

P. 77: John Poteet estate, Adm. widow Phebe & John C. Alron. Year's allowance to widow.

P. 77a: Mary Ann Peersons, bastard by Robert McClewrath.

P. 79a: Will of Thomas Williams proved.

P. 79a: Will of Richard Gibbs proved.

P. 81a: James Marcus, orphan at George Michael Redding's, Smokey Cr., & Rebaccah Marcus, orphan, at Wm. Bradsher's, & Diannah Crook's 3 children, Polly, Nancy, Elisabeth to be at next court.

JULY, 1809, p. 86: Polly Frazier's illegitimate son for next court.

P. 86a: William Tucker's will proved.

P. 87: Hiram Durken(?), 10 bound to 21 to Wm. Gibbs to be taught (etc.)

45

P. 87: Ambrose Hoard estate; Adm. granted Peggy Hoard& William Sherrill. Year's allowance to widow.

P. 90: John Petillo, dec'd, heirs: Elizabeth Petillo (now Currethers); Susannah Petillo (now Lytle); Littleton, Millington & John Petillo. Robert Currethers & wife; Thomas Lytle & Wife vs Heirs of John, dec'd.,: re: division of land.

P. 93: Miles Higgins to Wm., John & Edmond Young, deed of 250 a. Sept.15, 1807, pr.Joel Higgins.

P. 94: Joseph Dobson to Westly Young & Wife, Agnes, deed of 700 a., Jan.1, 1803.

APRIL, 1809: p. 95a: George Carter estate Adm. granted to Wid., Nancy. Year's allowance.

P. 96: James Marcus, 9, orphan, bound to Wm. Ryel to learn wagon making.

JULY, 1809, P. 109 & 109a: Chilren of colour bound.

P. 109a: Thos. Higdon estate to be settled.

P. 110a: Wm. Walton Admrs.

P. 111: Peggy Jackson's bastard by Alexander Hopkins.

P. 115: Thos. Higdon, dec'd., Jean as heirs of, about her dowery.

P. 119: Thomas Curtis' to Benj. Curtis, deed gift of property, "March 2, 1809," pr.by Joshua Curtis.

OCTOBER, 1809, p. 120: James Durham estate, Adm. granted Mastin Durham. Year's allowance to widow.

P. 120: Samuel Hoofman (Hoffman) will pr., widow, Dice.

P. 120a: Thos. Green, dec'd., to settle with Richard, Exer. of.

P.120a: Ruth Green, 10, orphan, bound to Jonathan Boon

P. 122a: Paul Anthony settlement with Executor.

P. 124a: John Brown, dec'd., Thos. Brown, Adm.

P. 124a: Wm. & David Cosby, sons of John Cosby who left his family, to be at next court.

P. 131a: Ally Smith, Barnet Decker, George Smith, deed of 100 a. to Henry Bailey, Sept 20, 1808, pr.Reuben Coffey.

JANUARY, 1810, p. 132a: William Probert will proved by Elijiah Patton & John Connoway.

P. 132a: Mary (?)Probert will proved by Jeremiah Walker, with Exrs. John Morrison & Elijah Patton.

P. 133a: Jean Reed, dec'd; Adm. to David Montgomery.

P. 134: GriefLindsey's guardian Lab(am) Estes to settle.

P. 134: John Dockry estate settlement with Adm. Wm. Webster.

P. 134: John Causby's son, David, 10, bound to Robert McElrath.

P. 136: John & Mary Hall given aid as old persons.

P. 138a: Grace Bailey's son, now with John Green, to next court.

P. 138a: Two boys, sons of Dickson, at Simpkens next court.

P. 138a: John Brown's estate to be settled with Adms.

P. 138a: Elizabeth Fox's son John, at Beverly Clark's, next court.

P. 139: Samuel Hoofman (Hoffman), dec'd., year's allowance to widow.

P. 139: Archibald Miller, 10 yr, 2 mos, bound to John McGuire.

P. 139: Widow Durham's year's allowance.
P. 139: Paul Anthony's settlement of estate returned.

P. 139: William Elrod, 6 yrs.& 3 mos, bound formerly to Charles McDowell, Jr., now to John McGuire.

P. 143: Antony & Rebecca Walton, 400 a. deeded to Phillip Johnson, Jan. 6, 1810, pr. Daniel Johnson.

P. 143: Benjamin & Ebberella Vickers deeded 150 a. to James Kearly, April 26, 1809, pr. Ebberella Vickers.

APRIL, 1810, p. 147: Elizabeth Pearcey will proved.

P. 148: Thomas Wiseman, dec'd., children: Glover Davenport Wiseman, Martin Wiseman, Dorothy Wiseman, Ann Wiseman's Gdn.

P. 148a: Thomas Higdon estate to be settled with Jean Higdon.

P. 149: Orphans, Wm., John, Ahab, & unknown Girl to next court.

P. 149a: Wm. Pearson, dec'd., year's allowance to widow.

P. 154a: David McDaniel & John Henecy vs Adms. of John Hughes.

P. 154a: Henry Hicks, Susannah Hicks, Sarah Wilson, ThomasBotts, Matthew Botts, 300 a. to Seth Botts Apr. 9, 1808, pr. Moses Collins.

P. 155a: Deed gift George Sealy, Sr., to George, Jr., for Negroes, June 17, 1808, pr. Wm. Jones.

JULY, 1810, p. 156a: Robert Hodge will proved.

P. 156a: Benjamin Allison will with Thomas Allison Executor.

P. 156a: Joseph Wilson, dec'd., Adm. granted Mary, Widow of & to Joseph Young.

P. 157: Year's allowance granted widow of Joseph Wilson.

P. 157a: Jacob Beck will proved. John & Elizabeth Beck, Exrs.

P. 158: Joseph Puit will proved.

P. 158a: Banjamin Bracket, dec'd., & Adm. granted widow, Ann Bracket.   Year's allowance to widow.

P. 160a: Wm. Pierson, dec'd., Adm. granted Susann Pierson & Michael Killion.

P. 160a: John Pearson estate and Adm.

P. 160a: Joseph Finley, orphan, to be at the next court.

P. 162: Mary Hartly, 15 yrs. 3 mos, bound to Ann Horshaw.

P. 162: Samuel Hoofman (Hoffman) will: Adm. granted to Conrad Hiletbrand, Jr., & John Martin.

P. 167a: Henry Miller, Sr., to Henry Miller, Jr., 162 a., July 23.

OCTOBER, 1810, p. 168: Robert Hodge will, with Susannah Hodge, Exrx.

P. 168a: James Henderson estate, with Adm. John Henderson.

P. 168a: Jacob Winkler estate to be settled.

P. 168a: Joseph Wilson, dec'd., Adm. to sell personal property.

P. 169: Nelly Lunceford's child, Nancy, 1 year 7 mos-bound to Thomas Capehart.

P. 169a: John Blackwell, gdn., to his children, Nancy, John H., Hamilton, Fanny, James Blackwell.

P. 176: John Good fined for bastardy.

P. 171: Crawford Wilson, dec'd., Wm. Wilson granted Adm.

P. 172: Elizabeth Cantrel's son at Wm. Mackey's, Toe River, to be at next court.

P. 172: Rody, Lida & George Vaughon living with Thomas Franklin to be at next court.

P. 172: Daniel, Samuel, John, George & Elisha Brown, orphans of John Brown, dec'd., living with Abby Brown on South Fork, to be at next court.

P. 172: Three Dickson children at Wm. Ainsworth's to be at next court.

P. 174a: Alexander McCombs of N. Y. State owns 89,000 acres in Burke Co., on Wilkes Co. line, head of Watauga.

P. 175a: John, Stephen, & Reuben Webb, 66 a. to James Webb, 1809, pr. Thomas Coleman.

(END C.R.14. 037)

48

Not read further except for a very valuable family record of the
Waightstill Avery - Caleb Poor line: April 1813.

p. 270: Polly Mira Avery, daughter of Waightstill Avery, m. (1)
Caleb Poor and had seven children as follows:

1- Edwin Poor, b. July 2, 1797
2- Polly Asgood, b. April 29, 1799
3- Leah Caroline, b. Dec. 17, 1800
4- Phoebe, b. Aug. 21, 1803
5- Wm. Probert, b. Jan. 19, 1806
6- Isaac Thomas, b. Feb. 20, 1808
7- Milton (?), b. Jan. 3, 1812

Divorce occurred in 1813; second marriage to Jacob Summey.

p. 287, Caleb Poor vs. Waightstill Avery for children.

(C.R.14.037)

Comment:
In reference to file numbers of Court Minutes, reference numbers may
have changed, since this research was completed many years ago.

Page
1 - John Parsons vs. Abraham Reece, Jan 20, 1783.
2 - Wm. Wofford & Lucia Spradling. Evidence to support charge,
     John Spradling, Wm. Johnson, Thos. Wommack. Sept, Court 1782.
     Jurors: John Walker, Wm. Penland, Jno. Blanton, John Dysart,
     William Willson, Wm. Sumter, Robert ----(?), Joseph Steel,
     Jonathan Hampton, George Brown , David Dickey, James Reed,
     Wm. Moore, ____(?_)(Not Legible), Sub. Sept. 3, 1782, State vs. above,
     returned to March 1783 term.   Bail: Wm. Spradling, Joseph
     Dobson, CSC.
3 - Mary Stuart vs. Will Moore re: slave, Jenny, 1780.
4 - Sub. to Sher. of Surry Co. for John Hare & James Ringgold behalf
     Jos. Winston, Esq., suit of John Blanton, Sept. 17, 1784.
5 - John Kemp vs. David Moore; Jas. Holland & Scroop Egerton, secs. of
     Rutherford Co., March 10, 1787 by Jon. Hampton, Sher., April 13,
     1787. Wits.: Elias Alexander, Wm. Twitty, Benj. Hider, And. Hampton.
6 - Will Gilbert vs. Will McCafferty of Meck. Co., Sept 10, 1784.
7 - William Walton, Sen., Notice of intention to take dep. on Tues.,
     Sept 18(1798) at James Britain's in Buncom(be) Co. of Jos. Tucker
     in suit of Walton vs, Wm. Dever. (signed) William Walton, Sher.
7 - Dep. of Abraham Levy, lawful age: "in case of Wm. Walton vs. Wm.
Dever...sd. Dever left fences in bad repair...resided on land.
          Taken at Pub. Whs. for Ins. Tob. at town of New Market, 1796."
8 - Bail Bond: Wm. McCafferty of Mecklenburg. Sec. Joseph Moore,
     Joseph Graham, Sher. of Mecklenburg Co. assigns to William Gilberts,
     pltff. Jan 20, 1785.
9 - Order to pay Benj. Knox & Adam Mack (other illeg., undated.)
10 - Mary Stewart vs William Moore, Esq., Sher, Adm. of estate of James
     (Price, Pierce ?) dec'd, March 1, 1786.
11 - James Holland, Antony Dicky & John Hampton, all of Rutherford Co.,
     secs. in suit of David Miller vs, Holland, Aug, 1784.
12 - Elizabeth Hogan vs. Wm. Duckworth bond:Pat Henecy.   Test: Jno.
Patton; Sher, Feb. 2, 1785.
13 - Dep. of Joel Ponton(?) in case of Wm. Walton vs. Wm. Dever, 59 a.,
Jan 1, 1790, at Pub. Whs. for Ins. Tobacco, Newmarket, Amherst Co., Va.
14 - Will Graham vs. Will Hill of Lincoln Co., Sept, 2, 1784.
15 - Elizabeth Hogan vs. John Creswell & wife, Jane, William & Jon.
     Duckworth, Sept. 1, 1784.
16- James Greenlee vs. Wm. Puet(?), platt & survey by Wm. Tate, Chb.
     Wm. Madaris & Sol. Crisp, 1784.
17 - Dep. of John Bridges & Phelis Walker re: controversy of William
     Bridges & Elizabeth Lloyd. Wit: David McKissick, John Steel,
     March 9, 1785.
18 - John Woods vs. Zacharieh Estes of Washington Co. (Tenn.), Nov. 2, 1789.
19 - Sub: to Tillman & John Walton in behalf of William, Sr. vs. William
     Deaver. March 2, 1797.
20 - Francis Price vs. John Bates of Lincoln Co., Sept. 10, 1784.

P. 21. To Samuel Hollansworth: behalf of William Deaver, Sr., March 3, 1797.

P. 22: Robert Miller vs. Andrew Taylor, July 4, 1799. Wits:: John Massey, Mark Mass(e)y, Henry Davis, Moses Ferguson.

P. 23.: Dep. of Henry Bibb, Thos. Fortune, John West in Amherst Co., (Va.) (Walton ‾ Dever Case). Nov. 1796.

P. 24: John Goodbread vs. Hugh Greenwood, 1785, Tar paper,

P. 25: Etheldred Sutton sub. & dys., Camden Co., S.C., before Isaac Alexander, J.P. In 1780 he was at John Parson's in Burke Co., N.C. re: mareof Abraham Reece, Jan 1, 1787.

P. 27: Subs. and Wits. to be examined in case of Lewis Bryan, Nathan Bryan, Emmanuel Simmons, Edwrd. Whitty, Kiteral Mimdone(?), Abraham Bisset Simmons, Wm. Randol, Esq., Justices of Jones Co., in controv. of Waightstill Avery, pl$ff, & sd. Justice deft., Sept. 10, 1783. Test. of Lewis Bryan by Frederick Harget & John Isler, J.P, of Jones Co., Jan 10, 1784. re: Taxes of Avery in Jones Co. Test. of Wm. Orme and Henry Marret, Jones Co.   ·

P. 28: State vs. George French of Lincoln Co., March, 1783. Alfred Moore, Att'y. Gen., assault on John Bradley of Burke Co.

P. 29: State vs. Isaac Martin, assault on W. Bryley, March term, 1783.

P. 31: James Greenlee vs. Elias Alexander, Dep. of John Lane & Joseph McDowell, June 19, 1785. J.P. Chas. McDowell, John Hardin.

P. 32: Thomas Camp, bail by Jones Hix & Richard Haney, Oct.11, 1784.

P. 33: Admrs. of Peter Cosner (Costner) vs. Robert Smith. Dep. Edward Hunter on April 4, 1787 at Michael Hoyl(e) where David Ellott, Robert Smith & others "came with Const., armed with guns and swords...came for their right , deprived by Michael Hoyl & Mary Cosoner (Costner), took them to Thomas McGills."

P. 34: Henry Dellinger vs. Robert Smith, March 10, 1787.

P. 35: Thomas Gourlay vs. Jacob Boyles, Sept. 9, 1796.

P. 36: Elizabeth Hogan vs. John Duckworth, bond: Thomas McTaggart, Feb. 3, 1785.

P. 37: Lincoln Co., Oct 25, 1782, prom. note of John Sloan . Wit: William Beatty, Arthur Graham.

P. 41: State vs. John Thompson & John Walbert, Wit: John Anderson, Sam'l. King, David Miller, 1783.

P. 43: William Walton to William Deaver who will take dep. of Edward Tilmer in Union Co., S.C. Feb. 1799.

P. 44: Sub. to Benjamin Woodson & William McCullock to examine wits. Edward Tillman "of Walton" vs. Deaver.

P. 45: John Bradburn vs. John Spencer, Mar 7, 1801. Bail: Robert Craig, John Jones, Jos. Burton, John Spears for Wm. Byrnes, March, 1799.

P. 48: Wm. Walton & Wm. Deaver, narrative case. Deaver in 1771 & Jan 1772 in Amherst Co., Va. in Walnut Cove of Rucker's Run. Feb. 2, 1799. (& see p. 56 narrative case.)

P. 49: Elizabeth Lloyd vs. Wm. Bridges, John Bridges, wit: Sept. 1785 term.

P. 50: Wm. Graham vs. John Bradburn, wit: Jacob Collins, March term, 1786.

P. 51: John Parsons vs. Abraham Reese, Sept. 3, 1782. Two Papers.

P. 51: John Blanton vs. Winston. Wit: Minor Smith of Winnsboro, Dst. of Cambden, S.C., 1784.

P. 54: Joseph Ashworth vs. David Miller, Mar. 1794 term.

P. 55: John Taylor vs. Joseph Dickson, wit: George Lampkin, Esq. Sept. 1, 1783.

P. 56: State vs. Thos. Miles of Rutherford Co., evidence by Wm. Gilbert, Ben Cleveland, Geo. Black, Sam'l Hunter, 1783.

P. 61: State vs. Laz. Tilley of Wilkes Co. by Benj. Coffee, March term, 1786.

P. 65: Jacob Beck vs. Stephen Potts. Dep. of James Potts, Jr. (Stephen, his father) to Ga... Michael Engle... Matthew Troy, Esq., March term, 1786.

P. 66: Cosner's Admrs. vs. David Elliott & Robert Smith, narrative case. 2 papers, March term, 1785.

UNPAGINATED:

Elias Morgan vs. Scrope Edgerton, Sarah Battle, Mumford Wilson & John Forgay, Exrs. of John Battle of Sussex Co., Va. who was in Rutherford Co, Jan. 4, 1774. Att'y. for pltff: Waightstill Avery.

Lincoln County, Sept 11, 1785. John Bridges examined in behalf of Wm. Bridges. Controversy: Elizabeth Lloyd, pltf. John Bridges, " about yr. 1759 or 1760 land now in dispute between Lloyd and Bridges... he held... as his claim " with his consent Wm. Hannah settled, "staid" few months till drove by Indians & never returned. After some years dispute between deponent & John Lloyd, lived further up creek...bounds...compromised by him and J.L. ... strong ridge 54p. above the improvement....was to divide them... settled by John Lyons... he sold ... to Henry Hill (who) staid about a year.. sold to Lyons again, 3a. cleared...Lyons sold to Elisha Baldwin (who) possessed it for 1 yr. & some months & deponent purch. it for 3 cows & calvs (Calves) ...Charles Walker & John Bridges, Jr., with deponent..not John Lawrence." Stephen Steel, Daniel McKissick, J.P.

John (X) Bridges

Elizabeth Lloyd vs. Wm. Bridges, Sept 5, 1785.
Sub. to John Bridges & Phillis Walker.

William Graham vs. John Barber, narrative case, Sept 1785.

William Gilbert vs, William Graham. Bond. James Holland, agent for Gilbert, John Smith & BenjaminOrmand, July 7, 1784.

William Walton, Sr., vs. Wm. Deaver, Sr., Mar. 1 1795. Another paper of Walton on Sept.13, 1796 to take dep. of Zacharies Taliaferro., Thomas Fortin (Fortune ?), John Pontin, John West,Abraham Seay & Henry Bibb at Publ. Whse. at Amherst, Va., in New Market.

James Howard dep, to Wm. Threadgill, J.P., called upon at "Superara"Court at Salsberey" in March, 1799 as wit to note of Reuben Smithers to Spencer Humphres, July 2, 1784. Two papers.

Benjamin Britt vs. David Barr, March 7, 1801)?),

William Walton vs. William Dever , Sen. Bond: Wm., Jr., James Hughey, H. Sher., Aug 17, 1795. Buncombe Co.

State vs. Adam Moore of Rutherford Co., ... paid Joseph White in counterfeit gold, Sept, 1784 Court.

State vs, James Blair, Sept•1783 court.

State vs. Jesse Gullet pros. by David Lorance, Wit: Agner Lorance, March term, 1783.

State vs. David McLosky, George Beneson & Alexander Bailey, Sept.2, 1782. Wits: John Pierson, Hannah Pierson, Averalla Clements, William Price, Thos. Kennedy.

State vs. John Camp of Rutherford Co. Wit: David Miller, William Grant, George Black, Sept 1782.

State vs. Will Witherer(?), pros. by Catherine Shuford. Wit: Conrad Rudolph, Charles McDowell, Sept.1782 term.

State vs. Andrew Hampton, Sept,4, 1784.

Alex. Carson vs. Samuel Greenlee, March 10, 1784.

Dep. of John Sigmon, March 7, 1787, in Dec.1784 at Michael Engles in Lincoln Co...saw Stephen Pots (Potts) deliver gelding. Dep. of John Lorance March 7, 1787 at Jacob Beck's in Burke Co. & saw Pots(Potts) & 3 unknown persons.

Thomas Gourley vs Jacob Boyles, narrative case, July 23, 1795. Waightstill Avery vs. Snead Davis, 1785.

John Bauldwin vs. Jesse Coffee, narrative case, March, 1786.

Jacob Beck vs. Stephen Potts, narrative case, Sept., 1786.

Will Graham vs. John Barber, Sept. 1785.

W. Graham Notice, on Nov 22, next at house of Wm. Brown near McCord's ferry on Congares in S.C., that John Carl Adams " and others" examined.

Camden Dist, S.C., Nov. 22, 1785:

J.P.,R.O. Brown for Rich Land(Richland) Co., ded. Joseph Dobson, C.C., Morgan Sup.Ct, Burke Co., N. C. to examine John Carroll Adams on contro. between Wm. Graham, Esq., pltff. & John Barber, deft.

March term, 1787, to James Blasingaim to examine wit: Jeremiah Smith in behalf of Wm. Graham & John Barber, deft.

Greenville Co., S.C., Aug 10, 1787, Jeremiah Smith, exam. re: Wm. Graham & John Barber... horse that James McAfee delivered to Graham as pay.

53

Samuel Oxford, 300 a., Burke Co. above Barnet Stevens, Oct. 11, 1783 (1-170)

Thomas Waggoner, 100a., Burke Co., Beaverdam Cr. & Little Cr. on Catawba River. ... John Waggoner line ... Lockerman's ... Pettys ...1780.(1-258)

Henry Pope, grant #907, 100 a., Burke Co., Lyles Cr., joining Wm. Simons & Devault Hunsucker, Meeks Hafner, Wm. Whittenburg, Aug. 1787. (1-335/6)

William Deal, grant #908, 180 a., Burke Co., Macklin's Cr., beg Geo. Minges ... along Phifers ... Cowans ... 1787. (1-335)

Wm. Bost, 1820, grant #249, Burke Co., Clark's Cr. ... John Cline ... Henry Propst's ... John Hartner's ... Gilbreath Falls ... Weaver's ... Smyers ... Meeting House Rd. ... Boston Cline's line ... Mar. 4, 1780. (1-464)

John Houk & wife, Catherine, "formerly Burke," Mar. 22, 1786, to Jacob Weaver, 226 a., (granted Oct., 11, 1783.... E. Jacobs Fork of Catawba R, ... Henry Whitner's corner. Wit: Martin Gronsmer(?). (2-22)

Geo. Pope of Burke (Geo. sig.), May 24, 1779 to Samuel Steele of Burke, 320 a., Elk Cr. ... George Smith ... (granted Bostian Cline, Feb 28, 1755, conveyed to Pope, Nov 15, 1771). Wit: Jos. Steel, Jacob Willcox. (2-543)

John Bradburn "in Burke Co." to Joseph Horton of Lincoln Co., June 1, 1787 ... Hills Iron works. William Sherrill, John Reed, Thomas Farley. (2-309)

(Vols. 4 and 5 are lost.)

Henry Pope, grant #191, 50 a. in Burke Co, Lyles Cr. ... Fred Shooks ... Melcar Hafner's ... Shooks ... Nov. 9, 1784. (6-76)

Paul Anthony of Burke to John Smier (Smyer) of Lincoln Co., 210 a. (granted April 28, 1768), S. br. of Clark's Cr. ... Crowders... Neaves-(?) ... April 30, 1790. Wit: Paul Antoni, Johannes Bass, and Jacob Starr. (16-12)

Paul Anthony of Burke to John Smier of Lincoln Co., 200 a. (granted April 25, 1767) ... Clerk's (Clark's) Cr. Br. ... William Bost , Bostian Cline ... Wit: Johannes Bast(Bost), Jacob Starz, Andrew Stockinger, April 30, 1790. (16-35)

John Horse (Haas) of Burke Co. ... (no particulars copied). (16-98)

Reuben Petty late of Rowan Co., 1778, Now Burke ... (no particulars copied.) (16-161)

John Cunningham of Lincoln Co. from Thomas Lyttle (of Burke Co., ... land. (no particulars copied.) (16-383)

John Brown & Sarah of Burke Co. to Henry Hill, 150 a. grant of "Dec. 30 in 16th year of Independence." Wit: Isaac Lowrance, Mary Edwards. (17-430)

Simon & George Hass (Haas) of Lincoln Co., to Jacob Lutz, Sr.,
Apr 1, 1796, land in Burke Co., E. Clark's Cr. ... Henry Bullinger's
Mill Br. ... Hasses Br. ... Bills Br. ... Jacob Eagnor ... Jos. Steele's
... Nich. Fry ... Jacob Lutz ... Rudolph Conrad ... Lewis Huyard's ...
granted jointly to Simon George & John Hass, Oct.11, 1783, Burke Co.,
John Hass, conveyed his part to Simon & George, May 30, 1781.(ger. sigs.)
(18-116)

John Bradburn, Esq. of Burke Co. to Conrad Waggoner, wheel wright
of Lincoln Co., 1794. ... Clark's Ford to McMullin's old place ...
Thomas Farley. (pat. #244, Aug 7, 1787). Wit: Michael Wagoner, 2 ger.
sigs.. (18-239)

John Smith of Burk(e) Co., planter, from Wm.Chambers ... 200 a.
1796 ... Indian Cr. ... Jacob Bullinger's & Bonhanes, Warrant #568,
Oct 13, 1795. ent. Jan. 8, 1793, granted Chambers, 1796. (18-574)

Thos. Litten of Burke Co. to Elijah Litten of Lincoln Co., 1802,
part tract granted Thos's. mother, #476, Oct 28, 1782. (21-187)

Samuel Oxford of Burke Co. to Uriah Davis of Iredell Co, 1801,
land on Matchet Cr. of S. Catawba R., grant of Dec 21, 1800   Wit: .
John Oxford, James Warren, Adam Coon. (21-193)   (NOTE:Uriah Davis' dau.,
m. James Warren & went to BumcombeCo. by 1804 as did Jon. Oxford.)
(22-41; 23-206)

Thomas Fisher to George Fisher, June 29, 1803, 80 a. farm in
Burke Co. on Falling Cr. (granted Joshua Perkins, 1790, & conveyed to
Thomas Fisher June 4, 1796). Wit: Joseph Fisher, Henry Hallman.(21-579)

Same to same - (Gr. Perkins 1787) same date. (21-583)

Phillip Killian of Burke Co., 1805, grant of 1800 sold. (22-365)

Michael Zimmerman of Burke Co, 1808 to David Whitener, Sr., 104
a. on S. Fork ... (granted Oct 16, 1796). (25-114)

Samuel Oxford, Jr. of Burke Co., 118 a. great Catawba R. Wit:
Jacob Oxford. (25-87) -Jan. 20, 1801 to Jonathan Oxford of Lincoln Co. -

George Deal, Sr., to Geo. Deal, Jr., 173 a. Mar. 21, 1815,
(grant to George, Sr. "then in Burke Co." Mar 14, 1780). Wit: Peter
Hoke, William Deel (Deal). (28-319)

Michael Zimmerman of Burke Co. to ShellWhitener of Lincoln Co.,
May 28, 1825 ... Hopps Cr. of S. fork of Hunsucker cor. (gr. John
Shell 1789). Wit: John Yoder, John Yount. (33-167)

"Zimmerman of Burke": David, John, Jacob, Ann, Elizabeth Sr. & Jr.
to Michael Zimmerman, Jr. Nov 19, 1825, our undivided parts decended
to us the legal reps. of Michael, Sr., dec'd., 100 a. Wit: Geo.
Bowman, Abraham Hauk (Houck). (33-173)

Thomas & Sarah James of Lincoln Co., 1830, heirs of Conrad Grider,
land on Elk Shoal Cr. Wit: Hugh Warren, (34-83)

Col. Hugh Brevard will in Burke Co. July 1781 Session, dau. Jane,
her son Hugh Brevard Stephenson. (34-267)

George Deal of Burke Co., 1829. (34-598)

Heirs of Wm. Deal, May 21, 1838 ... wid. Mary. one of heirs was
George Deal of Burke Co. (37-497)

Michael Keller of Burke Co. to John & George Yount of Lincoln Co.,
210 a. Apr 14, 1813, W. Catawba R. ... Cowan's Corner...John Mathewson
... up R. ..., part of grant #20002, Dec 20, 1803. Wit:William Heanan,
John Keller. (25-560)

Many of these deed abstracts are incomplete, since at the time of reasearch for my ancestors, I had not planned a Burke County, N.C., book. No index on microfilm was available at the time and many hundreds of papers were read.

EWH

1786 - 1787 CENSUS

The Census of 1786 as reported by Walter Clark in The State Records of North Carolina, Volume XVIII, pages 433-434, January 2, 1787:

"Mr. Wyatt Hawkins, from the Committee to whom was referred the returns made from the different counties in pursuant of an Act entitled: 'An Act ascertaining the number of white and black Inhabitants and the citizens of every age and condition in the State' ". Reported that due returns are made from about eighteen counties....."
Burke County was not among the counties named.
Returns for white males from 21 years to 60, white males under 21 and over 60, white females of every age, blacks from 12 to 60, and blacks from 12 and over 50.
Mr. Hawkins further stated, "..Partial returns are made from about twenty-five other counties, which said returns are so promiscuously thrown together, and being irregularly drawn, occasions them to be in so confused a manner as to be almost unintelligible to your Committee, neither is the names of the counties expressed, which has caused your Committee to state them as follows...".
And, again, Burke County was not listed among the twenty-five other unknown counties. In this last arrangement the categories were slightly different: white males from 21 years to 60, white males under 20 and over 60, white females of every age, blacks from 12 to 50, blacks under 12 and over 50.
In the 1784-1787 State Census Returns (File GO-130) the following Burke County militia captains in 1787 gave the number of "Souls" in their districts: Vance, Carson (by Jos. McDowell), John Bradburn, and William Neill.
John Bradburn, for instance: (211) "white females of all sorts and conditions." The other captains were less blunt about the females, merely stating "white females of every age" or "of all ages," as on the returns mentioned by Wyatt Hawkins.
Captain William Neill, was the only one of the above men to have even a partial list of names preserved, under date of April 5, 1787. This appears to be part of the Tenth Company. (see 1790 Census).

Captain's Neill's list is as follows: (April 5, 1787)

.... Wofford	2	4	5	3
.... Ainsworth	1	2	4	3
John Sisco. Sr.	1	3	4	0
John Sisco, Jr.	1	0	3	0
...ob Sisco	1	0	2	0
...n Van(n)	1	1	1	0
...ha Oakley	1	0	2	0
...... Crowell	1	2	4	0
.... Wilson	1	0	1	0
...... Wilson	1	2	6	0
... ...dlock	1	3	3	0
... (Wilson ?) 1 son)	1	4	5	0
....mas Young	1	3	1	0
William Phillips	1	4	3	0
.... lilah McFalls	0	3	1	0
Frederick Miller	2	1	0	0
James Lee	1	3	2	0
William Moodie	1	4	1	0
......es Bennett	1	2	2	0
.... Hensley	1	3	2	0
.... Hensley	1	3	4	0
.... Hensley	1	2	4	0
.........instaff	2	0	2	0
....	1	2	4	0
....taker	1	2	4	0
......mas Bright	0	5	4	0
.... Hensley	2	3	1	0
.... Pickeral	1	3	4	0
....e Raddock	1	4	7	0
....ert Turner	1	2	4	0
Samuel Gray	1	2	3	0
Jonas Griffith	1	2	4	0
George Holbrok	2	0	6	0
David McCraken	1	3	5	0
Thomas Baker	1	0	1	0
John Armstrong	0	5	4	0
Harold Gillespie	0	2	2	0
Richard Jacks	1	2	5	0
Tho.... ....arnard	1	0	1	0
....tgomery	2	2	2	1
....ling	0	2	3	0
....way	1	1	1	0
....right	1	1	1	0

(Differs slightly from G. O. 130)

1790 CENSUS

Three versions of the 1790 Census are as follows:

(1) Vol. XXVI, State Records of North Carolina, by Walter Clark, 1905. See following pages for this census.

(2) First Census of the United States, Federal, 1908.

(3) Microfilm of the original 1790 Census from The National Archives, Washinton, D. C.

All of the above may differ, sometimes radically, however in the files of Huggins will be found all three census records for a comparison in the sometimes "impossible search" for your ancestor.

See the following pages in order of appearance on this page.

No names from the above three census records will appear in the index of this book.

STATE RECORDS. By: 319.

Walter Clark, 1905

FIRST FEDERAL CENSUS, 1790—Continued.

BURKE COUNTY.

COUNTY, CITY. TOWN. PARISH, HUNDRED. ETC.	NAMES OF HEADS OF FAMILIES.	Free white males of sixteen years and upwards, including heads of families	Free white males under sixteen years.	Free white females, including heads of families.	All other free persons.	Slaves.
BURKE COUNTY	Jos. Dobson, Jr.	3	3	5	..	1
	Joshua Young	1	5	4	..	..
	George Davidson	1	3	1	..	1
	Matthew Washburn.	1	1	1	..	..
	Josiah Bradshaw	1	1	2	.	..
	Peter Stroud	1	5	2	.	3
	Peter Stroud. Jr.	1	.	1	..	..
	Jesse Stroud	1	3	1	..	..
	David Washburn	2	..	6	..	..
	Drury Washburn.	1	1	2	..	..
	Wm. Patton	1	.	2	..	..
	Sam Patton.	1	3	2	..	..
	Jas. McWilliams.	1	2	5	..	..
	Precilla McCracon.	1	2	5	..	1
	Robert Reed	1	4	3	..	1
	Jno. Trammell	1	3	4	..	..
	Jos. Brown.	4	..	5	..	..
	Jas. McDowell	1	2	2	..	2
	Wm. Cathey	3	4	5	..	3
	And'w McClure.	3	5	5	..	..
	Wm. Durr	3	2	4	..	3
	Thos. Welch	1	3	1	..	1
	Tho. H. Hannah	1	..	1	..	..
	Cathr'n Dickson	1	1	5	..	..
	John Melony	1	..	1	..	..
	Francis McClure	3	..	4	..	..
	Jno. Jones	1	3	3	..	..
	Rhoda Edenton	2	5	2	..	..
	Wm. Collet	1	2	2	..	..
	Thos. Bibo	1	1	3	..	..
	Mish Burchfield.	1	1	4	.	5
	John McDowell.	1	1	1	..	1
	Sterling Carol.	1	..	1	..	..
	George Carol.	1	1	8	..	..
	Jos. McDowell, Jun.	1	2	1	..	9
	Jno. Carson	2	5	2	..	12
	Jno Welsh, Sen	3	3	5	..	..
	Wat. O'Neal	2	1	3		..
	Morris Webster.	1	2	4	..	..
	Jon'thn McPeters	1	1	2	..	..
	Jos. McPeters.	1	3	5	..	..
	Wm. Plumley	3	1	3	..	..
	Nicholas Thorps	3	3	3	..	..
	Jacob Shuke	1	6	3	..	..
	Jno. Davidson	3	5	6	..	6
	Wm. Neal	4	1	4	..	..

First Federal Census, 1790—Continued.

COUNTY, CITY, TOWN, PARISH, HUNDRED, ETC.	NAMES OF HEADS OF FAMILIES	Free white males of sixteen years and upwards, including heads of families.	Free white males under six teen years.	Free white females, includ ing heads of families.	All other free persons.	Slaves.
BURKE COUNTY	Elijah Patten............	1	2	6	..	2
	Mary Hobs.	..	..	2	..	..
	Pounce Mitchell	1	2	2	..	..
	Sam'l Inman..	1	2	1	..	..
	Henry Inman	1	..	1	..	..
	Stephen Plumley........	1	1	2	..	..
	Henry Williams	1	1	3	..	..
	Sam'l Stout.	2	5	3	..	..
	Jno. Reed.....	1	..	3	..	..
	Jas. Neall.............	1	4	2	..	1
	Abram Wiggins.	1	2	2	..	1
	Aron Britton.	1	..	2	..	..
	Martin Brandon	2	4	7	.	..
	George Cathey	2	3	4	..	5
	Chas. Brown..	1	..	3	..	..
	Marget Cathey	..	1	4	..	..
	And'w Neall............	1	1	4	..	..
	Wm. Lewis	1	2	4	..	..
	Wm. Kelton	1	4	6	..	7
	Abram Floid	1	3	2	..	..
	Jno. McGonigle.	1	1	3	..	..
	Francis Posey.	1	4	2	..	..
	Thos. Wilson.......	5	..	2	..	12
	Robert Hill........ ...	1	1	1	..	..
	Rose Rees	1	3	5	..	..
	Ben Davis.............	5	3	4	...	..
	Dav'd Culberson......	1	3	4	.	..
	Tobias Bright........ ..	1	1	1	..	..
	Robt. Blakeley..	1	1	6	..	..
	Dav'd Washburn........	1	..	2	..	..
	Jno. Jetton.	1	1	4	..	2
	Wm Higgins	3	2	6	..	..
First Company.	Missor Norton	1	3	5	..	..
	Arche Templeton.......	4	2	4	..	..
	Jno. Martin	3	4	5	..	..
	James Hix.	1	1	2	..	..
	Isaac Atwater.....	1	..	..	..	..
	Edw'd Malony..........	1	2	6	..	..
	Ben Davidson....	2	1	9	..	..
	David McBride...... ...	1	2	1	..	..
	Thos. Glass.	2	..	6	..	..
	Henry Glass	1	2	1	..	..
	Wm. McGonigle	1	1	3	..	..
	Jane Logan.	2	1	3	..	..
	Wm. Kelly.	3	5	3	..	..
	Ben Bird, Sen	2	..	2	..	2
	Ben Bird, Jr	1	1	2	..	..
	Tho. Bird	1	3	1	..	.
	Zeb Brevard, Jr.........	1	2	3	..	.

FIRST FEDERAL CENSUS, 1790—Continued.

COUNTY, CITY, TOWN, PARISH, HUNDRED, ETC.	NAMES OF HEADS OF FAMILIES.	Free white males of sixteen years and upwards, including heads of families.	Free white males under sixteen years.	Free white females, including heads of families.	All other free persons.	Slaves.
BURKE COUNTY	Thos. Hemphill........	3	2	7	..	11
	Jno Adkins...........	3	3	6	..	..
	Thos. Ellison..........	1	1	5	..	..
	Henry Ellison..........,	1	4	1	..	..
	Rob. Hambrick........:	1	2	2	..	..
	Zach Thompson........	1	..	1	..	..
	Jno. Pinely...........	1	2	2	..	..
	Thos. Regan...........	2	4	4	..	..
	Luke Vickry...........	1	1	3	..	..
	Ben Ellison	2	2	3	..	.
	Jane Young............	..	2	5	..	..
	Jno. Wilson	1	1	1	..	..
	Jared Smith	1	..	1	..	..
	Augusta Gunter........	1	1	1	..	..
	Jno. McClisky.........	1	..	1	..	..
	Alex Ham Kelly.... ..	1	2	2	..	..
	Charles O'Neal.	1	..	1	..	..
	Mourning Rogers......	2	3	2	..	..
	George Adams.........	1	1	2	..	..
	Wilm Givins...........	1	2	4	..	..
SECOND COMPANY.	John Conally..........	1	3	5	..	10
	Jno. Shell	2	4	4	..	..
	Isaac Martin....	1	6	3	..	..
	Abram Hashaw.........	1	4	3	..	..
	Relekah Dudly,........	..	..	3	..	..
	Marget Martin.........	..	2	1	..	..
	Marget Wagoner	..	..	1	..	..
	Wm. Francum	1	3	3	..	..
	Jno. Francum....... ...	1	..	1	..	..
	Tho. Martin	1	2	4	..	..
	James Moore.	2	..	5 .	..	..
	Wm. Conally...........	2	2	2	..	..
	Abram Fliming....... .	1	3	3	..	8
	Conrod Winkloe.......	1	1	3	..	..
	Jno. Spencer, Jr	1	3	5	..	..
	Zadock Smith.........	1	5	3	..	..
	Jno. Murray...........	1	2	4	..	..
	David Murray	1	5	2	..	..
	Ben Clarke	1	..	1	..	..
	Wm. Bradshaw........	1	..	7	..	..
	Edward Boman....... .	1	..	3	..	3
	Gilbert Boman	1	2	6	..	..
	Jno. Fips	1	3	7	..	..
	Jos. Bellon.	2	..	3	..	..
	Benerly Clarke	1	..	3	..	..
	Stephen Bellon.	1	1	4	..	..
	George Hawk......	2	2	6	..	..
	Ben Tilloteon....... ..	1	2	5	..	..
	Nathan Turner.........	1	1	4	..	..

22 —21

FIRST FEDERAL CENSUS, 1790—Continued.

COUNTY, CITY, TOWN, PARISH, HUNDRED, ETC.	NAMES OF HEADS OF FAMILIES.	Free white males of sixteen years and upwards, including heads of families.	Free white males under sixteen years.	Free white females, including heads of families.	All other free persons.	Slaves.
BURKE COUNTY	Rebekah Francum......	1	1	1	..	..
	Jas. Conally	1	3	4	..	..
	Hugh Conally	1	1	3	..	..
	Jno. Barnhart.	1	2	3	..	..
	Jacob Doreberry........	1	4	3	..	..
	Mich'l Dorebury....	1	3	4	..	..
	Wm. Pain.....	1	2	7	..	..
	Joshua Perkins........	3	3	2	..	..
	Wm. Taylor	1	..	1	..	..
	Henry Stoner..........	3	2	7	..	..
	Wilm Clarke	1	..	4	..	..
	Mich'l Grinslaff........	1	1	4	..	..
	Mary Whitehead.......	..	..	3	..	..
	Thos. Winklirt	1	1	2	..	..
	Adam Sutilmire........	2	3	3	..	..
	Wil'm Bellon..........	1	9	3	..	..
	Henry Master..........	1	1	5	..	..
	Ame Williams.....	1	1	2	..	..
	H. Barton Baker	1	3	5	..	..
	Danl. Brown.....	1	2	4	..	..
	Joseph Berry...........	2	3	6	..	..
	Jas. Berry	1	1	1	..	..
	Jno. Berry...........	1	1	4	..	..
	Lot Berry.............	1	2	2	..	..
	Wm. Baldwin	1	4	4	..	..
	Sam'l Giles	1	2	2	..	..
	Joseph Winkler..... ...	1	1	2	..	..
	Jno. Wilson	1	..	2	..	..
	Thos. Smith	2	1	4	..	..
	Agnes Irwin...........	..	1	1	..	..
	Jas. Martin............	1	1	1	..	..
	Jno. Spencer, Jr........	1	..	3	..	..
	Jas. King	1	1	3	..	..
	Robt. Mason...........	1	1	5	..	..
	Laurenc Marcle	1	1	3	..	..
	Eliza Pack..............	2	..	2	..	..
	Michael Hart	1	3	7	.	..
	Thos. Winkler, Jr.	1	1	2	..	..
	Jno. Gibs......	1	6	3	..	..
	James Baker...........	1	1	4	..	..
	Sherwood Boma.	1	1	2	..	..
	Jno Parmer.............	2	..	..	..	..
	Jno. Pruitt	1	2	5	..	..
	Martin Grider	1	1	6	..	..
	Leah Williams	1	1	2	..	..
	Henry Pruitt	1	..	1	..	..
	James Innes...........	3	2	3	..	..
	Jonah Bradsha..........	1	3	3	..	..
	Mary Grasty......	..	1	3	..	..

FIRST FEDERAL CENSUS, 1790—Continued.

COUNTY, CITY, TOWN, PARISH, HUNDRED, ETC.	NAMES OF HEADS OF FAMILIES.	Free white males of sixteen years and upwards, including heads of families.	Free white males under sixteen years.	Free white females, including heads of families.	All other free persons.	Slaves.
BURKE COUNTY, 2D Co.	George Morgan..........	1	5	2	..	..
THIRD COMPANY.	David Baker....	1	3	3	..	..
	Robt. Penland.........	1	4	6	..	1
	George Penland.........	3	2	5	..	..
	Bartlet Henson.....	3	4	3	..	6
	Ben White.	2	3	3	..	..
	Paul Antony, Sr	2	2	2	..	1
	Jas. Baker	1	..	..	..	..
	Jas. Baxter........	1	4	2	..	..
	Jno. Browning	3	4	5	..	..
	Thos. White, Jr........	1	6	4	..	..
	Ben Parks..............	1	4	4	..	3
	Jacob Antony, Sr......	3	..	4	..	..
	Reuben White..........	1	2	2	..	..
	Jno Baker	1	2	3	..	..
	Eliza Mason	..	..	4	..	..
	Jacob Beck	3	6	5	..	..
	Stephen Rogers.........	1	1	2	..	..
	Philip Shefela...........	2	..	1	..	..
	Wm. Penland	5	2	3	1	..
	Charles Baker	1	..	2	..	..
	Jas. Prichard.......	1	2	7	..	..
	Edw'd Fowler.	2	1	3	..	..
	Thos. Walker	1	..	..	..	..
	Jos. Medley........ ...	1	1	1	..	..
	Thos White, Sr.	1	..	2	..	5
	Simon Sbell	1	..	1	..	..
	Fred Shell	1	3	6	..	..
	Fred Shell, Jr	2	1	2	..	..
	James Sherrile..........	1	1	3	..	..
	David McDaniel.......	1	1	3	..	..
	Thos. Mitchiner........	1	3	2	..	1
	Jno. McGahey..........	1	1	2	..	..
	Arthur Erwin	3	..	2	..	9
	Waight Avery	1	1	6	..	24
	Jno. Colwill Brown.....	1	3	5	..	7
	Jos. Pruitt....	2	4	2	..	7
	George Mosely....	1	2	5	..	2
	Stephen Pirrey..	1	2	5	..	..
	Dan Wright.............	1	..	1	..	..
	Titus Fox	1	2	3	..	..
	George Scott	1	..	7	7	..
	Henry Baker.	1	3	4	..	6
	Jacob Gyer....	2	3	4	..	..
	Alex Cole	1	1	3	..	..
	Jno. Fox	1	3	2	..	..
	Henry Wakefield..	1	2	4	..	2
	Jno. Simpson	1	2	3	..	..
	Alex Harbison	3	3	3	..	..

FIRST FEDERAL CENSUS, 1790—Continued.

COUNTY. CITY, TOWN, PARISH, HUNDRED, ETC.	NAMES OF HEADS OF FAMILIES.	Free white males of sixteen years and upwards, including heads of families.	Free white males under sixteen years.	Free white females, including heads of families.	All other free persons.	Slaves.
BURKE COUNTY	Jno Stilwell	1	3	3	..	..
	Reuben Odel	1	1	1	..	..
	Ben Rose	1	1	2	..	..
	Joshua Pinly	1	3	4	..	..
	Thos. Parks	2	3	6	..	1
	Eliza Alexander	1	..	2	..	..
	Paul Antony. Jr	1	..	..	..	..
	Jno. Brasfield	1	1	1	..	..
	Philip Antony	1	.	4	..	..
	Jno. Tramwell	2	1	2	..	..
	Jno. Painter	2	2	3	..	..
	James Alexander	1	5	4	..	..
	Jacob Alestony, Jr	1	..	1	..	..
	Allen Fox	1	2	2	..	..
	Sam'l Branch	1	2	4	..	..
	Meriah Scott	2	1	3	..	..
	Robt. Gilmore	1	2	2	..	..
	Larhon Parks	1	..	2	..	..
	Lazarus Phillips	1	3	3	..	..
	Willm Pinly, Jr	3	..	1	..	..
	Wm. Pinly, Sr	2	3	3	..	..
	Jno. Hall	2	2	2	..	..
	Rollin Burkes	4	4	4	..	..
	Robt. Church	1	2	1	..	..
	Thom Church	1	1	1	..	..
	Big Denis Tramele	2	2	3	..	..
	James Simpson	1	1	1	..	..
	John Wakefield	1	4	3	..	..
	Wiley Scott	1	..	6	..	..
	Eliza Piorcy	1	3	3	..	..
	Wm. Uslam	1	1	2	..	..
	Little Denis Tramele	1	1	3	..	..
	Jemima Allen	..	2	3	..	..
	Ute Sherrill	1	4	4	..	..
	Jno. Wagley	2	..	4	..	..
	Jno. Duke	1	2	2	..	..
FOURTH COMPANY.	James Forgay	3	3	4	..	..
	Jas. Edmison	3	3	3	..	..
	Sam Holinsworth	2	2	9	..	..
	Hozill Adams	1	1	2	..	..
	Mark Hailey	1	..	5	..	..
	Kizzie Raybon	..	..	1	..	..
	Harison McConico	1	2	8	..	..
	Wm. Green	2	4	1	..	..
	Elijah Green	1	2	5	..	..
	Wilm Morris	2	4	3	..	1
	Rd Haily	2	3	4	..	..
	Thom Williams	1	2	2	..	..
	Hodge Raybon	1	2	1	..	1

FIRST FEDERAL CENSUS, 1790—Continued.

COUNTY, CITY, TOWN, PARISH, HUNDRED, ETC.	NAMES OF HEADS OF FAMILIES.	Free white males of sixteen years and upwards, including heads of families.	Free white males under sixteen years.	Free white females, including heads of families.	All other free persons.	Slaves.
BURKE COUNTY	Wooetn Harris.........	2	1	3	..	..
	Luke Huggins	1	4	3	..	..
	Else Wadkins	..	2	1	..	..
	Ben Adams............	1	1	3	..	1
	Jno. Fleming..........	1	2	3	..	..
	Peter Fleming	1	3	4	..	..
	Clem Davis.	1	4	1	..	..
	Thom Fleming.	1	3	4	..	..
	Ben Pickerel..........	1	4	3	..	..
	Wm. Hailey..........	1	4	4	..	..
	Jas. Humphris	1	..	1	..	..
	Jas. Smith............	1	..	1	..	..
	Philip Goodbread	1	1	3	..	..
	Jos Goodbread..........	1	2	4	..	..
	Phillip Huggins	2	..	1	..	..
	James Stoker.	1	1	2	..	..
	Tho Wheeler....... ...	1	4	1	..	..
	Thos James	1	..	2	..	..
	Jno Wallace............	1	2	1	..	..
	Joshua Oans............	1	2	3	..	..
	Obadiah Bradsha	1	1	5	..	..
	Thom Bryan............	1	..	1	..	..
	Jesse Mendinall...... ..	1	2	2	..	..
	Ben Burgin............	2	6	1	..	..
	Wilm Hermby........ ..	3	..	2	..	..
	John Cozby	2	2	5	..	..
	Thos Nicols........... .	1	3	6	..	..
	Wm Portman.	1	..	1	..	..
	Wm Jax.	1	1	2	..	..
	James Wilson..........	1	..	2	..	..
	Jno Noblit.............	1	2	2	..	..
	Jos Chaffin, Jr........ ..	3	..	3	..	..
	Jno Petitto, Sen... ...	2	..	2	..	3
	Robt Hodge, Jr..........	1	..	6	..	..
	Wm Porter, Sen.........	2	..	4	..	..
	Jacob Haws.	2	3	1	..	..
	James Horrill	1	..	1	..	3
	Mary Chafin.....	.	..	2	..	..
	Sam Hughes............	2	..	1	..	..
	Edward Jackson........	2	5	3	..	..
	Eliza Fekes	1	1	1	..	..
	Thom Litle...........	1	3	1	..	..
	Midleton Petitto	1	1	1	..	..
	Thos Brown	2	..	3	..	..
	Ellis Bloonfin...........	1	1	1	..	..
	Nicholas Ledford.......	1	..	1	..	..
	Wm. Porter, Jr.........	1	1	8	..	..
	Henry Strain	1	4	1	..	..
	James Elliott	1	..	8	..	..

FIRST FEDERAL CENSUS, 1790—Continued.

COUNTY, CITY, TOWN, PARISH, HUNDRED, ETC.	NAMES OF HEADS OF FAMILIES.	Free white males of sixteen years and upwards, including heads of families.	Free white males under sixteen years.	Free white females, including heads of families.	All other free persons.	Slaves.
BURKE COUNTY	Elias Chaffin	1	..	1	..	.
FOURTH COMPANY.	Mary Dimint	2	2	2	..	..
	Jacob Kelloe	1	2	3	..	..
	Robt. Hodge, Jr	1	2	1	..	.
	Jos Wood	1	..	1	..	.
	Jno. Doaty	1	2	2	.	.
	Thom. Davis	1	2	1	..	.
	William Engld	1	2	3	..	.
	Joseph Scolds	1	..	2	..	.
	Ben Wallace	1	4	4	..	.
	Zeb Brevard, Jr.	1	..	2	..	..
	Ben Julin	1	1	4	..	..
	William Julin	1	2	6	..	..
	Michal Pinnly	1	1	1	..	..
	Cornelius Ridick	1	..	..	..	..
	Amos Chaffin	1	1	3	..	..
	Jno. Gilleland	1	4	4	..	..
	Prudence Collins	..	..	..	..	..
FIFTH COMPANY	Robt. Fitzpatrick	1	5	4	..	..
	Jasbret Webb	4	2	1	..	..
	Wilm. Minphey	1	3	1	..	3
	Joseph White	1	2	4	..	7
	Wm. Johnson	1	3	6	..	.
	Jesse Boone	1	3	5	..	.
	John Hankins	1	3	2	..	..
	George Holliway	1	1	2	..	..
	Wilm Lovin	1	1	4	..	..
	George Hickman	3	4	5	..	1
	Charles Weakfield	1	..	3	..	..
	Isaac Emings	1	..	1	..	..
	Reuben Fletcher	1	2	3	..	..
	John Church	1	1	4	..	..
	Jos. James	1	..	2	..	..
	Wm. Williams	1	3	2	..	..
	Reed Hite	2	..	5	..	7
	Jno. Moore, Ser	2	2	4	..	..
	Jno. Moore	1	1	4	..	1
	Ben Adkins	1	5	3	..	..
	Reuben Eastriss	1	4	3	..	9
	Lewis Harris	2	5	4	..	..
	Edward Haris	2	1	13	..	..
	George Miller	1	1	3	..	..
	Deep Waters	1	..	3	..	..
	Abram Waters	1	3	5	..	..
	Leonard Coner	1	1	1	..	..
	Charles Coner, Sr	2	2	3	..	..
	Charles Coner	1	1	2	..	..
	Wm. Coner	1	2	1	..	..
	Jesse Moore, Sr	2	..	7	..	..

FIRST FEDERAL CENSUS, 1790 –Continued.

COUNTY, CITY, TOWN, PARISH, HUNDRED, ETC.	NAMES OF HEADS OF FAMILIES.	Free white males of sixteen years and upwards, including heads of families	Free white males under sixteen years.	Free white females, including heads of families.	All other free persons.	Slaves.
BURKE COUNTY	Jesse Moore	1	..	3	..	..
FIFTH COMPANY.	Danl Moore	1	..	4	..	2
	Reuben Coffee	1	1	3	..	1
	John Coffey	1	1	1	..	..
	Jas. Coffy	1	1	3	..	1
	Jas. Holland	2	4	5	..	..
	Joseph Coker	1	..	2	..	..
	Jas. Moorhead	1	2	2	..	..
	Danl Mullin	1	1	5	..	..
	Richd. Calliway	1	..	1	..	1
	David Hicks	2	2	3	..	..
	Ezekiel Beard	2	3	2	..	..
	Saml Beard	3	2	2	..	..
	Ben Ward	2	4	2	..	..
	Joshua Ward	1	1	2	..	..
	James Giddins	1	1	4	..	..
	Robt. Searsey	2	3	3	..	..
	Wm. Edmison	1	2	4	..	1
	Thom. Hays	3	3	3	..	1
	George Hays	1	1	1	..	..
	Ben Webb	1	1	2	..	..
	Jas. Webb, Jr.	1	..	1	..	..
	Reynard Walker	1	5	2	..	..
	Jonathn Boon	1	3	5	..	..
	George Donell	2	3	3	..	..
	Moses Hille	2	..	4	..	..
	Thomas Anderson, Jr.	2	2	6	1	..
	Jessey Powers	1	1	5	..	..
	Thom. Powers	2	1	2	..	..
	John Rice	3	..	2	..	..
	Nathan Smith	1	1	2	..	..
	Rice Medecarst	1	2	5	..	..
	Moses Stafp	1	3	3	..	..
	Jas. Neely	1	4	6	..	..
	Michal Wilson	1	3	3	..	..
	Wm F. Jewell	1	3	7	..	..
	James Wilson	1	..	2	..	..
	Rollin James	1	..	6	..	..
	William Renault	1	..	1	..	..
	George Hutchins	1	3	3	..	..
	Thom. Church, Jr.	2	1	4	..	..
	Leonard Eastriss	1	..	2	..	..
	Wm. Wilson	1	1	3	..	..
	Jacob Snead	3	..	8	..	..
	George Carter	2	4	5	..	..
	Robt. Church	1	2	1	..	..
	Laybon Eastriss	2	..	2	..	..
	John Brown	1	3	3	..	..
	Baker King	1	2	2	..	..

FIRST FEDERAL CENSUS, 1790—Continued.

COUNTY, CITY, TOWN, PARISH, HUNDRED, ETC.	NAMES OF HEADS OF FAMILIES.	Free white males of sixteen years and upwards, including heads of families.	Free white males under sixteen years.	Free-white females, including heads of families.	All other free persons.	Slaves.
BURKE COUNTY	Jno Whittenton......	1	3	2	..	..
FIFTH COMPANY.	Champion Guir........	1	..	1	..	..
	Wm. White, Sen	5	..	2	..	12
SIXTH COMPANY.	Joseph Conan..........	2	1	3	..	..
	Jno. Reed	1	..	3	..	..
	Greenberry Wilson......	1	1	4	..	3
	Caleb Barr............	1	5	4	..	..
	Agnes Sellers..	1	1	4	..	..
	Jno Hall..............	1	3	6	..	1
	Moses Wilkinson...	1	..	3	..	3
	Jno Sellers	1	2	1	..	..
	Michael Pearson........	1	..	1	..	..
	Patrick O'Neal, Jr.	1	..	1	..	..
	John Dizard...........	1	6	4	..	..
	Robt. Sellers, Jr.	1	2	3	..	..
	Robt. Sellers	1	..	5	..	..
	Jas. Rutherford...... ..	1	2	3	..	2
	Marget Dizard	1	..	1	..	..
	John Allen, Jr..........	4	2	4	..	..
	Hezekiah Hiatt........	3	2	6	..	1
	Wm. Morrison.........	5	1	4	..	..
	Dane Andrews...... ...	3	4	4	..	..
	Wm. Rutherford........	2	..	3	..	5
	Enos Rust	4	3	2	..	..
	Peter Rust.....	1	3	3	..	..
	Wm. Moore.......	1	3	5	..	6
	Claybon Gunter	1	1	1	..	..
	Abram Plumly..........	1	1	5	..	1
	James Devine.	1	1	2	..	..
	Eliza Denton......	2	..	4	..	..
	Jas. Canly	1	1	2	..	..
	Harry Hanly	1	4	2	..	..
	Danl. Sullivan...... ...	1	..	3	..	..
	Issac Grant............	1	..	2	..	..
	Patrick O'Neal..........	3	..	2	..	..
	John Montgomery......	3	..	3	..	..
	Jas. Montgomery..	1	3	4	..	5
	Jas. Blag..	1	..	3	..	..
	Edwd. Leatherwood....	1	3	5	..	..
	Bridget Montgomery....	..	..	2	2	2
	Andrew Hunter........	1	..	4	..	..
	Jos. Justice............	2	2	1	..	..
	Rd. Simmons...........	1	2	1	..	..
	Lydia Gray.......	3	1	3	..	5
	Feld Bradshaw..........	1	4	3	..	2
	Edwd. Hyett.....	1	3	3	..	..
	Jacob Tenison	1	..	1	..	..
	Henry Chanler.........	1	4	3	..	..
	John McDowell	3	2	4	..	5

FIRST FEDERAL CENSUS, 1790—Continued.

COUNTY, CITY, TOWN, PARISH, HUNDRED, ETC.	NAMES OF HEADS OF FAMILIES.	Free white males of sixteen years and upwards, including heads of families.	Free white males under sixteen years.	Free white females, including heads of families.	All other free persons.	Slaves.
BURKE COUNTY	Robt. Montgomery	2	4	3	..	7
SIXTH COMPANY.	Thos. Beall............	1	4	5	..	1
~	Simon Hyett	..	1	3	..	1
	Isaac Terrill	..	5	4	..	1
	Alex. Robison	1	..	2	..	..
	Abizella Burchfld......	1	3	3	..	..
	Robt. Bellew..	3	1	5	..	..
	David Rust.	2	3	3	..	..
	Jno. Mays	1	3	2	..	..
	Charis Finley.	1	6	3	..	..
	John Rutherford.......	2	2	3	..	2
	Wm Gardner...........	2	3	7	..	3
	John Polk............	2	4	3	..	..
	Jno. Downing.	2	3	2	..	..
	Alex. Long	2	..	2	..	..
	James McAdams	3	3	4	..	..
	Ben Jones	1	3	2	..	..
	Frank Worley	1	3	2	..	..
	Jno. Summers.........	5	2	4	..	..
	Saml. Wood	3	3	6	..	..
	Jno, Reno...........	1	2	5	..	..
	Wm. Monson, Jr.......	1	..	4	..	..
	Churul Jackson	1	1	8	..	..
	Wm. Probit.	1	..	1	..	3
	Elijah Patten, Jr...	1	1	2	..	..
	Jas. Hemphill	3	4	4	..	..
	Eliza Monson...........	..	1	6	..	..
	David Lorrels.....	1	..	1	..	..
	Henry Martin	2	1	5	..	..
	Jas. Jenell............	2	1	3	..	..
	Wm. Cosby............	3	..	4	..	..
	Zacheus Hicks..........	1	1	2	..	..
	Wm. Greg...:.........	1	3	2	..	..
	Andrew Elder	1	2	1	..	..
	Andw. Woods	2	1	5	..	..
	Robt. Patten.........	1	1	3	..	..
	Frank Patten.........	3	1	6	..	2
	Marget Conan......	..	..	1	..	..
	Jno. Daniel.......	1	..	5	..	..
	Lodo Blankirsh, Jr......	2	4	3	..	..
	Frank Hodge..........	1	..	1	..	..
	George Hodge..........	1	1	3	..	...
	John Hall, Jr	1	..	1	..	..
	Joshua Hall.......	1	2	1	..	..
	Andrew Hughey	1	1	4	..	..
	Basdel Baker...........	1	..	2	..	..
	David McElwrath.	2	5	7	..	.
	Robt. Woods..	1	..	1	..	..
	George Evits	1	..	3	..	..

FIRST FEDERAL CENSUS, 1790—Continued.

COUNTY, CITY, TOWN, PARISH, HUNDRED, ETC.	NAMES OF HEADS OF FAMILIES.	Free white males of sixteen years and upwards, including heads of families.	Free white males under sixteen years.	Free white females, including heads of families.	All other free persons.	Slaves.
BURKE COUNTY	Naomi Hall		2	2	..	..
	Jno. Walker	1	3	2	..	..
	Jno. Smith	1	3	3	..	..
SEVENTH COMPANY.	Albert Conpening	1	4	4	..	..
	Jno. Franklin, Jr	2	1	6	..	..
	Martin Antony	2	5	2	..	..
	Micajah Sansom	1	2	4	..	..
	Edmund Fairs	1	3	5	..	..
	Eli Littlejohn	1	3	3	..	..
	Jos McDowell, Col.	2	..	5	..	10
	Henry McKinny	1	..	1	..	2
	Jeremiah Tomson	2	2	4	..	7
	Jno. Erwin	1	6	3	..	3
	Jno. Maxwell	2	1	2	..	..
	Jno. Lane	1	2	2	..	..
	Jno. McGimsey	2	..	1	..	3
	Robt. Fleming	1	2	8	..	..
	Thos. Wilsters	1	1	6	..	9
	Ben Coffee	1	3	2	..	..
	Jas. Murphey	1	1	1	..	5
	Jno. Harper	1	..	2	..	..
	Jno. Harper, Jr	2	3	3	..	..
	Alex. Erwin	1	3	7	..	11
	Jacob Fonay	1	..	..	..	6
	Ben Kelly	1	3	1	..	..
	Sam'l Tummins	1	2	2	..	..
	Christ'r Isom	2	3	3	..	..
	Thos Case	1	..	2	..	..
	Hugh Macay	1	2	2	..	..
	Wm. Fismire	1	1	3	..	..
	Adam Cook	2	..	3	..	..
	Isaac Maxwell	1	2	2	..	..
	Esau Dotson	1	..	1	..	..
	Elisha McKinny	1	..	4	..	1
	Bennet Bradford	3	2	4	..	1
	Wm. Carter	1	1	2	..	..
	Elza Husband	..	1	3	..	..
	Sam'l Turmire	1	..	1	..	..
	Jno. Goble	1	..	1	..	..
	Nancy Clarke	2	4	5	..	..
	Joana Clarke	1	3	3	..	..
	Jno. Clarke	1	..	3	..	..
	Jozane Arny	1	..	3	..	..
	Chrish Wagoner	1	3	2	..	..
	Adam Sutser	1	4	2	..	..
	George Cook	1	..	5	..	..
	Chesly Dobs	2	4	4	..	..
	Adam Winkler	1	1	3	..	..
	Thos. Winkler, Jr	2	..	3	..	..

FIRST FEDERAL CENSUS, 1790—Continued.

COUNTY, CITY, TOWN, PARISH, HUNDRED, ETC.	NAMES OF HEADS OF FAMILIES	Free white males of sixteen years and upwards, including heads of families.	Free white males under sixteen years.	Free white females, including heads of families.	All other free persons.	Slaves
BURKE COUNTY	David Winkler......	1	..	3	..	..
SEVENTH COMPANY.	Insy Conrad Winkler ..	1	1	2	..	..
	Big Conrad Winkler. ..	1	2	2	..	..
	Mich'l Howk	1	1	4	..	..
	Thos. Moody	2	3	2	..	..
	Jas. Moody	1	1	1	..	..
	Gilbert Sweat	1	1	2	..	..
	Ephraim Sweat........	1	2	3	..	..
	Hana Hughes.........	..	1	4	..	..
	Philip Martin...........	2	1	5	..	..
	George Martin	1	2	1	..	..
	Wm. Little...........	1	2	2	..	..
	Jno. Little....	1	1	2	..	..
	Thos. Day.........	3	1	6	..	..
	Abram Stallins	3	..	1	..	..
	Phil Stephens...... : ..	1	3	7	..	..
	Wm. Davis.............	2	2	2	..	..
	Jonathan Tears	1	2	2	..	..
	Nathan Hobs	1	3	2	..	..
	Thos. Lane	1	4	3	..	..
	Jno. Treble...........	2		2	..	..
	Charles McDowell......	1	2	5	..	10
	Elisha Perkins	2	2	2	..	9
	Silas Murphy........ ...	1	5	2	..	..
	Wm. Pelm.............	2	1	3	..	..
	Wm. Lozanca..........	1	..	1	..	..
	Adam Direberg	1	3	5	..	..
	Veasy Husband....	1	..	2	..	..
	Jacob Tips	1	4	3	..	..
	John Franklin, Jr.	1	1	3	..	..
	Thos. Cragg...	1	..	2	..	..
	Sam'l Cragg.............	1	..	2	..	..
	Meredith Harper.... ...	1	1	2	..	..
	Jacob Baldwin........	1	1	3	..	..
	Sam Crawford	1	..	1	..	..
	David Gibson........	1	2	4	..	..
	William Gibson...	1	3	2	..	..
	Harmon Gibson.	1	..	1	..	..
	Joab Crag	2	1	2	..	..
	John Stafford..........	3	2	2	..	..
	Rd Barns......	1	1	2	..	..
	Cleveland Coffee......	1	2	4	..	..
	Christ'r Crag...........	1	3	2	..	..
	Jno Hughes...........	1	1	2	..	..
	Dan'l Bolinger....... ..	1	3	2	..	..
	John Henesy	2	..	2	..	..
	Marget Little	..	..	2	..	..
	Ambrouse Jones........	1	..	1	..	..
	Wm. Crisp..	1	..	2	..	..

First Federal Census, 1790—Continued.

COUNTY. CITY, TOWN, PARISH, HUNDRED, ETC.	NAMES OF HEADS OF FAMILIES.	Free white males of sixteen years and upwards, including heads of families.	Free white males under sixteen years.	Free white females, including heads of families.	All other free persons.	Slaves.
BURKE COUNTY	Jno. Baldwin, Sen.	1	..	1	..	..
SEVENTH COMPANY.	Jno. Landers	1	1	4	..	..
	Jas. Richards, Sr....	2	2	2	..	..
	Joshua Gilbert	..	..	..	..	..
EIGHTH COMPANY.	Henry Reid.	1	2	3	..	..
	James Reid.	1	1	3	..	..
	Lewis Mayberry	1	2	1	..	2
	George Barns...........	1	1	6	..	..
	Stephen Gibson........	..	2	1	..	1
	Lewis Reetor	1	1	1	..	..
	Thos. Bradburn...	1	..	1	..	4
	Robt. Warren..........	2	3	6	..	..
	Wm. Warren..........	1	3	1	..	..
	George Pane	3	1	3	..	..
	Wm. Reid	1	4	3	..	..
	And'w Steel	3	..	2	..	3
	Matthew Burgess..	1	5	3	..	..
	Alex. West.	1	2	4	..	..
	Thos. Scott	1	4	4	..	..
	Rd. Emmit............	1	1	5	..	..
	John Bradford...	1	2	2	..	..
	Thos Green	4	3	6	..	..
	Rich'd Russell....	1	2	3	..	..
	Bray Crisp.....	1	1	2	..	..
	Alex. West, Sr..........	2	1	6	..	..
	Jno. Horse...(Hous)..	3	1	1	..	..
	Jas. Collire.	1	1	1	..	..
	Jno. Smith	2	1	2	..	..
	Matthew Cox........ ...	3	1	1	..	4
	Wm. Roberts, Jr	1	..	1	..	..
	Robt. Moore..........	1	1	2	..	..
	George Brown, Jr.. ...	1	1	3	..	..
	Rd. Brown............	1	2	2	..	..
	Sam'l Steel	1	2	3	..	..
	Jacob Winkler..........	5	..	1	..	..
	Amos Tuttle..........	2	2	2	..	..
	Wm. Sherrill	1	4	5	..	..
	John Headley.	1	2	3	..	..
	Ben Austin....	1	2	6	..	..
	Abr'm Hunsucker......	2	..	1	..	..
	Abr'm Hunsucker, Jr...	1	..	5	..	..
	Jno. Hunsucker.	1	2	4	..	..
	Barnet Pain.	1	4	3	..	4
	Jas. Fletcher	1	2	5	..	.
	Niclas Medlock	2	..	3	..	..
	Nicols Medlock, Jr.....	1	1	2	..	..
	John Falls	1	1	4	..	..
	John Barns.............	1	2	3,	..	..
	Hugh Reid..	1	6	2	..	..

STATE RECORDS.

First Federal Census, 1790—Continued.

County City, Town, Parish, Hundred, Etc.	NAMES OF HEADS OF FAMILIES.	Free white males of sixteen years and upwards, including heads of families	Free white males under sixteen years.	Free white females, including heads of families.	All other free persons.	Slaves.
BURKE COUNTY EIGHTH COMPANY.	Elijah Banks	1	3	2	..	..
	Hugh Fox	3	4	7	..	..
	Henry Baker	1	3	4	..	..
	Jacob Keller	1	1	2	..	..
	Martin Keller	2	3	2	..	..
	John Yeats Price	1	..	4	..	..
	Luke White	1	3	7	..	..
	Nicholas Jones	1	4	2	..	..
	Dailey Walker	1	2	5	..	..
	Edw'd Teague	1	2	6	..	2
	Jno. Teague	1	4	3	..	..
	Joshua Hadley	1	..	..	..	..
	Elijah Green	1	..	4	..	..
	Wm Roberts, Sr	2	1	6	..	..
	Christina Keller	1	1	1	..	..
	James Tenny	1	3	3	..	..
	Wm. Colwell	1	1	1	..	..
	Jos. Gibson	1	1	1	..	..
	Jno. Hooker	1	..	2	..	..
	Wm. Dockery	1	2	2	..	..
	Jno. Conrod	2	1	1	..	..
	Jno. Roberts	1	1	4	..	..
	Jas. Cunningham	1	5	2	..	..
	Jas. Dockery	1	2	4	..	..
	Sam'l Stenard	1	..	2	..	..
	Absalom Pinitor	1	..	2	..	..
	John McEntire	1	3	4	..	..
	Jonas White	1	1	2	..	..
	Jno. Hood	1	1	2	..	..
	Thos. Reed	2	..	3	..	..
	Absalom Brown	1	3	2	..	..
	Daniel Pain	1	1	1	..	..
	Phillip Hepbaer	1	..	1	..	..
	Isaac Grenslaff	2	2	4	..	..
	Isom Gibson	1	..	2	..	..
	John Parmin	2	1	2	..	..
	Wm. Fullerton	1	..	1	..	..
	James Clarke	1	5	2	..	..
	James Thomas	1	1	4	..	..
	Jane Grenstaff	..	2	2	..	..
	Charles Walker	1	1	5	.	2
	Simon Walker	1	3	4	.	..
	John Medlock	2	..	3	.	..
	Ben Austin, Sr	3	1	5	..	..
	Major Gibson	2	..	3	..	..
	Jesse Spradling	1	1	2	..	1
	Wilburn Gibson	1	1	2	.	..
	Jno. Scott	1	..	3	..	..
	John Dockery	1	1	2	..	..

73

FIRST FEDERAL CENSUS, 1790—Continued.

COUNTY, CITY, TOWN, PARISH, HUNDRED, ETC.	NAMES OF HEADS OF FAMILIES.	Free white males of sixteen years and upwards, including heads of families.	Free white males under sixteen years.	Free white females, including heads of families.	All other free persons.	Slaves.
BURKE COUNTY	Jonathan Barrett	2	..	2	..	..
EIGHTH COMPANY.	Jno. Yokely	1	..	3	..	..
	Jas. Fox	1	3	2	..	..
	Alex. Graham	1	1	2	..	..
	Jas. Presly	1	..	4	..	..
	James Steward	1	..	4	..	..
	Uriah Davis	3	5	3	..	..
	Elizabeth Green	..	..	1	..	..
	Rd. Price	1	4	3	..	..
	Phillip Price	2	3	4	..	..
	Eliza Dishazer	..	2	2	..	..
	Wm. Irons	1	3	3	..	..
	Wm. Smith	1	1	3	..	..
	Adam Troutman	1	2	7	..	..
	Jno. Cumming	2	1	3	..	..
	Jno. Allen	2	1	3	..	..
	Wm. Alexander	1	..	1	..	..
	Wm. Macay	1	1	2	..	..
	Alex. Matthewson	3	2	2	..	..
NINTH COMPANY.	Peter Thomson	3	4	4	..	1
	Jas Sumpter	1	..	3	..	..
	Jno. Bartley	1	4	4	..	..
	Jno. Hays	2	4	6	..	..
	Joshua Murray	2	1	3	..	..
	Nicolas Howk	1	4	4	..	..
	George Tucker	1	..	2	..	..
	Joseph Baker	2	1	3	..	..
	Wm. Moore	3	..	2	..	..
	Jos. McCrary	4	5	4	..	..
	Jno. Murray	1	..	1	..	..
	Jno. Murray, Jr	1	1	3	..	..
	Fred Grider, Jr	1	5	3	..	..
	Fred Grider, Sr	2	..	1	..	..
	Barbara Murray	..	1	4	..	..
	Sam'l Smith	1	3	3	..	..
	Thos. Powell	1	1	2	..	..
	Peter Angely	1	2	1	..	..
	George Hartley	2	2	2	..	..
	Johnson Lathrum	1	1	3	..	..
	Jno. Fincannon	1	5	3	..	..
	Jno. Grider	1	4	2	..	..
	Jacob Grider	1	..	2	..	..
	Abner Smally	1	3	5	..	..
	Wm. Repets	1	4	4	..	..
	Ezekl Wilson	1	..	4	..	..
	Jno. Wood	1	7	4	..	..
	Eliza Garlin	.	.	2	..	..
	Wm. Periman	1	2	4	..	..
	Saybort Shoat	1	..	3	..	..

FIRST FEDERAL CENSUS, 1790—Continued.

COUNTY, CITY, TOWN, PARISH, HUNDRED, ETC.	NAMES OF HEADS OF FAMILIES.	Free white males of sixteen years and upwards, including heads of families	Free white males under sixteen years	Free white females, including heads of families.	All other free persons.	Slaves.
BURKE COUNTY	Eliza Gilmore..........	1	1	1	..	..
NINTH COMPANY.	Rd. Green	1	4	6	..	..
	Christ'n Abshire.......	1	4	3	..	..
	Sam'l Swaringin	1		6	..	..
	Jerome Stilwell	1	..	2	..	..
	Solomon Smith	1	3	4	..	..
	Jas. Penly....	1	1	1	..	..
	Edward Wilson........	2	1	1		..
	Jno. Hines.............	2	4	5	..	..
	James Potts.	1		8	..	1
	Jas. Nailor.............	1	..	1		
	Jno. Coffee	1	4	4	..	..
	Mark Amons..........	1	..	3	..	..
	Micajah Allen..........	1	1	1	..	..
	George Tucker, Sen ...	1	1	1	..	...
	Sam'l Ramsy	1	1	1	..	..
	Wm. Davis	2		2	..	..
	Wm Thornton	1	1	3	..	..
	Jno. Allen...	2	1	2	..	..
	Henry Hottsclaw.... ...	4	..	4	..	..
	Edward Owins...... ...	1	..	3	..	..
	Isaac Muyson	1	1	4	..	..
	Hezekiah Struton.......	1	..	3	..	..
	Wm Hartley..........	1	1	3	..	..
	Sarah Hartley	1	3	4	..	..
	Jno. Blair	1	3	2	..	1
	James Hons............	1	..	2	..	..
	Sam'l Owins	1	4	5	..	..
	Jno. Day......	1	3	3	..	..
	Nicholas Day....	1	3	5	..	..
	James Day..	2	1	2	..	..
	Willis Hicks	2	..	8	..	..
	Jacob Green..........	1	..	1	..	..
	Jos. Wisdom...........	1	3	5	..	..
	Fred Hignsaw....... ...	2	2	3	..	..
	Susana Strutton........	1	2	5	..	..
	John Harris	1	2	2	..	..
	Elijah Hammons	1	2	3	..	..
	Thom. Randolph	2	1	3	..	..
	Wm. Horrin.	2	1	3	..	..
	Colward Blair.	1	1	2	..	3
	Wm. Sumpter	3	..	2	..	..
	Thos. Sumpter	2	..	3	..	..
	Abram Sotherd.	1	2	2	..	..
	Jno. Noely	1	1	1	..	..
	Jonath'n Allen	1	..	2	..	..
	Jonth'n Allen, Sen......	1	..	1	..	..
	Rd. Dennis.	1	..	2	..	..
	Jno. Crisp......	2	5	4	..	..

FIRST FEDERAL CENSUS, 1790—Continued.

COUNTY, CITY, TOWN, PARISH, HUNDRED, ETC.	NAMES OF HEADS OF FAMILIES.	Free white males of sixteen years and upwards, including heads of families.	Free white males under sixteen years.	Free white females, including heads of families.	All other free persons.	Slaves.
BURKE COUNTY	Wm. Crisp............	1	..	2	..	..
NINTH COMPANY.	Rich'd Ramsey..	1	3	4	..	..
	Linzy Constable	1	3	2	..	..
	Eliza Ramsy..	..	.	2	..	..
	Peter Hott	1	4	5	..	2
	Jacob Hott	2	..	2	..	1
	Aaron Reily...........	1	1	1	..	..
	Check Swaringin	1	1	2	..	..
	Ambrose Powell	2	4	5	.	1
	Elias Powell ...	1	3	3	..	1
	Jno. Townsend. ...	4	1	2	..	6
	Wm. Grissom.	1	1	1	..	..
	Jno. McDaniel	1	3	3	..	..
	Sam'l McDaniel........	1	:	2	..	..
	Wm. Thrasher	1	3	4	..	..
	Gerral Wilson.	1	3	2	..	..
	Joseph Greenaway	1	.	1	..	..
	Jos. Greenaway. Sr	2	1	3	..	..
	Thos. James...	1	..	2	..	..
	Wm. James............	1	..	1	..	..
	Mary James..........	..	..	2	..	3
	John Taylor	4	1	3	..	..
	Robt John Miller.......	1	2	2	..	2
	Temple McDaniel.......	..	1	4	..	..
	Sarah Smith	..	2	2	..	..
	Sam'l Swaringin	1	..	1	..	..
	Isaac Phillips..........	1	2	2	..	..
	Thos. Powell....	1	1	4	..	..
	Eljan Powell..........	1	..	1	..	2
	Isaac Cox.....	2	2	4	..	..
	Edward Long..........	1	4	3	..	..
	Isaac Earthman........	1	4	4	..	1
	Robt. Northerly	2	5	2	..	..
	Elias Powell, Sen	1	..	.	..	1
	Lewis Powell..........	1	..	1	..	..
TENTH COMPANY.	Joseph Young	1	..	2	..	..
	George Dimerlin........	1	4	2	..	4
	Wm. Wofford.	2	..	2	..	..
	Amy Bolin	..	1	4	..	..
	Jacob Holinsworth......	1	5	1	..	..
	Ben Wofford...........	1	..	1	..	..
	George Hopper	1	2	7	..	..
	Sam'l Holinsworth......	1	..	3	..	1
	Jos. Nation...........	2	4	4	.	..
	Wm. Nation	2	1	4	..	..
	Joel Hancock.	1	..	2	..	..
	Wm. Spoons......... ...	1	..	2	..	2
	John Hall	1	2	5	..	..
	Agnes Burlison	1	1	2	..	..

FIRST FEDERAL CENSUS, 1790—Continued.

COUNTY, CITY, TOWN, PARISH, HUNDRED, ETC.	NAMES OF HEADS OF FAMILIES.	Free white males of sixteen years and upwards, including heads of families.	Free white males under sixteen years.	Free white females, including heads of families.	All other free persons	Slaves.
BURKE COUNTY	Charles Phillips........	1	..	1	..	..
TENTH COMPANY.	John Vann........	2	1	3	..	..
	Wm. Phillips........	3	5	4	..	..
	Dan'l Holefield	1	..	3	..	..
	Isaiah Rose.	2	2	4	..	..
	Wm. Bridges.......	1	1	3	..	..
	Delila McFalls..........	..	3	1	..	..
	Charles Hopper.........	2	4	5	..	..
	James Carson.......	2	2	6	..	..
	Jno. Robison	1	3	3	..	..
	Marget Bell.	.	..	3	..	..
	Ben Hensly.	3	3	3	..	..
	James Lee	1	3	3	..	..
	Louisa Johnson....	..	1	1	..	..
	Wm. McKinny	1	3	6	..	..
	Thom. McKinny. ...	1	..	2	..	..
	Rd. Medlock...	1	3	4	..	..
	Jno. Gouge.	1	1	2	..	..
	Jno. Rose, Sen	1	2	3	..	..
	Jno. Rose, Jr	1	..	2	..	..
	Jas. Wilson,..........	2	1	4	..	..
	Jno. Harden	2	2	4	..	..
	James Morrow	1	5	2	..	..
	Jas. Ainsworth..	2	4	3	..	8
	Wm. Moody	1	5	2	..	..
	Wm. Bellins	1	2	4	..	..
	Jacob Forsythe.........	1	1	3	..	..
	Jno. McFalls..........	1	1	1	..	..
	Dan'l Brown ...	1	1	1	..	..
	Robt. Turner, Sr.......	1	..	1	..	..
	Robt. Turner..........	1	1	3	..	..
	Wm. Moore.	1	3	3	..	..
	Jno Wilson, Jr..	1	2	1	..	..
	David McCracon....	2	1	7	..	..
	Jno. Wilson	3	2	4	..	..
	Thos. Night	3	3	2	..	..
	Thos. Night, Jr..	1	1	4	..	..
	Neathn Deaton	1	..	2	..	..
	Thos. Moore............	1	..	1	..	..
	Sam Wilson	1	1	1	..	..
	George Wilson	2	2	7	..	..
	Thom. Young...........	2	1	2	..	2
	Joshua Young	1	..	1	..	.
	Abigail Kinsey..........	..	2	1	..	..
	Sally Hall	..	1	1	..	..
	Martin Devinport......	3	4	3	..	4
	Sam'l Bright...........'........	1	2	2	..	..
	Wm. Wiseman..........	4	4	5	..	..
	Thos. Wiseman.	2	1	3	..	..

22—22

FIRST FEDERAL CENSUS, 1790—Continued.

COUNTY, CITY, TOWN, PARISH, HUNDRED, ETC.	NAMES OF HEADS OF FAMILIES.	Free white males of sixteen years and upwards, including heads of families.	Free white males under sixteen years.	Free white females, including heads of families.	All other free persons.	Slaves.
BURKE COUNTY	Jos. Jones	1	3	4	..	..
TENTH COMPANY.	James Price	1	1	5	..	..
	Wm. Bright	1	1	2	..	..
	Wm. Hill.	2	1	6	..	..
	Jas. Taylor.	1	1	4	..	..
	Wm Hill, Sen....	2	..	1	..	..
	Thos. Beckenstaff.	1	1	1	..	..
	John Loller.... ...	1	2	2	..	..
	Jno. Mullins....	1	3	3	..	..
	Arthur McFalls.........	1	3	1	..	..
	Henry Gillespy	3	..	2	..	..
ELEVENTH COMPANY.	David Vance	2	1	5	..	3
	Wm. Deevir....	6	..	4	..	..
	Jo. Smith...............	2	..	6	..	..
	Nat. Smith.............	1	1	1	..	..
	Jacob Beifle.........	1	1	2	..	..
	Adam Dansmore	2	2	2	..	..
	Jno. Gilbert	3	2	3	..	..
	Henry Heatly...........	2	1	6	..	..
	Sam Renfrin	3	1	6	..	..
	David Rogers...........	1	4	3	..	..
	Jas Cunnigam...	1	..	6	..	1
	Nathan Bartlet..	2	2	3	..	..
	Jno. Bartlet......	1	..	1	..	..
	Wm. McAfer	2	3	5	..	..
	Wm. Young............	1	1	2	..	..
	Matthew Patten.	1	..	3	..	..
	Jno. Moore	1	..	3	..	..
	Wm. Greaham	3	1	4	..	..
	Jno. Lacky..	1	..	5	..	..
	Jonson Summers	2	..	1	..	..
	James Davidson.........	2	6	3	..	..
	Sam'l Davidson.	1	..	1	..	..
	Ben McWhorter.	2	..	1	..	1
	Robt. Patten, sad	1	2	5	..	2
	Wm. Long..	1	2	1	..	..
	Thos. Patten	3	1	3	..	..
	Hump Cunigam	1	..	3	..	..
	Jas. Patten.	1	..	5	..	..
	Jas. Climments........ ...	1	1	3	..	..
	Jno. Alexander.	3	..	4	..	..
	Jas. Alexander.........	1	3	2	..	..
	Matthew Patten, Sen....	3	..	2	..	1
	Aron Patten	1	..	3	..	..
	Matt. Patten, Jr	1	..	1	..	..
	Wm. Davidson	4	2	4	..	8
	Tas. McMahan..........	3	1	2	..	..
	Jno. Smith.............	1	1	1	..	..
	Jho. Davidson	2	..	2	..	..

FIRST FEDERAL CENSUS, 1790—Continued.

COUNTY, CITY, TOWN, PARISH, HUNDRED, ETC.	NAMES OF HEADS OF FAMILIES.	Free white males of sixteen years and upwards, including heads of families.	Free white males under sixteen years.	Free white females, including heads of families.	All other free persons.	Slaves.
BURKE COUNTY	Jas. Ritchy.	1	2	4	..	1
ELEVENTH COMPANY.	Jas. McNabb	1	4	2	..	3
	Wm. Jones.	2	1	3	..	..
	Joseph Rice.	1		3	..	..
	George Cunigam	2	4	3	..	..
	Ben Gudger.	2		1	..	..
	Arche Neal	2	..	4	..	..
	Sam Forgay.	1	2	4	..	4
	Wm. Kerr.	1		2	..	..
	Jno. Patten.	1	1	4	..	2
	Gabrl Ragsdel	1	2	1	..	3
	Elinor Lee.	..	..	5	..	..
	Jno. West.	1	1	3	..	..
	Wm. Gudger.	1	2	6	..	1
	Jos Randolph	1	1	1	..	..
	Ezra Phillips	1	1	2	..	..
	Wm. Whitson	1	5	2	..	2
	Phil Smith	1	1	2	..	..
	Dan'l Killian.	1	2	1	..	..
	John Phillips.	1	2	1	..	..
	James Boys.	1	1	4	..	1
	Wm Ryant.	1	5	3	..	..
	Abram Case.	2	4	5	..	..
	Jno. Bufle.	1	1	2	..	..
	Jno. Davis	1	..	6	..	..
	Wm. Ingrum.	1	1	6	..	..
	Thos Jinkins	2	..	4	.	..
	Jno. Jinkins	1	..	2	..	..
	George Ramsy	1	3	4	..	..
	Baxter Davis.	3	6	1	..	..
	Jnothn Blevin	1	1	3	..	..
	Jas. Cravins	2	3	3	..	..
	Jno. Gillahan.	1	1	3	..	..
	Jas. George.	2	2	4	..	..
	Connell Kennedy.	1	1	1	..	..
	Adam Beifle	1	..	1	..	1
	Jno. Roberts	1	2	3	..	..
	Jno. Weaver	1	1	3	..	1
	Jacob Wagoner	1	5	2	..	..
	Wm. Roberts.	2	..	4	..	..
	John Rounds.	1	3	2	..	..
	Wm. Brittain.	1	2	2	..	..
	Jno. Dillard.	1	3	5	..	..
	Wm. Gregory.	3	4	3	..	..
	Wm. Baily	1		3	..	..
	Jane Guin.	1	1	2	..	..
	Jas. Stanfield.	1	2	6	..	..
	Chas. Guin.	1	1	3	..	..
	Jno. Chambers.	2	2	2	..	.

79

First Federal Census, 1790—Continued.

County, City, Town, Parish, Hundred, Etc.	NAMES OF HEADS OF FAMILIES.	Free white males of sixteen years and upwards, including heads of families.	Free white males under sixteen years.	Free white females, including heads of families.	All other free persons.	Slaves.
BURKE COUNTY TWELFTH COMPANY.	John Gregory	1	..	1	..	..
	Edmund Parmer	1	3	4	..	..
	Charles Edes	2	1	3	..	..
	Jno. Ramsy	1	..	1	..	..
	Wm. Bartley 央 F. ...	2	..	1	..	..
	Jno. Bradley	1	1	3	..	..
	Jacob Boiler, Sen	5	1	3	..	..
	Jno. Keller	1	2	5	..	..
	Aron Treadaway	2	2	5	..	..
	Henry Atkinson	1	3	4	..	..
	Jos. Bounds	1	3	1	..	..
	Nicolas Keller	1	1	3	..	..
	Tim Barnett	3	3	3	..	..
	Wm. Treadaway	1	1	4	..	..
	Robert Treadaway	1	1	3	..	..
	Wm Finley	1	1	1	..	..
	Jno. Terry	3	3	3	..	..
	Jno. Likens	1	..	1	..	..
	Christ. Shoat	1	..	1	..	1
	Moses Shoat	1	2	1	..	..
	Henry Divers	2	5	2	..	..
	Christ Shoat, Jr	1	..	1	..	..
	Jacob Pyburn	3	1	5	..	..
	James Pialms	1	4	6	..	..
	Jno. Tinker	2	5	5	..	..
	Jos. Forsythe	1	..	1	..	..
	Josh'a Chanler	1	2	2	..	..
	Jno. Blacwell	1	1	3	..	..
	Mcredith Webb	3	4	5	..	5
	Martha Win	..	..	4	..	..
	Jas. Bounds	1	..	2	..	..
	Austin Shoat	1	6	2	..	..
	Wm. Rice	1	8	2	..	..
	Gabriel Elkins	2	1	2	..	2
	Wm. Pialms	1	4	3	..	1
	Edmund Pialms	1	4	3	..	1
	Jno. Street	1	2	2	..	..
	Holand Higins	1	3	..	..	..
	Elijah Bunis	1	2	4	..	..
	Henry Hensly	1	5	5	..	..
	Jno. Renfrew	1	2	8	..	..
	Jno. Hensly	1	..	3	..	..
	James Langford	1	1	2	..	..
	Wm. Edwards	1	..	2	..	..
	David Hinton	1	1	2	..	..
	Jno. Stanton	1	3	4	..	..
	Isaac Angling	1	4	3	..	..
	Phil. Hoddon, pyc	1	3	5	..	..
	Charles Caliway	1	3	2	..	..

FIRST FEDERAL CENSUS, 1790—Continued.

COUNTY, CITY, TOWN, PARISH, HUNDRED, ETC.	NAMES OF HEADS OF FAMILIES.	Free white males of sixteen years and upwards, including heads of families.	Free white males under sixteen years.	Free white females, including heads of families.	All other free persons.	Slaves.
BURKE COUNTY	Allen Summers	1	2	1	..	..
TWELFTH COMPANY.	Hana Phips	..	1	2	..	..
	Wm. Hinton	1	1	2	..	4
	Julius Robison	1	4	4	..	..
	Abner Marcum	1	5	4	..	..
	Phil Williams	1	3	3	..	..
	Obadiah Hamons	1	..	3	..	..
	Robt. Baker, Jr.	2	..	2	..	..
	Jas. Hensly	1	2	4	..	..
	Thos. Ray	3	3	2	..	..
	Jno. Carrol	1	2	4	..	..
	Peter Hamons	1	3	2	..	..
	Jas. Bennett	2	1	3	..	..
	Hicman Hensly	1	4	3	..	..
	George Baker	1	3	4	..	.
	Jno. Edwards	2	4	6	..	..
	Jas. Arrington	1	1	5	..	..
	Jno. Baker	1	5	3	..	..
	Mark Foster	1	3	5	..	..
	Mark Foster, Jr.	4	1	4	..	..
	Jno. Hughes	1	4	1	..	..
	Jane Paterson	..	1	2	..	..
	Peter Hughes	1	2	1	..	..
	Lettice Dyer	..	1	2.	..	..
	Austin Haworth	1	3	4	..	1
THIRTEENTH COMPANY	Jno. M. Galliard	1	1	6	..	..
	Mary Eagen	2	..	2	..	..
	Dan'l England	3	2	6	..	..
	Jo. England	1	2	3	..	..
	Conrod Hitlebrand	1	2	1	..	..
	George Bellow	1	..	2	..	..
	Jno. Bradburn	1	..	..	..	..
	Peter Muse	3	1	3	..	1
	Joseph Morgan	4	2	3	..	..
	Wm. Welsh	1	3	2	..	1
	Ann Direberry	2	..	1	..	..
	Jno. Duckworth	1	2	4	..	..
	West Walker	1	..	2	..	..
	Andrew Direberry	1	..	1	..	..
	Thom. Langin	1	3	5	..	..
	Jno. Hartley	2	..	2	..	..
	James Lock	1	1	1	..	..
	John Macky	3	2	5	..	..
	Jno. England, Sr	2	2	7	..	..
	Jno. Hughes	2	4	3	..	1
	Sam'l Macay	2	1	6	..	..
	David Tomson	2	2	3	..	..
	Daniel Beall	2	1	5	..	3
	Zach. Dorrs	2	..	2	..	..

First Federal Census, 1790—Continued.

County, City, Town, Parish, Hundred. Etc.	Names of heads of families.	Free white males of sixteen years and upwards, including heads of families.	Free white males under sixteen years.	Free white females, including heads of families.	All other free persons.	Slaves.
BURKE COUNTY	Thos. Macay	2	..	4	..	..
THIRTEENTH COMPANY	Jno Tate	5	..	3	..	3
	Ben Nulin	1	2	1	..	..
	Erasmus May	2	..	1	..	..
	Patrick Hensey	1	1	1	..	3
	Jno. Quein	1	..	2	..	..
	Wm. Duckworth	2	1	1	..	..
	Henry Wood	2	4	3	..	..
	Joseph Dobson	1	..	1	..	3
	Jo Priest	1	..	1	..	..
	Zach Dorrs, Jr	2	1	2	..	..
	Phillip Brettn.	1	1	5	..	..
	Jno. Cooper	1	2	3	..	..
	Leonard Lyon	1	..	5	..	1
	Wm. West	1	3	3	..	..
	Eliza Young	..	..	3	..	..
	Jno. Spears	2	2	1	..	..
	Wm. James	2	..	4	..	..
	Robt. Craige	1	2	1	..	..
	Debo. Guin	2	..	2	..	..
	Wm. McDowell	1	4	4	..	..
	Jno. Henry Sturly	3	..	1	..	..
	Isaac Thompson	1	1	2	..	..
	Alex Baily	2	3	3	..	1
	Robt. Wood	1	1	3	..	1
	Alex Cunings	1	..	1	..	..
	Thos. Kell	1	..	1	..	2
	Thom. Smith	1	..	2	..	..
	Jas. Greencle	1	5	..	..	24
	Jas. Mackey	1	1	1	..	..
	Sally Worthy	..	1	3	..	..
	Waller Sorrels	1	3	4	..	..
	Lewis Lonman	1	2	2	..	..
	Martha Anderson	..	1	3	..	..
	Jas. Pearson	1	1	2	..	..
	Edwd Botial	1	2	1	..	..
	Joseph Hawkins	1	1	3	..	..
	Robt. Kell	1	3	6	..	..
	George Walker	3	2	6	..	..
	Reuben Walker	1	3	2	..	..
	Wm. Southerton	2	2	7	..	..
	Reeson Howard	1	1	2	..	..
	Thos. England	1	..	..	..	..
	Austin Hawkins	1	2	3	..	..
	Wm. Boteat	1	1	2	..	..
	Thos. Kell, Jr	1	1	1	..	..
	Wm. Kell	1	..	2	..	..
	Sam Haufman	1	3	3	..	..
	Jno. McTagert	5	..	8	..	..

FIRST FEDERAL CENSUS, 1790—Continued.

COUNTY CITY, TOWN, PARISH, HUNDRED, ETC.	NAMES OF HEADS OF FAMILIES.	Free white males of sixteen years and upwards, including heads of families	Free white males under sixteen years.	Free white females, including heads of families.	All other free persons.	Slaves.
BURKE COUNTY THIRTEENTH COMPANY	Sam C. Brown.........	2	1	4	..	..
	Thos Higden..........	?	2	2	..	..
	Nicolas Chapman.......	1	2	2	..	..
	Tindel Southerlin......	1	..	1	..	..
	Adam Wise.............	1	1	4	..	..
	Ed Dougherty..........	1	2	6	..	..
	Josiah Hart............	1	1	2	..	..
	Nicolas Burns.........|	1	..	..	..	..
	Phillip Burns..........	1	1	3	..	..
	James Roper...........	1	.	2	..	..
	Jno. Craig.............	1	2	1	..	..
	Jamima Brittn..........	1	1	1	..	..
	Jacob Stillwell.........	2	1	1	..	1
	Henry Box.............	1	3	4	..	..
	Dan Morrow...........	3	..	3	..	..
	James Ross............	1	1	5	..	.
	Jno. England, Jr........	1	5	1	.	..
	Christ'n Bortles.........	1	1	1	..	1
	Jno. Jeferis.............	..	2	4	..	1
	Rd Gibbs	1	1	4	..	..
	Wm. White	1	2	3	..	..
	Wm. Hawkins..........	1	1	2	..	..
	Stephen Rogers.........	1	1	1	..	..
	Dan'l Carol............	1	..	1	..	..
	Adam Smith............	1	1	3	..	..
	Ruth Craig	1	1	1	..	..
	George Daily...........	1	1	4	..	..
	Eloner Clarke...........	.	2	2	..	..
	George Sealy...........	1	1	4	..	..
	Jno. Oxford	1	1	1	..	..
	Sam'l Oxford...........	1	..	1	..	..
	Sarah Elmore...........	..	2	4	..	..
	Robt. Howard..........	1	3	3	..	..
	Rd. Mouser............	1	2	2	..	..
	Henry Miller.	1	1	3	..	..
	Adm Overwort.........	1	..	1	..	..
	Thos. Walker, Jr........	1	1	2	..	..
	George Walker..........	1	3	2	..	..
	Eliza Hughey	1	2	1	..	..
	Jos. Hughey...........	2	..	2	..	..
	George Scott...........	1	2	3	..	..
	Wm. Jones.............	1	5	4	..	..
	Jas. McIntire..........	4	3	4	.	5
	Jno. Gibbs.............	1	3	4	.	..
	Henry Garrison.........	2	3	2	..	..
	Wm. Erwin	1	2	1	..	11
	Wm. Hays.............	1	3	7	..	..
	Wm. Orr..............	2	1	5	..	..
	Stophl Layman.........	1	..	2	..	..

First Federal Census, 1790—Continued.

County, City, Town, Parish, Hundred, Etc.	NAMES OF HEADS OF FAMILIES.	Free white males of sixteen years and upwards, including heads of families.	Free white males under sixteen years.	Free white females, including heads of families.	All other free persons.	Slaves.
BURKE COUNTY	Mary Adams............	..	2	1	..	..
Thirteenth Company	Jno. Smith.............	3	3	4	..	..
	Jos. Scott.............	1	4	7	..	1
	Jno. Neall.............	2	2	2	..	..
	Wm. Baily.............	2	3	6	..	3
	Sam'l McMurry........	1	5	4	..	.
	Jas. Rucker............	3	5	2	..	..
	Thos. Pearson..........	2	..	2	..	..
	Christ'r Pearson	1	..	2	.	..
	Jacob Hips	1	2	4	..	..
	Thos. Gallion..........	1	3	5	.	1
	George Hips, Sr........	3	2	2	..	..
	George Hips...........	2	..	4	..	..
	Jno. Cammell..........	1	1	2	..	..
	Bartlett Anderson..... .	1	..	1	..	..
	Jas. Hartly	1	1	1	..	..
	Jas. Templeton.........	2	2	3	..	..
	George Scott...........	1	2	3	..	..
	Hana Direberry........	1	2	1	..	..
	Thos. Patten...........	2	3	6	..	..
	Jno. Burgess...........	1	2	3	..	..
	Jno. Pearson...........	4	3	8	..	1
	Rd. Burgess...........	1	1	5	..	..
	Thos. Dorrs	1	3	1	.	..
	Jno. Carswell..........	2	2	2	..	..
	Solomon Good.........	1	1	6	..	..
	John Boteat, Sr	3	2	3	..	..
	Jno. Boteat, Jr.........	1	..	1	..	..
	Anguish Camil	1	3	4	..	..
	Abram Wrenshaw	2	..	3	..	..
	John Gunter...........	2	1	2	..	..

1257 heads of families in Burke County.

FIRST CENSUS OF THE UNITED STATES.

FEDERAL, 1908

MORGAN DISTRICT, BURKE COUNTY.

Column headers (applies to all three sections below):
- A = Free white males of 16 years and upward, including heads of families.
- B = Free white males under 16 years.
- C = Free white females, including heads of families.
- D = All other free persons.
- E = Slaves.

FIRST COMPANY.

Name of head of family.	A	B	C	D	E
Dobson, Jos., Jr.	3	3	5		1
Young, Joshua	1	5	4		
Davidson, George	1	3	1		1
Washburn, Matthew	1	1	1		
Bradshaw, Isaiah	1	1	2		
Stroud, Peter	1	5	2		3
Stroud, Peter, Jr.	1		1		
Stroud, Jesse	1	3	1		
Washburn, David	2		6		
Washburn, Drury	1	1	2		
Patten, Wm	1		2		
Patten, Sam	1	3	2		
McWilliams, Jas	1	2	5		
McCracon, Quilla	1	2	5		1
Reed, Robt	1	4	3		1
Trammell, Jno	1	3	4		
Brown, Jos	4		5		
McDowell, Jas	1	2	2		2
Cathey, Wm	3	4	5		3
McClure, Andw	3	5	5		
Durr, Wm	3	2	4		3
Welsh, Thos	1	3	1		
Hannah, The H	1		1		
Dickeson, Cathrn	1	1	5		
Melony, John	1		1		
McClure, Francis	3		4		
Jones, Jno	1	3	3		
Edenton, Rhoda	2	5	2		
Collet, Wm	1	2	2		
Bibo, Thos	1	1	3		
Burchfield, Mialth	1	1	4		3
McDowell, Jno	1	1	1		1
Carol, Sterling	1		1		
Carol, George	1	1	8		
McDowell, Jos, Jun	1	2	1		9
Carson, Jno	2	5	2		12
Welsh, Jno, Senr	3	3	5		
O'Neal, Wat	2		3		
Webster, Moses	1	2	4		
McPeters, Jonathan	1	1	2		
McPeters, Jos	1	3	5		
Plumley, Wm	3	1	3		
Trorps, Nicholas	3	3	3		
Shuke, Jacob	1		3		
Davidson, Jno	3	5	6		6
Neall, Wm	4	1	4		
Patten, Elijah	1	2	6		2

FIRST COMPANY—con.

Name of head of family.	A	B	C	D	E
Hobs, Mary			2		
Mitchell, Pounce	1	2	2		
Innan, Saml	1	2	1		
Innan, Henry	1		1		
Plumly, Stephen	1	1	2		
Williams, Henry	1	1	3		
Stout, Saml	2	5	3		
Reid, Jno	1		3		
Neall, Jas	1	4	2		1
Wiggins, Abram	1	2	2		1
Brittain, Aron	1		2		
Branden, Martin	2		2		
Cathey, George	2	3	4		5
Brown, Chas	1		3		
Cathey, Marget		1	4		
Neall, Andw	1	1	4		
Lewis, Wm	1	2	4		
Kelton, Wm	1	4	6		7
Flord, Abram	1	3	2		
McGonigle, Jno	1	1	3		
Posey, Francis	1	4	2		
Wilson, Thos	5	1	2		12
Hill, Robt	1	1	1		
Rus, Rose	1	3	5		
Davis, Ben	5	3	4		
Culberson, David	1	3	4		
Bright, Tobias	1	1	1		
Blakely, Robt	1	1	6		
Mashburn, David	1		2		
Jetton, Jno	1	1	4		2
Higgins, Wm	3	2	6		
Norton, Messer	1	3	5		
Templeton, Arche	4	2	4		
Martin, Jno	3	4	5		
Hix, James	1	1	2		
Atwater, Isaac	1				
Melony, Edwd	1	2	6		
Davidson, Ben	2	1	9		
McBride, David	1	2	1		
Glass, Thos	2		2		
Glass, Henry	1	2	1		
McGonigle, Wm	1	1	3		
Logan, Jane	2	1	3		
Kelly, Wm	3	5	3		
Bird, Ben, Sen	2		2		2
Bird, Ben, Jr	1	1	2		
Brevard, Zeb, Jr	1	2	3		

FIRST COMPANY—con.

Name of head of family.	A	B	C	D	E
Hemphill, Thos	2	2	7		11
Adkins, Jno	3	2	6		
Ellison, Thos	1	1	6		
Ellison, Henry	1	4	1		
Hambrick, Robt	1	2	2		
Thompson, Zach	1		1		
Penhly, Jno	1	2	2		
Regan, Thos	2	4	4		
Vickry, Luke	1	1	3		
Ellison, Ben	2	2	8		
Young, Jane			6		
Wilson, Jno	1	1	1		
Smith, Jared	1		1		
Gunter, Agusta	1	1	1		
McClisky, Jno	1		1		
Kelly, Alex. Ham	1	2	2		
Oneal, Charles	1		1		
Rogers, Mourning	2	3	2		
Adams, George	1	1	2		
Givins, Wim	1	2	4		

SECOND COMPANY.

Name of head of family.	A	B	C	D	E
Conally, John	1	3	5		10
Shell, Jno	2	4	4		
Martin, Isaac	1	6	3		
Hashan, Abram	1	4	3		1
Dudly, Rebekah			3		
Martin, Marget		2	1		
Wagoner, Marget			2		
Francum, Wm	1	3	3		
Francum, Jno	1		1		
Martin, Thos	1	2	4		
Moore, James	2		5		
Conally, Wm	2	2	2		
Fleming, Abram	1	3	3		8
Winkler, Conrod	1	1	3		
Spencer, Jno, Sr	1	3	5		
Smith, Zadock	1	5	3		
Murray, Jno	1	2	1		
Murray, David	1	5	2		
Clarke, Ben	1		1		
Suttlemire, Jacob	1	3	4		
Bradshaw, Wm	1		7		
Homan, Edwd	1		3		3
Homan, Gilbert	1	2	8		
Fips, Jno	1	3	7		

Continued on next page, 107.

From :First Census of the United States, Federal, 1908.

At the end of this version, a comparison of the two census records will be shown as taken from the National Archives in Washington, from film.

MORGAN DISTRICT, BURKE COUNTY—Continued.

Column headers for each section:
- Free white males of 16 years and upward, including heads of families.
- Free white males under 16 years.
- Free white females, including heads of families.
- All other free persons.
- Slaves.

SECOND COMPANY—con.

NAME OF HEAD OF FAMILY.	16+ M	<16 M	F	Other	Slaves
Bellew, Jos	2		3		
Clarke, Beverly	1		3		
Bellew, Stephen	1	1	4		
Hawk, George	2	2	6		
Tillotson, Ben	1	2	5		
Turner, Nathan	1	1	4		
Francum, Rebekah	1	1	1		
Conally, Jas	1	3	4		
Conally, Hugh	1	1	3		
Barnhart, Jno	1	2	3		
Dereberry, Jacob	1	4	4		
Dereberry, Mich'l	1	3	4		
Pain, Wm	1	2	7		2
Perkins, Joshua	3	3	2		
Taylor, Wm	1		1		
Stoner, Henry	3	2	7		
Clarke, Wilm	1		4		
Grenstaff, Michl	1	1	4		
Whitehead, Mary			3		
Winkler, Thos, Sr	1		3		
Sottlemire, Adam	2	3	3		
Bellew, Willm	1	9	2		
Master, Henry	1	1	5		
Williams, Anne	1	1	2		
Baker, H. Barton	1	3	5		
Brown, Dan'l	1	2	6		
Berry, Joseph	2	3	6		
Berry, Jas	1	1	1		
Berry, Jno	1	1	4		
Berry, Lot	1	2	2		
Baldwin, Wm	1	4	4		
Giles, Saml	1	2	2		
Winkler, Joseph	1	1	2		
Wilson, Jno	1		2		
Smith, Thos	2	1	4		
Erwin, Agnes		1	1		
Martin, Jas		1	1		
Spencer, Jno, Jr	1	1	3		
King, Jas	1	1	3		
Mason, Robt	1	1	5		
Marcle, Laurene	1	1	3		
Pack, Elisa	2		2		
Hart, Michal	1	3	7		
Winkler, Thos, Jr	1	1	3		
Giles, Jno	1	6	4		
Baker, James	1	1	4		
Boone, Sherwood	1	1	2		
Parmer, Jno	2				
Pruett, Jno	1	2	5		
Grider, Martin	1	1	6		
Williams, Leah	1	1	2		
Pruett, Henry	1		2		
Innes, James	3	2	2		
Bradsha, Josiah	1	3	3		
Grasty, Mary		1	2		
Morgan, George	1	5	2		

THIRD COMPANY.

NAME OF HEAD OF FAMILY.	16+ M	<16 M	F	Other	Slaves
Baker, Davd	1	3	3		
Penland, Robt	1	4	6		1
Penland, George	3	2	5		
Hanson, Bartlet	3	4	3		6
White, Ben	2	3	3		
Antony, Paul, Sr.x	2	2	2		1
Baker, Jas	1				
Baxter, Jas	1	4	2		
Browning, Jno	3	4	5		
White, Tho, Jr	1	6	4		
Parks, Ben	1	4	4		3
Antony, James, Sr	3	4	4		
White, Reuben	1	2	2		
Baker, Jno	1	2	3		
Mason, Elisa			4		
Beck, Jacob	3	6	5		
Rogers, Stephen	1	1	2		
Shelela, Philip	2		1		
Penland, Wm	5	2	3		1
Baker, Charles	1		2		
Prichard, Jas	1	2	7		
Fowler, Edwd	2	1	3		
Walker, Thos	1		1		
Medly, Jos	1	1			
White, Tho, Sr	1		2		
Shell, Simon	1		2		
Shell, Fred	1	3	6		
Shell, Fred, Jr	2	1	2		
Shenito, James	1	1	3		
McDonell, Davd	1	1	3		
Mitchenor, Thos	1	1	2		
McGahey, Jno	1	1	2		
Erwin, Arthur	1		2		
Avery, Waight	1	1	6		24
Brown, Jno Colwill	1	3	5		7
Pruett, Jos	2	4	2		7

THIRD COMPANY—con.

NAME OF HEAD OF FAMILY.	16+ M	<16 M	F	Other	Slaves
Mosely, George	1	2	5		2
Piney, Stephen	1	2	5		
Wright, Dan	1		1		
Fox, Titus	1	2	3		
Scott, George	1		7	7	
Baker, Henry	1	3	4	6	
Gyer, Jacob	2	3	4		
Cole, Alex	1	1	3		
Fox, Jno	1	3	2		
Wakefield, Henry	1	2	4	2	
Simpson, Jno	1	2	3		
Harbison, Alex	3	3	3		
Stilwell, Jno	1	3	3		
Odel, Reuben	1	1	1		
Rose, Ben	1	1	4		
Penly, Joshua	1	3	4		
Parks, Thos	2	3	6		1
Alexander, Elisa	1		2		
Antony, Paul, Jr	1				
Brasfield, Jno	1	1	1		
Antony, Philip	1		4		
Trammell, Jno	2	1	2		
Painter, Jno	2	2	3		
Alexander, James	1	5	4		
Antony, Jacob, Jr	1		1		
Fox, Allen	1	2	2		
Branch, Saml	1	2	4		
Scott, Miriah	2	1	3		
Gilmore, Robt	1	2	2		
Parks, Larkin	1		2		
Phillips, Laraaus	1	3	1		
Penly, Willm, Jr	3		1		
Penly, Wm, Senr	2	3	3		
Hall, John	2	2	2		
Burkes, Rolln	1	4	4		
Church, Robt	1	2	1		
Church, Thom	1	1	1		
Tramel, Big Denis	2	2	3		
Simpson, James	1	1	1		
Wakefield, John	1	4	3		
Scott, Wiley	1		6		
Piercy, Elisa	3	1	2		
Ustam, Wm	1	1	2		
Trancle, Little Denis	1		3		
Allen, Juima		2	2		
Sherrll, Ute	1		4		
Wagiey, Jno	2	4	4		
Duk, Jno	1	2	2		

FOURTH COMPANY.

NAME OF HEAD OF FAMILY.	16+ M	<16 M	F	Other	Slaves
Forgayn, James	3	3	4		
Edmison, Jas	3	3	3		
Hollnsworth, Sam	2	2	9		
Adams, Howell	1	1	2		
Halley, Mark	1		5		
Raybon, Kizzi			4		
Conizo, Harison W	2	2	8		
Green, Wm	2	4	4		
Green, Elijah	1	2	5		
Morris, Wilm	2	4	4		1
Hally, Rd	2	2	4		
Williams, Thom	1	2	9		
Raybon, Hodge	1	2	1		
Harris, Wooton	2	1	3		
Huggins, Luke	1	4	4		
Wadkins, Else		2	1		
Adams, Ben	1	2	3		
Fleming, Jno	1	3	1		
Fleming, Peter	1	3	4		
Davis, Clem	1	4	1		
Fleming, Thom	1	3	4		
Pickeral, Ben	1	3	4		
Halley, Jas	1	4	4		
Humphris, Jas	1		4		
Smith, Jas	1		3		
Goodbread, Philip	1	1	3		
Goodbread, Jos	1	2	4		
Huggins, Phillip	2		1		
Stoker, Jas	1	1	2		
Wrester, Thos	1	4	1		
Janis, Jno	1	2	1		
Wallace, Jno	1	2	3		
Oaks, Joshua	1	2	3		
Brndsha, Obadiah	1	1	5		
Bryan, Thom	1		3		
Mendinall, Jesse	1		5		
Burgin, Ben	2	6	1		
Hamby, Wilm	3	2	3		
Corby, John	2	2	5		
Nicols, Thos	1	3	6		1
Portman, Wm	1		5		
Jax, Wm	1	1	5		
Wilson, James	1	2	6		
Noblet, Jno	1	2	2		

FOURTH COMPANY—con.

NAME OF HEAD OF FAMILY.	16+ M	<16 M	F	Other	Slaves
Chafen, Jas, Jr	3		3		
Petillo, Jno, Sen	2		2		3
Hodge, Robt, Sr	1		6		
Porter, Wilm, Sr	1		4		
Haws, Jacob	2	3	4		
Horrill, James	1		1		3
Chafen, Mary			3		
Hughes, Sam	2		2		
Jackson, Edward	2	5	3		
Fikes, Elisha	2		1		
Litle, Thom	1	3	1		
Petillo, Midleton	1		1	1	
Brown, Thos	2		3		
Cormpin, Ellis	1		1		
Ledford, Nicholas	1		1		
Porter, Wm, Jr	1	1	3		
Strain, Henry	1	4	1		
Elliot, James	1		3		
Chaffen, Elias	1		1		
Diment, Mary	2	2	2		
Keller, Jacob	1	2	1		
Hodge, Robt, Jr	1	2	1		
Wood, Jos	1		3		
Doaty, Jno	1	2	2		
Davis, Thom	1	2	2		
Engld, William	—1	2	3		
Scolds, Joseph	1		4		
Wallace, Jno		4	4		
Heward, Zeb, Jr	1		2		
Julin, Ben	1	1	4		
Julin, William	1	2	6		
Penkly, Michal	1	1	1		
Redick, Cornelius	1		3		
Chaffen, Amos	1	1	3		
Gilliland, Jno	1	4	4		
Collins, Frudence			2		

FIFTH COMPANY.

NAME OF HEAD OF FAMILY.	16+ M	<16 M	F	Other	Slaves
Kilpatrick, Robt	4	5	4		
Webb, Jas. Crit	2	2	2		
Murphey, Wilm	1	3	2		3
White, Joseph	1	2	4		7
Johnson, Wm	1	3	6		
Bonne, Jesse	1	3	5		
Hankins, John	1	3	2		
Holliway, George	1	1	4		
Lovin, Wilm	1	1	4		
Hickman, George	1	4	5		1
Weakfield, Charles	4		5		3
Wakefield, Thom	1		3		
Ewings, Isaac	1		2		
Fletcher, Reubin	1	2	3		
Church, Jno	1	1	4		
James, Jos	2		2		
Williams, Wm	1	3	2		
Hite, Reid	2		7		7
Moore, Jas, Senr	2		4		
Moore, Jno	2	1	4		1
Adkins, Ben	1	1	5		
Eastress, Reubin	1	4	3		9
Lewis, Lewis	2	5	4		
Harris, Edward	2	1	13		
Miller, George	1	1	3		
Waters, Deep	1		3		
Waters, Abram	1	3	5		
Coker, Leonard	1		3		
Coker, Charles, Sr	2	2	3		
Coker, Charles	1		2		
Coker, Wm	1	2	1		
Moore, Jesse, Sr	2		3		
Moore, Jesse	1		3		
Moore, Danl	1		4		2
Coffee, Reubin	1	1	3		3
Coffey, John	1	1	2		
Coffy, Jas	1	1	3		1
Holland, Jas	2	4	5		
Coker, Joseph	1		2		
Moorhead, Jas	1	2	2		
Whitbeck, Matha	2	2	5		
Mullin, Danl	1		5		
Callaway, Ricd	1	1	1		
Hicks, David	3	2	3		
Beard, Ezekiel	1	3	2		
Beard, Saml	3	2	2		
Ward, Byn	1	1	2		
Ward, Joshua	1	1	1		
Giddins, James	2		4		
Searsey, Robt	1	3	4		
Edmison, Wm	1	3	3		
Hays, Thom	3	3	3		1
Hays, George	1	1			
Webb, Ben	1	2	2		
Webb, Jas, Jr	1		1		
Walker, Reynard	1	5	3		

FIRST CENSUS OF THE UNITED STATES.

NAME OF HEAD OF FAMILY.	Free white males of 16 years and upward, including heads of families.	Free white males under 16 years.	Free white females, including heads of families.	All other free persons.	Slaves.
FIFTH COMPANY—con.					
Boon, Jonathn	1	3	5		
Dowell, George	2	3	3		
Helle, Moses	2		4		
Anderson, Thos, Jr	2	2	6		1
Powers, Jessey	1	1	5		
Powers, Thom	2	1	2		
Rice, Jno	3		2		
Smith, Nathan	1	1	2		
Medecarst, Rice	1	2	5		
Stud, Moses	1	3	3		
Neely, Jas	1	4	6		
Wilson, Michal	1	3	5		
Jenell, Wm. F	1	3	4		
Wilson, James	1		2		
James, Rolin	1		6		
Renault, Wm	1		1		
Hutchins, George	1	3	3		
Eastriss, Leonard	1		2		
Wilson, Wm	1	1	3		
Church, Thom, Sr	2		4		
Snead, Jacob	3		8		
Carter, George	2	4	5		
Church, Robt	1	2	1		
Eastriss, Layton	2		2		
Brown, Jno	1	2	3		
King, Baker	1	2	2		
Whittenton, Jno	1	3	2		
Guin, Champion	1		1		
White, Wm, Senr	6		2		12
SIXTH COMPANY.					
Cowan, Joseph	2	1	3		
Reed, Jno	1		3		
Wilson, Greenberry	1	1	4		3
Bars, Caleb	1	5	4		
Sellers, James	1	1	4		
Hall, Jno	1	3	6		1
Wilkinson, Moses	1		3		3
Sellers, Jno	1	2	1		
Pearson, Michal	1		1		
O'Neal, Patrick, Jr	1		1		
Dizard, Jno	1	6	4		
Sellers, Robt., Sr	1	2	3		
Sellors, Robt	1		5		
Rutherford, Jno	1	2	3		2
Dizard, Marget	1		3		
Allen, Jno, Sr	4	2	4		
Hytle, Hezekiah	2	2	6		1
Morrison, Wm	5	4	4		
Andrews, Danl	3	4	4		
Rutherford, Wm	2		2		5
Rust, Enos	4	3	2		
Rust, Peter	2	2	3		
Moore, Wm	1	3	5		6
Gunter, Clayton	1	5	1		
Plundy, Aham	1	1	5		1
Devian, Jas	2		2		
Denton, Elisa	2		4		
Curely, Jas	1	1	2		
Caroly, Henry	1	4	2		
Sullivan, Danl	1		2		
Grant, Isaac	1		2		
O'Neal's, Patrick	2		2		
Montgomery, Jno	2		3		
Montgomery, Jas	1	3	4		5
Bing, Jas	1		9		
Leatherwood, Edw'd	1	3	5		2
Montgomery, Bridg'	2	2	2		2
Hunter, Andrew	1		4		
Justice, Jos	2	2	1		
Simmons, Rd	1	1	2		
Gray, Lydia	2	1	5		5
Bradshaw, Field	1	4	3		2
Hytle, Edwd	1	3	3		
Tennison, Jacob	1		3		
Chanler, Henry	1	4	3		
McDowell, Jno	2	2	4		5
Montgomery, Robt	2	4	3		7
Beall, Thos	1	4	4		
Hyett, Simon	1		3	1	
Ferrila, Isaac	1	5	4		
Robison, Alex	1		2		
Burchild, Aberilla	3	3	5		
Bellew, Robt	3	1	5		
Rust, David	1	3	3		
Maya, Jno	1	3	6		
Finley, Charles	1	6	3		
Rutherford, Jno	2	2	3		2
Gardner, Wm	2	4	7		3
Polk, Jno	2	4	3		
Downing, Jno	2	2	3		
Long, Alex	3		4		
McAdams, Jno	1	3	4		
Jones, Ben	1		2		
Worley, Frank	1	3	2		
Summers, Jno	1	5	4		

NAME OF HEAD OF FAMILY.	Free white males of 16 years and upward, including heads of families.	Free white males under 16 years.	Free white females, including heads of families.	All other free persons.	Slaves.
SIXTH COMPANY—con.					
Wood, Saml	3	3	6		
Reno, Jno	1	2	5		
Morison, Wm, Jr	1		4		
Jackson, Chaswl	1	1	8		
Probit, Wm	1		1		3
Patten, Elijah, Jr	1	1	2		
Hemphill, Jas	3	4	4		
Morison, Eliza		1	6		
Loneis, David	1		1		
Martin, Henry	2	1	5		
Jewell, Jas	2	1	3		
Corby, Wm	1	1	3		
Hicks, Zacheus	1	1	2		
Greg, Wm	1	3	2		
Elder, Andrew	1	2	1		
Woods, Andw	1	1	5		
Patten, Robt	1	1	3		
Patten, Frank	3	1	6		2
Cowan, Marget			1		5
Dunel, Jno	1		5		
Blankenship, Lodo	2	4	3		
Hodge, Frank	1		1		
Hodge, George	1	1	3		
Hall, Jas, Jr	1		2		
Hall, Joshua	1	2	1		
Hughes, Andrew	1	1	4		
Baker, Bardel	1		2		
McElwrath, David	2	5	7		
Woods, Robt	1		1		
Evits, George			3		
Hall, Naomi		2	2		
Walker, Jno	1	3	2		
Smith, Jno	1	3	3		
SEVENTH COMPANY.					
Coreponong, Albert	1	4	4		
Franklin, Jno, Sr	2	1	6		
Antony, Martin	2	5	2		
Sansom, Micaja	1	2	4		
Fais, Edmund	1	3	5		
Littlejohn, Eli	1		3		
McDowell, Col. Jos	2		5		10
McKinny, Henry	1	1	2		2
Tomson, Jeremiah	2	2	4		17
Erwin, Jno	1	6	3		3
Maxwell, Jno	1	2	2		
Lane, Jno	1	2	2		
McGimsey, Jno	2		1		3
Fleming, Robt	1	2	8		
Wisloen, Thos	1	1	6		9
Coffee, Ben	1	3	2		
Murphey, Jas	1	1	1		5
Harper, Jno	1		2		
Harper, Jno, Jr	2	3	3		
Erwin, Alex	1	3	7		11
Fonay, Jacob	1	2			6
Kelly, Ben	1		2		
Tummins, Saml	1	2	2		
Isom, Christa	2	3	3		
Case, Thos	1	2	2		
Macay, Hugh	1	2	3		
Flamire, Wm	1		3		
Cook, Adam	1	2	2		
Maxwell, Isaac	1		2		
Dotson, Esau	1		3		
McKinny, Elisa	1	1	4		1
Bradford, Benet	3	2	4		
Carter, Wm	1	1	3		
Husband, Elas	1		3		
Turnire, Saml	1		1		
Goble, Jno	1		1		
Clarke, Nancy	2	4	3		
Clarke, Joaba	1		3		
Clarke, Jno	1	2	2		
Arney, Lorane			2		
Wagoner, Christd	1	3	2		
Sutser, Adam	1		2		
Cook, George	1	2	4		
Dobs, Chesly	2	1	4		
Winkler, Adam	2		2		
Winkler, Thos, Sr	2		2		
Winkler, David	1		2		
Winkler, Jersey Conrod	1	2	2		
Winkler, Big Conrad	1	1	4		
Howk, Mich	2	3	2		
Moody, Tho	2	3	2		
Moody, Jno	1		1		
Sweat, Gilbert	1	1	3		
Sweat, Ephraim	1	2	2		
Hughes, Hana	1	1	5		
Martin, Phillip	2		3		
Martin, George	1	2	2		
Little, Wm	1	2	2		
Little, Jno	1	1	2		
Day, Thos	3	1			
Stallins, Abram	3		6		

NAME OF HEAD OF FAMILY.	Free white males of 16 years and upward, including heads of families.	Free white males under 16 years.	Free white females, including heads of families.	All other free persons.	Slaves.
SEVENTH COMPANY—continued.					
Stephens, Phil	1	3	7		
Davis, Wm	2	2	2		
Flass, Jonathan	1	2	2		
Hobs, Nathan	1	3	2		
Lane, Thos	1	4	3		
Trible, Jno	2		2		
McDowell, Charles	1	2	5		10
Perkins, Elisha	2	2	2		9
Murphy, Silas	1	5	2		
Pitin, Wm	2	1	3		
Lorance, Wm	1		5		
Dinbery, Adam	1	3	5		
Husband, Vesay	1		2		
Tips, Jacob	1	4	3		
Franklin, John, Jr	1	1	3		
Cragg, Thos	1		3		
Crag, Saml	1		2		
Harper, Meredith	1	4	2		
Baldin, Jacob	1	1	1		
Crawford, Tom	1		3		
Gibson, David	1	2	4		
Gibson, William	1	3	1		
Gibson, Harmon	1		1		
Cray, Joab	2	1	2		
Stafford, Jno	3	2	2		
Barns, Rd	1	1	2		
Coffe, Cleveland	1	2	4		
Crag, Christn	1	3	2		
Hughes, Jno	1	1	2		
Bolinger, Jno	1		2		
Henery, John	2		3		
Little, Marget			2		
Jones, Ambrous	1		1		
Crisp, Wm	1		2		
Baldin, Jno, Senr	1		1		
Landers, Jno	1	1	4		
Prichard, Jas, Sr	2	2	2		
Gilbert, Joshua	1		3		
EIGHTH COMPANY.					
Reid, Henry	1	2	3		
Reid, James	1	1	3		
Mayberry, Lewis	1	2	4		2
Barns, George	1		6		
Gibson, Stephen	2	1	1		1
Rutor, Lewis	1		1		
Bradburn, Thos	1	1	3		
Warren, Robt	3	3	6		
Warren, Wm	3	3	1		
Pane, George	1	1	3		
Reid, Wm	1	4	3		
Stuel, Andw	3		2		3
Burgess, Matthew	1	5	3		
West, Alex	1	2	4		
Scott, Thos	1	4	4		
Ennuit, Rd	1	2	5		
Bradford, Jno	1	2	2		
Green, Thos	4	3	6		
Russell, Ried	1	1	4		
Crisp, Bray	1	1	3		
West, Alex, Sr	1	1	8		
Horse, Jno	3	1	1		
Collier, Jas	1	1	2		
Smith, Jno	3	1	1		
Cox, Matthew	3	1	1		
Roberts, Wm, Jun	1		1		
Moon, Robt	1	1	3		
Brown, George, Jr	1	2	3		
Brown, Rd	1	2	2		
Steel, Saml	1	2	2		
Winkler, Jacob	5		1		
Tuttle, Amos	2	2	2		
Sherril, Wm	1	4	5		
Headley, Jno	1	2	3		
Austin, Ben	1	2	6		
Hunsucker, Abrm	2		1		
Hunsucker, Abrm, Jr	1		2		
Hunsucker, Jno	1	2			
Pain, Barnet	1	4	5		
Fletcher, Jas	1	2	3		
Medlock, Nicolas	2		4		
Medlock, Nicols, Jr	1	1	2		
Falls, John	1	2	2		
Bains, John	1	2	3		
Reid, Hugh	1	6	4		
Banks, Elijah	1	2	4		
Fox, Hugh	1	2	7		
Baker, Henry	1	3	4		
Kellor, Jacob	1	3	4		
Kellor, Martin	3	3	4		
Price, Jno Yeats	1	2	7		
White, Luke	1		4		
Jones, Nicholas	1	4	4		
Walker, Dulley	1	2	5		
Teague, Edwd	1		4		2
Teague, Jno	1	2	3		

MORGAN DISTRICT, BURKE COUNTY—Continued.

NAME OF HEAD OF FAMILY.	Free white males of 16 years and upward, including heads of families.	Free white males under 16 years.	Free white females, including heads of families.	All other free persons.	Slaves.
EIGHTH COMPANY—con.					
Hadly, Joshua	1				
Green, Elijah	1		4		
Roberts, Wm, Sr	2	1	6		
Keller, Christina	1		1		
Tenny, James	1	3	3		
Colwell, Wm	1	1	1		
Gibson, Jos	1				
Hooker, Jno	1		2		
Dockery, Wm	1	2	2		
Conrod, Jno	2	1	1		
Roberts, Jno	1		4		
Cuningham, Jas	1	5	2		
Dockery, Jas	1	2	4		
Steward, Saml	1		2		
Feniton, Absalom	1		2		
McErtin, Jno	1	3	4		
White, Jonas	1	1	2		
Hood, Jno	1		2		
Reed, Tho	2		3		
Brown, Absalom	1	3	2		
Pain, Danl	1	1	1		
Hephaer, Phillip	1		1		
Grenstaff, Isaac	2	2	4		
Gibson, Isom	1		2		
Farmes, Jno	2	1	2		
Fullerton, Wm	1		1		
Clarke, James	1	5	2		
Thomas, James	1	1	4		
Grenstaff, Jane		2	2		
Walker, Charlow	1	1	5		2
Walker, Simon	1	3	4		
Medlock, John	2		3		
Austin, Ben, Sr	3	1	5		
Gibson, Major	2		3		
Spradling, Jesse	1	1	2		1
Gibson, Wilburn	1	1	2		
Scott, Jno	1		3		
Dockery, Jno	1	1	2		
Banell, Jonathan	2		2		
Yokely, Jno	1		3		
Fox, Jas	1	3	2		
Graham, Abs	1	1	2		
Prisly, Jas	1		4		
Steward, James	1		4		
Davis, Uriah	3	5	3		
Green, Elizabeth	1		3		5
Price, Rd	1	4	3		
Prew, Phillip	2	3	4		
Dishazer, Eliza		2	2		
Irons, Wm	1	3	3		
Smith, Wm	1	1	3		
Troutman, Adam	1	2	7		
Cumming, Jno	2	1	3		
Allen, Jno	2		3		
Alexander, Wm	1		1		
Macay, Wm	1	1	2		
Matthewson, Alex	3	2	2		
NINTH COMPANY.					
Thomson, Peter	3	4	4		1
Sumpter, Jas	1		3		
Bartley, Jno	2	4	4		
Hays, Jno	2	4	6		
Murray, Joshua	2	1	3		
Howk, Nicolas	1	4	4		
Tucker, George	1		2		
Baker, Joseph	2	1	3		
Moony, Win	3		2		
McCrary, Jno	4	5	1		
Murray, Jas	1		3		
Murray, Jno, Jr	1	1	3		
Grider, Fred, Jr	1	5	3		
Grider, Fred, Sr	2		3		
Murry, Barbara		1	4		
Smith, Saml	1	3	3		
Prowell, Thos	1		2		
Angely, Peter	1	2	1		
Hartley, George	2	1	3		
Lathrum, Johnson	1	1	3		
Fincannon, Jno	1	5	3		
Grider, Jno	1	4	2		
Grider, Jacob	1		2		
Smally, Abner	1	3	5		
Repofo, Wm	1	4	4		
Wilson, Ezekl			4		
Wood, Jno	1	7	4		
Garlin, Eliza			2		
Perlman, Wm		2	4		
Shoat, Saybort	1		3		
Gilmore, Eliza			1		
Green, Rd	1	4	5		
Abshiro, Christn	1	4	3		
Swaringin, Saml	1		6		

NAME OF HEAD OF FAMILY.	Free white males of 16 years and upward, including heads of families.	Free white males under 16 years.	Free white females, including heads of families.	All other free persons.	Slaves.
NINTH COMPANY—con.					
Stilwell, Jeremy	1		2		
Smith, Solomon	1	3	4		
Penly, Jas	1	1	1		
Wilson, Edward	2		1		
Hines, Jno	2	4	5		
Pots, James	1		3		1
Nailor, Jas	1		3		
Coffce, Jno	1	4	4		
Amons, Mark	1		3		
Allen, Micajah	1	1	1		
Tucker, George, Sen	1	1	1		
Ramsey, Saml	1	1	1		
Davis, Wm	2		2		
Thornton, Wm	1	1	3		
Allen, Jno	2	1	2		
Hottsshaw, Henry	4		4		
Owens, Edwd	1		4		
Mayson, Isaac	1	1	4		
Streeton, Hezekiah	1		3		
Hartley, Wm	1	1	3		
Hartley, Sarah	1	3	4		
Blair, Jno	1	3	2		1
Hons, James	1		2		
Onions, Saml	1	4	5		
Day, Jno	1	3	3		
Day, Nicholas	1	3	5		
Day, James	2	1	2		
Hicks, Willis	2		8		
Green, Jacob	1		1		
Wisdom, Jos	1	3	3		
Highsaw, Fred	2	2	3		
Stroetton, Susana	1	2	2		
Harris, Jno	1	2	2		
Hammons, Elijah	1	2	3		
Randolph, Thom	2	1	3		
Herrin, Wm	1		3		
Blair, Colvard	1	1	2		2
Sumpter, Wm	3		2		
Sumpter, Thos	1		3		
Setherd, Abram	1	2	2		1
Neely, Jno	1	1	2		
Allen, Jonathn	1		2		
Allen, Jonthn, Sr	1		3		
Dennis, Rd	1		4		
Crisp, Jno	2	5	4		
Crisp, Wm	1		1		
Ramsey, Richd	1	3	4		
Constable, Liney	1	3	2		
Ramsay, Eliza			2		
Hott, Peter	1	4	5		2
Hott, Jacob	2		1		1
Relly, Arom	1	1	1		
Swaringin, Check	1	1	2		
Powell, Ambros	2	4	5		
Powell, Elias	1	3	3		1
Townsend, Jno	4	1	2		6
Grisom, Wm	1		1		
McDaniel, Jno	1	1	3		
McDaniel, Saml	1		3		
Thrasher, Wm	1	3	4		
Wilson, Ginral	1	3	2		
Greenaway, Joseph	1		3		
Greenaway, Jos, Sr	2	1	3		
James, Thos	1		2		
James, Wm	1		1		
James, Mary			2	3	
Taylor, Jno	4	1	3		
Miller, Robt, Jesse	1	2	2		2
McDaniel, Tempe			2		
Smith, Sarah			2		
Swaringen, Saml	1		1		
Phillips, Isaac	1	2	2		
Powell, Thos	1	1	4		
Powell, Elias	1		2		2
Cox, Isaac	2	2	4		
Long, Edward	1	4	3		
Eashtman, Isaac	1	4	4		1
Notherly, Robt	2	5	2		
Powell, Ellas, Sr	1				1
Powell, Lewis	1		1		
TENTH COMPANY.					
Young, Joseph	1		2		
Demerlin, George	1	4	2		4
Wofford, Wm	2		2		
Bolin, Amy			4		
Holinsworth, Jacob	1	1	4		
Wofford, Ben	1		2		
Hopper, George	1	2	7		
Holinsworth, Saml	1	3	4		1
Nation, Jos	2	3	4		
Nation, Wm	2	1	2		
Hancock, Joel	1		2		

NAME OF HEAD OF FAMILY.	Free white males of 16 years and upward, including heads of families.	Free white males under 16 years.	Free white females, including heads of families.	All other free persons.	Slaves.
TENTH COMPANY—con.					
Spoons, Wm	1		2		2
Hall, Jno	1	2	5		
Burleson, Agnes	1	1	2		
Phillips, Charles	1		2		
Vann, Jno	2	1	3		
Phillips, Wm	2	1	4		
Holefield, Danl	1	5	4		
Rose, Isaiah	2	2	4		
Bridges, Wm	1	1	3		
McFalls, Delila			3		
Hopper, Charls	2	4	5		
Carson, James	2	2	6		
Robison, Jno	1	2	3		
Bell, Margot			2		
Hensly, Ben	3	3	3		
Lee, James	1	3	3		
Johnson, Louisa		1	1		
McKinny, Wm	1		3		
McKinny, Thom	1		2		
Medlock, Rd	1	3	4		
Gouge, Jno	1	1	2		
Rose, Jno, Senr	1	2	3		
Rose, Jno, Junr	1		2		
Wilson, Jas	2	1	4		
Hanlen, Jno	2	1	2		
Morron, James	1	5	3		
Ainsworth, Jas	2	4	3		8
Moody, Wm	1	5	4		
Billins, Wm	1	2	4		
Forsythe, Jacob	1	1	3		
McFalls, Jno	1	1	1		
Brown, Danl	1	1	1		
Turner, Rost, Sr	1	1	1		
Turner, Robt	1	1	2		
Moore, Wm	1	3	3		
Wilson, Jno, Jr	1	2	1		
McCracon, David	2		7		
Wilson, Jno	3	2	4		
Night, Thos	3	3	4		
Night, Thos, Jr	1		2		
Deaton, Neathn	1		4		
Moore, Tho	1	1	1		
Wilson, Sam	1	1	4		
Wilson, George	2	2	7		
Young, Thos	2	1	2		2
Young, Joshua	1		1		
Kensy, Abigail		2	1		
Hull, Sally		1	1		
Devenport, Martin	3	4	3		4
Bright, Saml	1	2	3		
Wiseman, Wm	4	4	5		
Wiseman, Thos	1		4		
Jones, Jos	1	3	4		
Price, James	1	1	5		
Bright, Wm	1	2	5		
Hill, Wm	2	1	6		
Taylor, Jas	1	1	4		
Hill, Wm, Senr	1		4		
Breckerstuff, Thos	1	1	1		
Loller, John	1	2	2		
Mullins, Jno	1	3	1		
McFalls, Arthur	1	3	1		
Gillespy, Henry	3		2		
ELEVENTH COMPANY.					
Vance, David	2	1	5		3
Deover, Wm	6		4		
Smith, Jno	1		5		
Smith, Nat	1	1	1		
Beefle, Jacob	1	1	2		
Dunsmore, Adam	1	2	2		
Gilbert, Jno	2	2	3		
Heatly, Henry	2	1	6		
Unfrin, Sam	1	1	6		
Rogers, David	1	4	3		
Cunnigan, Jas	1		6		1
Bartlet, Nathn	2	2	5		
Bartlet, Jno	1		4		
McAfee, Wm	2	3	5		
Young, Wm	1	1	1		
Patten, Matthew	1		3		
Moore, Jno	1		3		
Graham, Wm	3	1	4		
Lacky, Jno	1		5		
Summers, Jonson	2		6		
Davidson, James	2		6		3
Davidson, Saml	1		4		
McWhorter, Ben	2		1		
Patten, Robt, Sad	1	2	5		1
Long, Wm	3	2	6		
Patten, Thos	3	1	3		
Cunigam, Hump	1		3		
Patten, Jas	1		5		

MORGAN DISTRICT, BURKE COUNTY—Continued.

NAME OF HEAD OF FAMILY.	Free white males of 16 years and upward, including heads of families.	Free white males under 16 years.	Free white females, including heads of families.	All other free persons.	Slaves.
ELEVENTH COMPANY—continued.					
Clemments, Jas	1	1	3		
Alexander, Jno	3		4		
Alexander, James	1	3	2		
Patten, Matthew, Sr	3		2		1
Patten, Aron			3		
Patten, Matt., Jr	1		1		
Davidson, Wm	4	2	4		8
McMahan, Jas	3	1	2		
Smith, Jno	1	1	1		
Davidson, Thos	2		2		
Ritchy, James	1	2	4		1
McNabb, Jas	1	4	2		3
Jones, Wm	2	1	3		
Rice, Joseph	1		3		
Cunigan, George	2	4	1		
Gudger, Ben	2		1		
Neall, Archie	2		4		
Furgay, Sam	1	2	4		4
Kow, Wm	1		2		
Patten, Jno	1	1	4		2
Ragsdil, Gabil	1	2	1		1
Lee, Eloner			5		
West, Jno	1	1	3		
Gudger, Wm	1	1	6		1
Randolph, Jos	1	1	4		
Phillips, Ezra	1		3		
Whitson, Wm	1	3	2		1
Smith, Phil	1	2	2		
Killian, Danl	1	2	1		
Phillips, Jno	1		4		1
Boys, James	1	5	4		
Byant, Wm	1	5	3		
Case, Abram	2	4	5		
Davis, Jno	1		6		
Butle, Jno	1		2		
Ingrum, Wm	1	1	2		
Jenkins, Thos	2		4		
Jenkins, Jno	1		2		
Ramsy, George	1	3	4		
Davis, Baxter	3	6	1		
Blevins, Jnthn	1		3		
Cravens, Jas	2	3	2		
Gillahan, Jno	1	3	3		
Godm, Jonas	2	2	4		
Kennedy, Connell	1		1		
Butle, Adam	1		1		1
Roberts, Jno	1	2	3		
Weaver, Jno	1	1	3		
Wagoner, Jacob	1	5	2		
Roberts, Wm	2		4		
Bound, Jno	1	3	2		
Brittain, Wm	1	2	2		
Dillard, Jno	1	3	3		
Gregory, Wm	3	4	3		
Bally, Wm	1		3		
Guin, Juke	1	1	2		
Stanfield, Jas	1	2	6		
Guin, Chas	1	1			3
Chambers, Jno	2	2	2		
Gregory, Jno	1		1		
TWELFTH COMPANY.					
Parmer, Edmund	1	3	4		
Edes, Chals	2	1	3		
Ramsy, Jno	1		1		
Bailey, Wm	2		1		
Bradly, Jno	1	1	3		
Buller, Jacob, Sen	5	1	3		
Killer, Jno	1	2	5		
Treadaway, Aron	1	3	4		
Atkison, Henry	1	3	1		
Bounds, Jos	1	3	3		
Keller, Nicolas	1	1	3		
Barnett, Tim	3	3	3		
Treadaway, Wm	1	1	4		
Treadaway, Robt	1	1	3		
Finley, Wm	1	1	1		
Tony, Jno	3	3	3		
Lekins, Jno	1		1		
Shoat, Christi	1		1		
Shoat, Moses	1	2	1		
Derm, Henry	2	5	1		
Shoat, Christi, Jr	1		1		
Pyburn, Jacob	3	1	5		
Pialus, James	1	4	6		
Tinker, Jno	2	5	5		
Forsythe, Jos	1		1		
Chandor, Josha	1	1	3		
Blazwell, Jno	1		4		
Webb, Mendoth	3	4	5		5
Win, Martha			4		
Bound, Jas	1		2		
Shoat, Austin	1		2		
Rice, Wm	1	6	2		
Elkins, Gabriel	2	1	2		2
Pialus, Wm	1	4	3		1
Pialus, Edmund	1	4	3		1

NAME OF HEAD OF FAMILY.	Free white males of 16 years and upward, including heads of families.	Free white males under 16 years.	Free white females, including heads of families.	All other free persons.	Slaves.
TWELFTH COMPANY—continued.					
Street, Jno	1	2	2		
Hgins, Roland	1	3			
Bunis, Elijah	1	2	4		
Hensly, Henry	1	5	5		
Renfren, Jno	1	2	8		
Hensly, Jno			3		
Langford, James	1	1	2		
Edward, Wm			2		
Hinton, David		1	2		
Stanton, Jno		3	4		
Angling, Isaac	1	4	3		
Hoodenpye, Phil	2	3	5		
Caleway, Charls	1	3	2		
Summers, Allen	1	2	1		
Phips, Hana			2		
Hinton, Wm		1	2		4
Robison, Julius	1		4		
Marcum, Abner	1	5	4		
Wilhams, Phil	1	3	3		
Hamons, Obadiah	1		3		
Baker, Robt., Jr	2		2		
Hensly, Jas	1		3		
Ray, Thos	3	3	2		
Carrol, Jno	1	2	4		
Hamons, Peter	1	3	2		
Bennett, Jas	2	1	3		
Hensly, Hirman	1	3	4		
Baker, George	2	4	6		
Edwards, Jno	2	4	6		
Arrington, Jas	1		5		
Baker, Jno	1	5	3		
Foster, Mark	1	3	5		
Foster, Mark, Jr	2	1	4		
Hughes, Jno	1	4	1		
Paterson, Jane		1	7		
Hughes, Peter	1		2		
Dyer, Lettice		1	2		
Haeworth, Austin	1	3	4		1
THIRTEENTH COMPANY.					
Galliard, Jno M	1	1	6		
Eagan, Mary	2		5		
England, Danl	3	2	6		
England, Jo	1	2	3		
Hilterbrand, Conrad	1	2	1		2
Bellen, George	1		2		
Bradburn, Jno	1		4		
Mull, Peter	3	1	3		1
Morgan, Josep	4	2	3		
Welsh, Wm	1	5	2		1
Direberry, Anne	2		1		
Duckworth, Jno	1	2	4		
Walker, West	1		1		
Direberry, Andrew	1		2		
Largin, Thom	1	3	2		
Hartley, Jno	2		2		
Lack, James	1	1	1		
Macky, John	3	2	5		
England, Jno, Sr	2		7		
Hughes, Jno	2	4	3		1
Macy, Saml	2	2	3		
Tomson, David	2	2	3		
Benll, Danl	2	1	5		3
Downs, Zach	2		2		
Macay, Thos	2		4		
Tate, Jno	5		3		3
Nolin, Ben	1	2	1		
May, Erasmus	2		1		
Hensy, Patrick	1	1	1		3
Justn, Jno	1		2		
Duckworth, Wm	2	1	1		
Wood, Henry	2	4	3		
Dobson, Joseph, Jr	1		3		3
Priest, Jo	1		1		
Downs, Zach., Jr	2	1	5		
Britta, Phillip	1	1	5		
Cooper, Jno	1	2	3		
Lyon, Leonard	3		5		1
West, Wm	1		3		
Young, Elias	1		3		
Spears, Jno	2	2	1		
James, Wm	2		4		
Craige, Robt	2	2	4		
Guin, Debo			4		
McDowell, Wm	1	4	4		
Skevely, Jno Henry	3		1		
Tompson, Isaac	1	3	3		
Bailey, Alex	2	3	3		
Wood, Robt	1		1		1
Cunings, Alex	1	1	1		
Kell, Thos	1		2		2
Smith, Thom	1		2		
Greenlea, Jas					24
Mackay, Jas		1	1		
Worthy, Sally	1	1	1		
Sorrlis, Walter	1	3	4		
Lowman, Lewis	1	2	2		

NAME OF HEAD OF FAMILY.	Free white males of 16 years and upward, including heads of families.	Free white males under 16 years.	Free white females, including heads of families.	All other free persons.	Slaves.
THIRTEENTH COMPANY—continued.					
Anderson, Martha		1	3		
Pearson, Jas	1	1	2		
Roteat, Edwd	1	2	2		
Hawkins, Joseph	1	1	3		
Kell, Robt	1	3	6		
Walker, George	3	2	6		
Walker, Reubin	1	3	2		
Southorlin, Wm	2	1	7		
Howard, Ruson	1		1		
England, Thos	1		1		
Hawkins, Austin	1	2	3		
Boteat, Wm	1	1	3		
Kell, Tho', Jr	1	1	2		
Kell, Wm	1		2		
Huffman, Sam	1	3	3		
McTagart, Jno	5		3		
Brown, Saml	1	1	4		
Higden, Thos	1	2	2		
Chapman, Nicolas	1	2	3		
Southorlin, Tisdol	1		3		
Wise, Adam	1	1	4		
Dougherty, Ed	1	2	6		
Hart, Josiah	1	2	1		
Burns, Nicolas	1		3		
Burns, Phillip	1	1	3		
Roper, James	1	2	1		
Craig, Jno	1	1	1		
Brittin, Junims	1	1	1		
Stilwell, Jacob	2	1	1		1
Box, Henry	1	3	4		
Morrow, Dan	3		3		
Ross, James	1	1	5		
England, Jno, Jr	1	5	1		
Bortles, Christn	1	1	4		1
Jeferis, Jno	1	2	4		
Gibs, Rd	1	1	4		
White, Wm	1	2	3		
Hawkins, Wm	1	1	2		
Rogers, Stepen	1		1		
Carol, Danl	1		3		
Smith, Adam		1	3		
Craig, Ruth		1	4		
Dally, George	1	2	4		
Clarke, Eloner		2	4		
Scaly, George	1	1	1		
Oxford, Jno	1		1		
Oxford, Saml	1				
Elmore, Sarah		2	4		
Howard, Robt	1	3	2		
Mousor, Rd	1		2		
Miller, Henry	1	1	1		
Overwon, Adm., Jr	1		2		
Walker, Tho', Jr	1	1	2		
Walker, George	1	3	2		
Hughey, Eliza	1	2	3		
Hughey, Jos	1		2		
Scott, George	1	2	3		
Jones, Wm	1	5	4		
McEntira, Jas	4	3	4		5
Gibs, Jno	1	3	4		
Garison, Henry	2	2	2		
Erwin, Jno	3	2	1		11
Hays, Wm	1	3	1		
Orr, Wm	2	1	5		
Layman, Stophi	1				
Adams, Mary		2	1		
Smith, Jno	3	3	4		1
Scott, Jos	1	4	7		
Neall, Jno	2	3	4		3
Bailey, Wm	2	3	6		
McMurry, Saml	1	5	4		
Rucker, Jos	3	5	2		
Pearson, Thos	2		2		
Pearson, Christe	1		2		
Hips, Jacob	1	2	4		
Galllou, Tho'	1	3	5		
Hips, George, Sr	3	2	4		
Hips, George	1		4		
Cammell, Jno	1		2		
Anderson, Bartlet	1	1	1		
Hartly, Jas	1	2	3		
Templeton, Jas	2	2	3		
Scott, George	1	2	3		
Direberry, Hana	1	2	5		
Patten, Tho'	2	2	9		
Burgess, Jno	1	3	5		
Pearson, Jno	2	2	2		1
Burgess, Rd	1	3	5		
Downs, Tho'	1	2	2		
Carswell, Jno	2	2	6		
Good, Solomon	2	1	2		
Boteat, Jno, Sr	3	1	1		
Boteat, Jno, Jr	1		2		
Camil, Augustn	1	3	4		
Wrenshaw, Abam	2		1		
Gunter, Jno	2	1	2		

ADDITIONS AND CORRECTIONS TO THE 1790 CENSUS OF BURKE COUNTY, N.C.

Compiled by William Perry Johnson(deceased), Professional Genealogist, Editor of The North Carolinian, A Quarterly Journal of Genealogy and History, Post Office Box 1770, Raleigh, North Carolina, and given to Edith Warren Huggins for her future use.

Two versions of the 1790 Census of North Carolina have been published. The first was by Walter Clark, Chief Justice of the Supreme Court of North Carolina, and was published in 1905; this is volume XXVI of The State Records of North Carolina. The second was published in 1908 by the Federal Government. A few discrepancies have been noted in the two volumes. The index of the former volume is incomplete, and an ancestor may appear in one volume and not the other. There are many variances in spelling of the same name. It is recommended that both volumes be consulted.

A microfilm of the original 1790 Census Schedules has been obtained from the National Archives in Washington, D.C., and compared with the two published versions. The major errors and omissions for Burke County, North Carolina, are listed below, one list for each of the two published volumes:

1790 Census of North Carolina (Volume XXVI of The State Records of North Carolina):

Page 319:
Change Matthew Washburn to Matthew Mashburn
Change Josiah Bradshaw to Isaiah Bradshaw
Change David Washburn to David Mashburn
Change Drury Washburn to Drury Mashburn
Change Precilla McCracon to Quilla McCracon
Change Mish Burchfield to Mesh'h Burchfield
Change Morris Webster to Moses Webster
Change Nicholas Thorps to Nicholas Trops

Page 320:
Change Dav'd Washburn to Dav'd Mashburn
Change Missor Norton to Messer Norton
Change Zeb Brevard, Jr. to Zeb Brevard, Sr.

Page 321:
Change tabulation for Thos. Hemphill from 3-2-7-0-11 to 2-2-7-0-11
Change Jno. Pinely to Jno. Pinkly
Change tabulation for Abram Hashaw from 1-4-3-0-0 to 1-4-3-0-1
Change Relekah Dudly to Rebekah Dudly
Change Conrod Winkloe to Conrod Winkler
Between the names of Ben Clarke and Wm Bradshaw insert Jacob Suttlemire
Change Jos. Bellon to Jos. Bellew
Change Benerly Clarke to Beverly Clarke

Page 321 (continued)
Change Stephen Bellon to Stephen Bellew
Change George Hawk to George Howk

Page 322:
Change Jacob Doreberry to Jacob Dereberry
Change Mich'l Doreberry to Mich'l Dereberry
Change tabulation for Wm Pain from 1-2-7-0-0 to 1-2-7-0-2
Change Mich'l Grinslaff to Mich'l Grinstaff
Change Thos. Winklirt to Thos. Winkler, Sr.
Change Adam Sutilmire to Adam Suttlmire
Change Wil'm Bellon to Wil'm Bellew
Change Ame Williams to Anne Williams
Change Agnes Irwin to Agnes Erwin
Change Sherwood Bome to Sherwood Bome(?)
Change Jonah Bradsha to Josiah Bradsha
Change tabulation for Mary Grasty from 0-1-3 to 0-1-2

Page 323:
Change tabulation for Wm Penland from 5-2-3-1-0 to 5-2-3-0-1
Change Stephen Pirrey to Stephen Piercy

Page 324:
Change Jno. Tramwell to Jno. Trammell
Change Jacob Alestony,Jrto Jacob Antony, Jr(?)
Change Larhon Parks to Larken Parks
Change Big Denis Tramele to Big Denis Tramel
Change Eliza Piorcy to Eliza Piercy
Change Little Denis Tramele to Little Denis Tramell
Change tabulation for Jemima Allen from 0-2-3 to 0-2-2
Change Jno. Duke to Jno. Duk
Change Hozill Adams to Howell Adams
Change Harison McConico to Harison McConico(?)

Page 325:
Change Wooetn Harris to Wooton Harris
Change Thos. James to Thos. Janes(?)
Change Joshua Oans to Joshua Oaks
Change Wilm Hermby to Wilm Hamby
Change Jno Petitto, Sen. to Jno Petillo, Sr.
Change Robt Hodge, Jr. to Robt Hodge, Sr.
Change tabulation for Thom Little from 1-3-1-0-0 to 1-3-1-0-1
Change Midleton Petitto to Midleton Petillo
As for the name "Ellis Bloonfin" the first part of the last name is
    illegible, but it may end in "fin"

Page 326:
Change Jacob Kelloe to Jacob Keller
Change Michal Pinnly to Michal Pinkly
Change Cornelius Ridick to Cornelius Ridick(?)

91

Page 326 (continued)
Change Robt. Fitzpatrick to Robt. Kilpatrick
Change Jasbret Webb to Jas. Crit.(?) Webb
Change Wilm. Minphrey to Wilm. Murphey
Change tabulation for Charles Weakfield from 1-0-3-0-0 to 4-0-3-0-3
Betweeen the names of Charles Weakfield and Isaac Emings insert:
    Thom Wakefield 1-0-3
Change Leonard Coner to Leonard Coker
Change Charles Coner, Sr. to Charles Coker, Sr.
Change Charles Coner to Charles Coker
Change Wm Coner to Wm. Coker

Page 327:
Between the names Jas. Holland and Joseph Coker insert: Mathw.
    Whitlock 2-2-3
Change George Donell to George Dowell
Change Moses Hille to Moses Helle(?)
Change Moses Stafp to Moses Stapp
Change Wm. F. Jewell to Wm. F. Jerrell (Fitzjerrell (?))

Page 328:
Change Champion Guir to Champion Guin
Change Joseph Conan to Joseph Cowan
Change Agnes Sellers to James Sellers
Change Robt. Sellers, Jr. to Robt. Sellers, Sr.
Change John Allen, Jr. to John Allen, Sr.
Change Hezekiah Hiatt to Hezekiah Hyett
Change Dane Andrews to Danl Andrews
Change Jas. Canly to Jas. Carely
Change Harry Hanly to Henry Carely
Change Patrick O'Neal to Patrick O'Neal, Sr.
Change tabulation for Bridgt. Montgomery from 0-0-2-2-2 to 0-0-2-0-2
Change Feld Bradshaw to Field Bradshaw

Page 329:
Change tabulation for Simon Hyett from 0-1-3-0-1 to 0-1-3-1-0
Change Isaac Terrill to Isaac Ferrill and tabulation from 0-5-4-0-1
    to 0-5-4-1-0
Change James McAdams to Jno. McAdams
Change Jno. Summers to Jno. Sumners
Change Wm. Monson, Jr. to Wm. Moreson, Jr.
Change Churul Jackson to Churwl. Jackson
Change Eliza Monson to Eliza Moreson
Change David Lorrels to David Sorrels
Change Jas. Jennell to Jas. Jewett(?) or Jewell(?)
Change Marget Conan to Marget Cowan
Change Lodo Blankirsh to Lodo Blankenship

Page 330:
Change Albert Conpening to Albert Corepening
Change Jno. Franklin, Jr. to Jno. Franklin, Sr(?)
Change Jno. Lane to Jno. Laws
Change tabulation for Jeremiah Tomson from 2-2-4-0-7 to 2-2-4-0-17
Change Thos. Wilsters to Thos. Wilshire
Change Jozane Arny to Loranc Arney
Change Chrish Wagomer to Christr. Wagoner
Change Thos. Winkler, Jr. to Thoas. Winkler, Sr.

Page 331:
Change tabulation for David Winkler from 1-0-3 to 1-0-2
Change Insy Conrad Winkler to Insy(?) Conrad Winkler
Change Jonathan Tears to Jonathan Fears
Change Jno. Treble to Jno. Trible(?)
Change Wm. Lozanca to Wm. Lorance
Change Adam Direberg to Adam Derebery
Change Jacob Baldwin to Jacob Baldin
Change Sam Crawford to Sam(?) Crawford

Page 332:
Change Jno. Baldwin to Jno. Baldin
Change Jas. Richards, Sr. to Jas. Prichard, Sr.
Change Lewis Reetor to Lewis Rector
Change Jas. Collire to Jas. Collier
Change John Barns to Jehu Barns

Page 333:
Change Sam'l Stenard to Sam'l Steward
Change Absalom Pinitor to Absalom Pineton(?)
Change Phillip Hephaer to Phillip Hephner
Change Isaac Grenslaff to Isaac Grinstaff
Change John Parmin to John Parmer(?)

Page 334:
Change tabulation for Elizabeth Green from 0-0-1-0-0 to 0-0-1-0-5
Change Wm. Moore to Wm. Moony
Change Fred Grider, Jr. to Fred Greider, Jr.
Change Thos. Powell to Thos. Prowell
Change Wm. Repets to Wm. Ri_pito

Page 335:
Change Christ'n Abshire to Christr. Abshire
Change Sam'l Swaringin to Sam'l Swaringim
Change Jerome Stilwell to Jeremy Stilwell
Change George Rucker, Sen., to George Tucker, Jr.
Change Henry Hottsclaw to Henry Holtsclaw
Change Isaac Muyson to Isaac Mayson
Change Hezekiah Struton to Hezekiah Streetor(?)
Change James Hons to James Hows

Page 335 (continued)
Change Fred Hignsaw ro Fred Highsaw
Change Susana Strutton to Susana Streetor(?)
Change Wm Horrin to Wm. Herrin
Change Colward Blair to Colvard Blair and tabulation from 1-1-2-0-3
    to 1-1-2-0-2
Change tabulation of Abram Sotherd from 1-2-2-0-0 to 1-2-2-0-1
Change Jno. Noely to Jno. Neely
Change Peter Hott to Peter Holt
Change Jacob Hott to Jacob Holt
Change Check Swaringin to Check Swaringim
Change Gerral Wilson to Genral Wilson
Change Robt   John Miller to Robt Josh(?) Miller
Change Temple McDaniel to Tempe McDaniel
Change Sam'l Swaringin to Sam'l Swaringim
Change Eljan Powell to Eljah(?)Powell
Change Robt. Northerly to Robt. Netherly

Page 337:
Change Abigail Kinsey to Abigail Kemsy
Change Sally Hall to Sally Hull

Page 338:
Change Thos. Beckenstaff to Thos. Beckerstaff
Change Jacob Beifle to Jacob BUfle
Change Adam Dansmore to Adam Dunsmore
Change Sam Renfrin to Sam Renfrew
Change Wm. McAfer to Wm. McAfee
Change tabulation for James Davidson from 2-6-3-0-0 to 2-0-6-0-3
Change Ben McWhorter to Ben McWherter
Change Tas. McMahan to Jas. McMahan
Change Jno. Davidson to Thos. Davidson

Page 339:
Change Wm. Kerr to Wm. Koon(??)
Change tabulation for Jos. Randolph from 1-1-1 to 1-1-4
Change Dan'l Killian to Dan'l Kellean
Change tabulation for Jas. Cravins from 2-3-3 to 2-3-2
Change Jas. George to Jones Gouge
Change Adam Beifle to Adam Bufle

Page 340:
Change Charles Edes to Chals Edes
Change Wm. Bartley to Wm. Bailey
Change tabulation for Henry Divers from 2-5-2 to 2-5-3
Change James Pialms to James Psalms
Change Wm. Pialms to Wm. Psalms
Change Edmund Pialms to Edmund Psalms
Change Elijah Bunis to Elijah Burris
Change Phil. Hoddon, pyc to Phil. Hoddenpye and tabulation from
    1-3-5 to 2-3-5

Page 341:
Change tabulation for Mark Foster, Jr. from 4-1-4 to 2-1-4
Change Austin Haworth to Austin Hacworth
Change Conrod Hitlebrand to Conrod Hiltebrand and tabulation from
    1-2-1-0-0 to 1-2-1-0-2
Change George Bellow to George Bellew
Change Peter Muse to Peter Mull
Change Thom. Langin to Thom. Largin
Change Zach. Dorrs to Zach. Downs

Page 342:
Change Jno. Quein to Jno. Queen
Change Joseph Dobson to Joseph Dobson, Jr.
Change Zach Dorrs, Jr. to Zach Downs, Jr.
Change Jno. Henry Sturly to Jno. Henry Stevely
Change Jas. Greencie to Jas. Greenlee
Change Waller Sorrels to Walter(?) Sorrels
Change Lewis Lonman to Lewis Lowman
Change Sam Haufman to Sam Hufman

Page 343:
Change Sam C. Brown to Saml. Brown
Change tabulation for Thos. Higden from 0-2-2 to 1-2-2
Change Adm Overwort to Adam Overwort(?)
Change tabulation for Eliza Hughey from 1-2-1 to 1-2-3

Page 344:
Change Thos. Dorrs to Thos. Downs

The letters "e" and "i" were used interchangeably, and even though
such use makes some of the names a little difficult to recognize,
there were so many instances that listing them here would not be
practical. WPJ

1790 Census of North Carolina (published by the Federal Government),1908:

Page 106 - 1st Column
Change Wasburn, Matthew to Mashburn, Matthew
Change Washburn, David to Mashburn, David
Change Washburn, Drury to Mashburn, Drury
Change Burchfield, Mishh to Burchfield, Mesh'h

Page 106 - 2nd column
Change Flord, Abram to Floid, Abram
Change Rus, Rose to Rees, Rose

Between the names, Bird, Ben, Jr., and Brevard, Zeb, Sr., insert
    the name Bird, Tho. - 1-3-1-0-0
Change Brevard, Zeb, Jr. to Brevard, Zeb, Sr.

Page 106 - 3rd column:
Change Pnnhly, Jno. to Pinkly, Jno.
Change Hashan, Abram to Hashaw, Abram

Page 107 - 1st column:
Change Suttlenmire, Adam to Suttlmire, Adam
The name Boone, Sherwood, may or may not be Boone -- looks like Bome
    (1800 Census of Burke lists a Shered Bowman)
Change Hanson, Bartlet to Henson, Bartlet
Change Shenite, James to Sherrile, James
Change McDonell, David to McDanell, David

Page 107 - 2nd column:
Change Pincy, Stephen to Piercy, Stephen
Change Phillips, Larasus to Phillips, Lazarus
Change Ustam, Wm. to Uslam, Wm.(1800 Census of Burke lists Usbun, Sally
Change Forgayn, James to Forgay, James
Change Conizo, Harrison W. to McConico(?), Harrison
Janis, Thos. could be Janes(?), Thos.

Page 107 - 3rd column:
Change Fikes, Elisha to Fikes, Eliza
Corpin, Ellis - last name is illegible (perhaps ends in "fin")
Change Kilpatrick, Robt. to Fitzpatrick, Robt.
Change Webb, Jas. Crit. to Webb, Jas. Bret.(?)
Change Ewings, Isaac to Emings, Isaac
Change Whitloch, Matha to Whitloch, Mathw.
Change Ward, Byn to Ward, Ben

Page 108 - 1st column:
Change Jenell, Wm F. to Jerrell, Wm F. (Fitzjerrell(?))
Change Bars, Caleb to Barr, Caleb
Change Sellers, James to Sellers Agnes
Change Hytle, Hezekiah to Hyett, Hezekiah
Change O'Neal's, Patrick to O'Neal, Patrick, Sr.
Change Hytle, Edwd. to Hyett, Edwd.
Change Barchfld, Aberilla to Burchfld, Abesilla
Change Finley, Charles to Finley, Chares

Page 108 - 2nd column:
Change Jackson, Chaswl. to Jackson, Churwl.
ChangeLonels, Davd. to Sorrels, David
Jewell, Jas. could be Jewett, Jas. or Jerrell, Jas.
Change Corby, Wm. to Cosby, Wm.
Change Hughes, Andrew to Hughey, Andrew

96

Change Baker, Bardel to Baker, Basdel
Change Coreponong, Albert to Corpening, Albert
Change Franklin, Jno., SR. to Franklin, Jno. F.(?)
Change Fais, Edmund to Fairs, Edmund
Change Lane, Jno. to Laws, Jno.
Change Wilsken, Thos. to Wilshire, Thos.
Change Isom, Christn to Isom, Christ'r
Change McKinny, Elisa to McKenny, Elisha
Winkler, Jersey Conrad could be Winkler, Insy(?) Conrad

Page 108 - 3rd column:
Change Fiass, Jonathan to Fears, Jonathan
Pilm, Wm. could be Pelm, Wm.
Change Dinbery, Adam to Derebery
Crawford, Tom could be Crawford, Sam
Change Cray, Joab to Crag, Joab
Change Crag, Christn to Crag, Christ'r
Change Henery, John to Hensy, John
Change Rutor, Lewis to Rector, Lewis
Change Russell, Ried to Russell, Ricd.
Change Moon, Robt. to Moore, Robt.
Change Bains, John to Barns, Jehu

Page 109 - 1st column:
Peniton, Absalom could be Pineton(?), Absalom
Change McErtin, Jno. to McEntire, Jno.
Change Hephaer, Phillip to Hephner, Phillip
Change Parmes, John to Parmer, John
Change Banell, Jonathan to Barrett, Jonathan
Change Graham, Aha to Graham, Alex
Change Prew, Phillip to Price, Phillip
Repeto, Wm. could be Ripito, Wm.

Page 109 - 2nd column:
Tucker, George, Sr. probably should be Tucker, George, Jr.
Change Hottsdaw, Henry to Holtsclaw, Henry
Streeton, Hezekiah could be Streetor, Hezekiah
Change Hons, James to Hows, James
Change Onions, Saml. to Owins, Saml.
Streetton, Susana could be Streetor, Susana
Change Hott, Peter to Holt, Peter
Change Hott, Jacob to Holt, Jacob
Miller, Robt., Jesse could be Miller, Robt. Josh(?)
Change Easthman, Isaac to Earthman, Isaac
Change Notherly, Robt. to Netherly, Robt.
Change Morron, James 1-5-3 to Morrow, James 1-5-2
Change Kensy, Abigail to Kemsy, Abigail
Change Beefle, Jacob to Bufle, Jacob
Change Unfrin, Sam to Renfrew, Sam
Change Cunnigan, to Cunnigam, Jas.
Change McWhorter, Ben to McWherter, Ben

Page 110 - 1st column:
Change McMahan, Jas. to McMahan, Tas.
Kow, Wm could be Kerr(?), Wm.
Change tabulation for Randolph, Jos. from 1-1-4 to 1-1-1
Change Guin, Jake to Guin, Jane
Change tabulation for Guin, Chas. from 1-1-0-0-3 to 1-1-3-0-0
Change Tony, Jno. to Terry, Jno.
Change Lekins, Jno. to Likens, Jno.
Change Devus, Henry to Devers, (or Divers), Henry
Change Pialms, James to Psalms, James
Change Webb, Mendoth to Webb, Meredith
Change Pialms , Wm. to Psalms, Wm.
Change Pialms, Edmund to Psalms, Edmund

Page 110 - 2nd column:
Change Higins, Koland to Hegins, Holand
Change Bunis , Elijah to Burris, Elijah
Change Renfren, Jno. to Renfrew, Jno.
Change Hensly, Hirman to Hensly, Hicman
Change Haeworth, Austin to Hacworth, Austin
Change Bellen , George to Bellew, George
Change Mull, Peter to Muse, Peter
Change Lack, James to Lock, James
Change Jucin, Jno. to Queen, Jno.
Change Skevely, Jno. Henry to Stevely, Jno. Henry
Change Greeneu, Jas. to Greenlee, Jas. and the tabulation from
    1-0-5-0-24 to 1-5-0-0-24
Change Sorrils, Walter to Sorrels, Waller

Page 110 - 3rd column:
Change Boteat, Edwd. to Boteal(?), Edwd.
Change Southorlin, Wm. to Southerton, Wm.
Change Howard, Ruson to Howard, Reeson
Change Boteat, Wm to Boteal(?), Wm
Change Southorlin, Tindel to Southerlin, Tindel
Change Brittu, Jumina to Brittn, Jumina
Change Overwon, Adm, Jr. to Overwort(?), Adam (Overwinter in 1800 ?)
Change Pearson, Christe to Pearson, Christ'r.
Change Wrenshaw, Aham to Wrenshaw, Abram

Note: These additions and corrections will not be found in the Index.

98

P. 720: Robert Alexander, Joseph Alexander, Daniel Andrew, John
Adams, Joseph Abets, John Allen, Mark Amonds, James Absher, John
Armstrong, Ananias Allen, John Allen, Jr., Lawrence Arney, James Allen,,
Jr., Lawrence Arney, Isaac Ammonds,James Allen, Jacob Anthony, Sr.,
Christopher Absher, James Alexander, Gideon Allen.

P. 721: Nobel Alexander, Paul Anthony, Samuel Alexander, Nelly
Aronel(?), Mar garet Alder, James Armstrong, Absolem Abbots, Jacob
Anthony, Thomas Allison, Benjamin (Austin ?). Nathaniel Osborn, Benjamin
Adams, Alexander Long, William Alexander, Nathaniel Armstrong, Josiah
A...(sew ?), Peter Angle, Leanea Amburn.

P. 722: John Alran, Robert Ayers, Rachel Anderson (?), Samuel
Austin, Jr., Phillip Austin, Wm. Arthur, Samuel Austin,, Sen.,
Elisha Adams, Wm. Austin, Nathan Austin, Elisha Austin, Jr., Dan
Alexander, Benjamin Allison , ... Adams, Francis Allison, Burch Allison,
PosseyAllison, Wm. Allison, Wm. Adams.

P. 723: Ezekiel Allison, Henry Allison, Benjamin Allison, Jonathan
Abbots, Waightstill Avery, Johnathan Bird, ThomasBoushill, Wm. Beach,
Jacob Baldwin, John Brown, Sr. Thomas Boon, Wm. Bowen, Mary Buckhannon,
James Buckhannon, Joshua Brown, Thomas Brown, Joseph Bowlin, Josiah
Bracher.

P. 724: Gilbert Bowman, Thomas S. Bratton, Benjamin Bratton, Thomas
Bird, Aaron Briton, Samuel Briton, Mark Briton, Robert Blue, Thomas Bell,
Field Bracher (Bradshaw ?), Littleberry Burnet, Elias Biven, Michael
Burchfield, James Brown, IsaiahBracher, Jacob Beck, John Barger.

P. 725: John Burke, George Booth, George Bilew, Anderson Branch,
Christian Bratels (?), Robert Lewis, Michael Baker, Lot Berry, Richard
Burges, Nicholas Burns, Phillip Briton John Bradford, Colbert Blair,
Reuben Bray, Thomas Brunt, Wm. Bailey, John Blair. Joshua Bilew.

P. 726: Jonathan Boon, Henry Baker, Jr., John Bolin, Sr., Wm.
Bracher, Sr. (Bradshaw), James Bucknor, Jesse Boon, Harry Baker,
Thomas Brevard, John Bailey,Sr., Benjamin Bird, Sr., Daniel Brown,
Caleb Burr, Sr. (Barr) ?), Wm. Blue, James Bone, Sr., Bennet Bradford,
Andrew Beard, Samuel Brown.

P. 727: David Barr, James Blair, John Burgess, Olive Branch,
Nathan Burchfield, Wm. Bradshaw, James Barns, John Brown, John Bradford,
Elijah Bruninger, Joseph Berry, John Brumley, Jean Brumley, Matthew Black,
Obadiah Bracher(Bradshaw ?), Robert Black, (Jacob Bergin under 'T'), Rachel Bowen.

P. 728: Wm. Greenfield Barr, Ancil Bailey, Samuel Bright, Rob't Burns,

John Browning, Sr., John Browning, Sr., Ancil Bailey, Samuel Bright, Robert Burns, Nathan Burchfield, David Burks, Thomas Burlison, James Buchannon, Joseph Buchannon, John Barnes, Ninivy Barnes, Quisey Brooks, Thomas Bradburn, Stephen Blew, Groves Bowman.

P. 729: Nancy Bowman, Peter Bean, Seth Bradsher (Bradshaw ?), John Beach, Thomas Bollin (?), Conrod Burns, Colbert Blaire (Blair), Thomas Bryant, John Bird, John Barrons, Henry Baker, Absolem Brown, John Bradburn, Wm. Brooks, Robert Bird, Josiah Brandon, Amos Brown, Benjamin Bergin.

P. 730: John Bird, Charles Bailey, John Burgen, Benoni Beming(?)), Wm. Blakely, Charles Brown, David Baker, Wm. Baker, Jacob Bowman, Abraham Bivens, Martin Browning, John Bryant, John Beard, Jonathan Boon, Jr., Polly Bilew, Shered Bowman, Mary Bradley, Joseph Bolin.

P. 731: Joseph Belew, Mary Brant, Benjamin Brant, Elisha Browning, David Biddle, Robert Craig, William Coruthers, Frederick Caphart, George Cook, John Cobble, David Chester, Joanna Clark, Joseph Cowan, Jeremiah Clark, William Culberson, Thomas Church, Paul Chren(Green), Michael Celler(Seller ?).

P. 732: Thomas Curtis, Thomas Coursey (?), Osburn Cox, George Crawford,Jackson Childers, Joshua Curtis, Isaac Cook, William Conley, Archibald Carman, Samuel Craige, Henry Craige, Thomas Cell, Joseph Curtis, John Cross, James Conely, John Curwell.

P. 733: Robert Curwell , Benjamin Coffe, Thomas Cell, Jr., Thomas Curtis, James Copelin, Thomas Craige, John Crider, Frederick Crider, James Chambers, James Crochlaw, James Colyar, Lewis Coffe , William Conely , Jr., Benjamin Cobb, Benjamin Clark, Volentine Crider, James C. Webb, Reuben Coffe .

P. 734: James Couden, Thomas Coleman, Michael Cook, Elijah Craige, Wm. Cole, Jacob Crider, John Cooper, Wm. Craige, Albert Copeny, Wm. Cerley(?), John Church, Wm. Crisp, Reuben Coffe , Joseph Coker, Elijah Chambers, Joel Coffe .

P. 735: Charles Collet, James Correll, Isaac Cox, James Carson, James Cerly , Brice Collins, Thomas Cox, Herman Cox, Henry Cerly,, Wm. Cry, John Capehart, David Crawford, John Cross, Charles Chill, Osborn Cox, Adam Cook, Alexander Clark.

P. 736: Benjamin Clark, Sr., Nancy Clark, Martin Clark, Wm.Carter, Samuel Clark, Ambrose Collon, Elisia Chas(E), Wm. Cosby, Josiah Cirby, Wm. Carter, Jr., Edward Curtis, Joseph Cooper, Charles Cantrel, Wm. Cantrel, Thomas Chester, Clisby Cobb, Wm. Crouse, John Cosby.

P. 737: Wm. Constable, Darby Connor, Larkin Cerly, Robert Church,

100

John Childers, Darby Connor, Larkin Cerley, Robert Church,
Matthew Cox, Nicholas Cellar, Martin Cellar, Christian Cellar, Jacob
Cellar, Richard Chapman, Adam Clim(?), Robert Coruthers, John Cellar,
Thomas Caldwell,Amos Chaffin, Alexander Celly, James Clark.

P. 738: Andrew Creson, Robert Celton, Wm. Curtis, Chanler
Cherenhapet(?), Abel Cox, Elizabeth Campbell, Thomas Chester, David
Cox, Alexander Cole, Archibald Cathey, Samuel Cathey, Andrew Crossett,
James Crouchlow, Rubin Coffe, , Joel Crisp, John Crisp, Charles Crisp,
James Chapman.

P. 739: Ruth Craige, John Craige, James Copelin, Hugh Conley,
John Childers, Wm. Clark, Susanna Clark, Benjamin Cochran, Thomas Day, Jr.,
Wm. Day, Thomas Day, Sr., Johnathan Day, Sr., Jon athan Duckworth,
Margaret Disart, Richard Davis, William D venport, John Deal, Andrew
Derberry.

P. 740: Nicholas Day, James Disart, Ann Derberry, Joseph Dobsonn,
Thomas Davis, Thomas D.evenport, Samuel Davis, Joshua Davis, Elijah
Dorsey, Wm. Davis, Chesle Dobs, Wm. Dobs, John Dunn, Daniel Derberry,
John Doeherty(?), George Duckworth, William Deese(?),.

P. 741: John Dowel, Wm. Durham, George Dowell, Laban Day, George
Detweker(?), Clement Dorset, Jo .nathan Dawson, James Day, John Day,
John Dyke,, MartinDeavenport, Jacob Derberry, George Dill, Richard
Dennis, Rachael Devine, John Dick, Mary Deal.

P. 742: George Deal, Michael Derberry, John Duckworth, Hannah
Derberry, George Derberry, Jacob Deal, John Dorsey, Wm. Dorsey,
Clement Davis, Robert Dickey, Jesse Dicks ....(?), Devinport(age 26-45),
Peter Duncan, Wm. Davis, Elisha Dehart, Rubin Dehart.

P. 743: Edward Day, Zachariah Downs, Edward Doherty, John Doherty,
Mary Duncan, Henry Dorsen, Jean Dean, Pattrick Davis, Francis Dorset,
Thomas Doherty, John Doherty, Wm. Doherty, George Doherty, John Doherty,
Mary Dement, William Davis, Sr.

P. 744: John Durham, John Dellinger, Nimrod Elliott, Daniel
England, John Engly, Joseph England, John Erwin, Alexander Erwin, Jr.,
John Ensly, Wm. England, Wm. England, Sr., Conrod Elrod, John Erwin, Sr.,
Ephraim Evans, Thomas England, Ezekiel Ennis, Leonard Eastis.

P. 745: Lot Eastis, John England, Laban Eastis, Joseph England,
Sr., William Edmondson, Arthur Erwin, Ezeriah Eanes, Henry Every,
James Erwin, John England, Nancy Erwin, Joseph Ecord, Wm. Erwin,
Alexander Erwin, John Erwin, James Edmisten.

P. 746: Richard Emmet, George Edmiston, Edmond Forest, John Franklin,
Robert Flemming Joseph Farr, William Fincannon, Prudence Fortune,
Abram Flemming Charles Finley, Jesse Fortune, John Fairley, William
Fizmire, Jacob Forney, John Franklin, Wm. Fortner.

P. 747: John Fipps, Peter Fincannon, Johnathan Franklin, Edey
Feril, Rubin Fletcher, Richard Fortune, Samuel Fox, Partinent Fleshman,
John Fincannon, Allen Fox, James Fox, Elijah Fox, Prudence Fortune,
John Forsyth, Moses Fox, Moses Franklin, Nathan Fox.

P. 748: John Fox, Charles Finley, William Fulwood, Ezekiel Fortune,
Wm. Francom, Ferreby Fouler, John Ford, Andrew Fox (Free ?), William
Fox, Adam Fullerton, Thomas Fort, Thomas Forster , James Fletcher,
John Frissel, Joseph Francom, David Francom.

P. 749: James Fox, Sally Ford, Hugh Fox, Jr., James Fox, Jr.,
Peter Freeman, Patrick Floriday, Wm. Grag, John Gilbert, Benjamin
Garish, Solomon Good, James Glass, Thomas Glass, Henry Glass, James Gage,
Clayburn Gunter, James Gunter, Ephraim Gray.

P. 750: Elijah Green, Peter Grear, John Giles, Joseph Gree(n),
Joseph Greenway, Joseph Griffey, John Grider, Alexander Gray, Solomon
Good, Henry Gerish(?), Richard Green, Mangard Gillom, John Green, Wm.
Gage, James Gilbert, Michael Gilbert.

P. 751: Alexander Glass, Jacob Grimes, Phillip Gier, Henry Gouger(?),
Richard Green, Peter Giger, Wilburn Gibson(?), Samuel Goldsmith, John
Greer, Samuel Goin, John Goldsmith, Henry Garrison, Wm. Grinway, Isaac
Griffey, James Gorman, William Golsby.

P. 752: Richard Giles, Elijah Gilbert, John Grissom, Phillip
Goodbread, Joseph Goodbread, Miles Green, Wm. Green, John Grissom, David
Gillespie, John Green, John Gouge, Isaac Grinstaff, George Groslea, Wm.
Gibson, Richard Gibbs, John Grible.

P. 753: Henry Gillespie, Wm. Gouge, James Garrison, John Griffey,
John Godfray, Jacob Grimes, Nathan Gibson, Mary Gibson, Joseph Gibson,
Wm. Givens, Thomas Green, Gust Gunter,, Wm.Grasy, Robert Gibson, Stephen
Gibson, Ann Hall.

P. 754: John Hughes, Esq., John Hughes, Jr., John Hicks, Andrew
Haslip, Windle Hinkle, John Harper, Jr., John Harper, Sr., Veasey Husbands,
Wm. Harper, George Holly, Alex. Hensy, Elizabeth Husbands, Alexander
Harbison, Wm. Harbison, , Bartlet Henson, Thomas Henson, John H. Slevile,
John Henry.

P. 755: James Henry, Jarman Heath, John Hall, Andrew Hunter,
Benjamin Hensel, Joseph Hughes, Jonathan Hains, Thomas Hemphill, Bartlet
Henson, Joseph Hawkins, David Houston, Matthew Harbison, Wm. Husbands,
George Hip, Peter Holt.

P. 756: Ezeriah Hight, Abram Harshaw, Jonathan Herod, James Hawkins,
Samuel Hufman, Henry Hiland, Joseph Hart, Elihu Hicks, McEgey Hall,
James Halley, John Hays, Wm. Hays, George Hays,Lewis Harse, John House,
Read Hight.

P. 757: James House, Andrew Highsaw, Thomas Hays, Rich Hill, Samuel Hickman, Isaac Hickman, Meridy Harper, Jacob Hartly , Friderick Highsaw, James Harden, Wm. Hawkins, Hary Hogans, John Hight, Leonard Higdon, David Harris.

P. 758: Joshua Hall, Robert Hunter, Conrad Hiltebrunt, John Harden, Robert Harris, Elisha Hudley, Barnet Huffman, Sally Harris, Ambrose Howard, Elijah Hall, James Hogans, Michael Houck, Thomas Higdon, Benjamin Hawkins, Henry Hill.

P. 759: John Harden, Matthias Hipp, Hezekiah Hicks, John Harden, Jr., Abraham Hulson, John Hogerly, James Hicks, John Hood, George Hodg, Josiah Hurd, Wm. Hagins, Mills Hagins, Samuel Harris, Peter Hunsucker, Jacob Hart, Jacob Hipp

P. 760: Peter Hose, Henry Hose, Buckrom)?) Hilton, Thomas Hilton, Margret Hilton, Michael Hart, Benjamin Hensley, David Henry, Henry Hatslow, Joseph- Hetslow, David Hall, Abner Hanely(?), Peter Holt, Sr., Thomas Hadley, Joshua Hadley, Joel Holt.

P. 761: John Hadley, John Hacker, ElishaHowell, Robert Hodg, Joshua Harden, Samuel Hughs, John Scott Hughs, Thomas Hemphill, Reuben Hannah, John Hall, John Moss, James Hemphill, James Horse, Benjamin Harris, Henry Hays, Elisha Headen.

P. 762: John Hunsucker, John Hunsucker, Sr., Wm. Hill, Swi field Hill, Thomas Hughs, Daniel Holyfield, John Hays, Charles Hopper, Robert Hodge, Jr., Wm. Heartley, George Harley, Augustine Hawkins, John Heddin, Peter Houk, George Houk, Hezekiah Jerman.

P. 763: Isbal Thompson (see "T"), Henry Jerman, Wm. Ingram, Nancy Jerman, Robert Inglish, Henry Inglish, John Jones, Nathaniel Jones, Gabrill Jackson, Henry Justice, Joseph Justice, Samuel Jameson, John Jitton, Joseph Jones,, Wm. Jones.

P. 764: John Jewell, Wm. James, Thomas James, Amon Joul(?), William James, Sr., Henry Justice, Killian Jarret, Wm. James, Samuel James, Stephen Jones, Wm. Jarrell, Polly Jones, Samuel Jiles, Edward James, John Justice, Lewis Johnston, Hezakiah Jerman.

P. 765: Thomas Justice, Elias Jackson, Edward Jackson, Amos Jackson, John Jackson, Isaac Jennings, John Kincaid, Archibald Kinkaid, James Kincaid, Thomas King, Thomas Knight, Henry Killian, James Kid, Johnston King, Thomas King(see Richard Knowles, under "N"), Robert Kincaid.

P. 766: Martin King, Abraham Leslie, John Wilm. Little, John Eli Little, Margret Little John, Martin Lewis, James Lock, Peter Ledford, John Letterman, Randle Lane, Leonard Lyons, Thomas Largin, Wm. Loving, William Lourance, Lohn Lutes (See Kellars, under "C")

P. 767: John Loving, Alexander Ledford, James Lowry, Wm. Lane,
Mary Lochran, Thomas Little, Archibald Luster, Ruben Lemman,John Little,
Elisha Largent, David Lynn, John Ledford, John Logan, Gabriel Loving,
James Loyd (see Alexander Long & Robert Lewis under "A").

P. 768: William Lowry, Jacob Lowdermilk, Wm. Loving, Sally Lee,
Stophel Lemon, Sally Ledford, Nelly Ledford, Samuel Love, Henry Leagle,
Richard Leigh, Lavis ᵂ Laumann, Nimrod Ledford, Peter Leigh , James
Musenline, James Muckey,Charles McDowell.

P. 769: Thomas McIntire, Jacob (or Joab) Morgan, Joseph McDowell,
Phillip Martin, George Martin, Thomas Moody, James Moody, Thomas Moody,
James Miles, David McDaniel, Elizabeth Mooney, James McCoy, David Montgomery,
Edward Moody, John McDowell, Jesse Martin, John Moody, Frederick Moore.

P. 770: George Moody, Peter Mull, Jr., Peter Mull, Sr. , Joseph
Morgan, James Morrow, John Meadows, Wm. Morrison, Andrew Morrison, James
Murphy, Wilson McCerny, Wm. McDowel , Wm. Murphy, Wm. McClure, John
Miller, John McLemore, Wm. Mashburn, Elizabeth Morrison, Alexander McClure.

P. 771: David Mashburn, Andrew McClure, David McClure, Drury
Mashburn, Henry Morris, Matthew Mashburn, Jacob Martin, James Mashburn,
Sr., Jacob Martin, James Mashburn, Sr., James Macoy, John Martin,
McCaye Moody, Wm.Mackey, David McElwrath.

P. 772: James Morris, James Mackey, Phillip Martin, Henry Miller,
Rose Moyers, Peter Mason, John Moore, Jeremiah Mooney, Joseph Moore,
James Moore, Jr., John McDaniel, Thomas Moore, George Mackey, David
McElroy, John Morton, Nathaniel Medlock, Robert Michael.

P. 773: Aaron Mitchell, John Migalyard, Rice Medaris, John Mitchell,
Josiah Moore, John Moyers, Daniel Moore, Thomas Mitchner, Malden Meyca,
John Murry, John Moyers, John Megonigel, Charles McKinney, Samuel McKinney,
John Mullins, Wm. Morrow, Kenneth McKinzey, Celia Martin, Wm. Morris.

P. 774: Nancy Moore, Mathias Mias(?), Wm. Moore, Jeremiah Macoy,
Joseph Medley, Jacob McElwrath, Frederick Mooney, Jean McNeal, Benjamin
Moore, ;...? Morgan, Robert Morrow,David Mashburn, Levi Mashburn,
Elisha Mashburn, Arthur McFalls,Arthur Mullin, Baker Mullins.

P. 775: John Mullins, Thomas McKinney, Samuel McKinney, John Mckinney,
Wm. McKinney, Richard Medlock, John Morrison, EdwardMoore, James Malin(?),
Temperance McDaniel, Samuel McDaniel, Randle Meades, Merreman McGee,
Wm.McDears, George McCenery,Thomas McCenery.

P. 776: John McFalls, John Mays, Edward Moorin, ...)?) McFalls,
Pattrick McGee, Henry Masters, Jacob Masters, Nancy Medlock, David
McRory, John Medlock, Charles Medlock, Stephen Medlock, James Moore, Jr.,
John Macke , James Morrow.

P. 777: James Melone, Jeremiah Monday, Thomas Mays, John Mays,
Frederick Miller , James Medley, George Miller, Nicholus Medlock, John
Mon...(?), Jesse Mendenhal, Robert Macefe, William Moffit,
Matthew Macorick, John Moffit, James Miller, Abraham Miller, Ann
McDowell, (See John Moss under "H").

P. 778: James Murlow, Julius Nucum, Gilbreath Neal, Samuel Neal,
James Neal, Joseph Noblet, David Newman, Benjamin Newland, Samuel Neal,
Cornelius Nice, John Neal, Robert Nether, George Noe, Wm. Neal,
James Nichols, Thomas Nele, Richard Knowles.

P. 779: Solomon Northern, Patrick Oneal, Eliu (?) Ogelsby,
Samuel Oldrage, Richard Oglethorpe, Samuel Obar, Samuel Owens, John Owens,
John Onstat, James Oxford, James Oaks, Adam Overwinter, Jacob Olmond
(see Nathaniel Osborn under "A"), John Piteat, Joseph Pruet, John Penenland,

P. 780: Samuel Painter, Jospiah Phipps, Thomas Pain, Joseph Perkins,
Catherine Patton, Francis Patton, Stephen Pearson, Elizabeth (Poteat ?),
Caleb Poore, Able Plumly, Wm. Pearson, John Pleman, Peter Pleman,
Samuel Pleman, Thomas Plemon , Samuel Pruet, Hugh Pruet.

P. 781: Samuel Patton, James Pritchard, John Pearson, Larkins
Parks, Benjamin Parks, Jean Purden, Phillip Pitts, James Potts, Lewis
Powel, Thomas Powel, Elisha Powel, Henry Panter , Daniel Paine, Josiah
Penly, William Pentland Robert Penland.

P. 782: John Pruit, Sen., Joseph Pruit, Jr., Simon Perkins,
Terah Prock, Barnet Paine, Tobias Peterson, Thomas Pearson, Wm. Parks,
Michael Pearson, Christopher Pearson, Thomas Parks, Lewis Powel,
Robert Patton, Elijah Patton, Daniel Page, Wm. Pertland, Wm. Paine.

P. 783: James Poteat, Elias Paul, Wm. Perriman, James Perriman,
Daniel Paine, John Panter, Robert Patterson, Elizabeth Percy, Wm. Penlee,
Joshua Penlee, Lawrence Phillips, George Parks, Samuel Parks, Nancy Penley,
Phillip Pearcy, Ezra Phillips, James Penland,

P. 784. Andrew Porter, Rachel Plumer, Elizabeth Plumer, Zechreah
Plumer, John Prince, Jesse Perkins, Ning Prita(?), John Peasly,
Christian Prock, Daniel Palmor, Joseph Pruitt, Jacob Bergin, George Paine,
Thomas Paine, Robert Paine, AbsolomPentlent, Wm. Peasley.

P. 785: Margaret Paul, Benjamin Paul, Elias Paul, Joseph Paine,
Caroline Paine, John Peasely, James Peasely, Jesse Puet., John Price, Jr.,
David Price, John Price, Sr., Redmon Perry, Wm. Porter, Sr., Millington
Patila, Rachel Patilla, Nathan Peaseley, Thornton Pendergras

P. 786: John Patilla, Henry Patilla, Rothel Pruet, Pat Palmer,
(fem), Michael Pinkley, John Quin, , Conrod Rether, John Redick, James
Reed, Sr., James Reed, Jr., Margaret Rust, Risdon Robinson, John Reed,

Francis Rose, Jospeh Robins, Ezra Rist, George Robonson.

P.787: James Roach, Samuel Reed, John Robinson, Peter Rust, Abraham Rencher, James Ramsey, Benjamin Rose, Wm. Repeto, Wm. Ramsey, Jr., Fredrick Rider, Benjamin Rose, Sr., Simon Ramsey Jacob Rider, Benjamin Rose, Sr., Wm. Roberts, John Wright, John Rutherford , Ephriam Roiler(?).

P. 788: David Rust, Richard Roads, Wm. Roads, John Ray, Wm. Ray, Hodge Reburn, George Reed, Arthur Robinson, Jonathan Rose, Jean Rincher(fem), Wm. Robinson, Alexander Robinson, Lovet Read, John Rose, Solomon Wright, Jacob Rose, Thomas Wright.

P. 789: David Rutherford , Richard Ramsey, James Roper, David Ramsey, John Ruter, John Reed, Frederick Robison, Wm. Reed, Sr., Wm Reed, James Reed, Thomas Reed, Jesse Reed, Thomas Randle, John Row, Henry Reed.

P.790: Cornelius Redick, Robert Rockets, John Robins, Benjamin Smith, John Spencer, John Spears, Frederick Shull, Andrew Smally, Walter Sorrels, Thomas Stowman, James Sherrill, William Sutherland, John Simmons, John Sellars, Thomas Summers, Margret Summers, Ridick Sorrels.

P. 791: George Scott, Wm. Sparks, Sr., Thomas Sharp, Jeremiah Sparks, Andrew Straghorn, Archibald Slone, Jorden Stroud, Peter Stroud, Pattrick Slone, John Scidmore, Abraham Stalyons, James Smith, Jaret Smith, James Sellars, Solomon Stunsbury, Isaac Simmons, Ameneria Scott.

P. 792: Nathan Smith, Shadrack Stilwell, Thomas Sherrill, Robert Sherman, George Sukman (Sigman ?), Edward Simons, Robert Sellars, Jonas Stokes, Allen Stokes, Thomas Sumpter, Henry Sumpter, Robert Sweden, Solomon Smith, John Step, Wm. Summers, Robert Sisk.

P. 793: John Spencer, Samuel Smith, Fielding Sumpter, Henry Smith, Livingston Sumpter, Henry Smith, George Smith, Abraham Scott, Joseph Scott, James Smith, Abner Smoty, Wm. Spencer, Pattrick Slone, Thomas Suthards, Simon Stacy, Zedekiah Smith, Wm. Sumter, Sr.

P. 794: Thomas Smith, Robert Sellars, James Sellars, Timothy Sink, James Shoote, Findel Sutherland, Wm. Sherrill, Peter Stalcup, Thomas Summers, Adam Setser ,Christopher Shifler, RubinStalyans, Ute Sherrill, John Stillwell, Abraham Southards, Wm. Selby, Peter Spinhour.

P. 795: Jeremiah Shake, Thomas Selby, Ralph Simpson, Margret Sorrels, Samuel Sorrels, Wm. Summers, Nancy Smith, Peter Stroud, Sr., Thomas Smith, Elizabeth Stephens, Henry Smith, John Sap, Samuel Spencer, R. Stanley, Joseph Stanley, Thomas Sutts, Able Simpkins.

P. 796: Samuel Scold, Jacob Sutimore (Settlemire ?), Andrew Steele, James Steele,John Steele, Samuel Steele, David Spadlim, Wm. Sherrill,

James Spadlim, Jesse Spadlim, Jacob Snead, John Spencer, Sr., Samuel Slone, John Sheppard, Wm. Sherrill, Robert Sellars, Jacob Silvers.

P. 797: Michael Souther, John Sterlary, Thomas Stanly, Wm. Stephenson, Sarah Simpkins, Sally Smith, Thomas Scott, Rubin Stanley, Charles Stanley, Wm. Slone, James Sumpter, Edward Sellars, George Sealey, John Smith, Jr., Abraham Smith, John Smith, John Swink (see John H. Stevile under "H").

P. 798: Shadrack Sanders, Adam Smith, Wm. Smith, Daniel Sullivan, Samuel Stout, Joseph Saratt, Daniel Smith, Henry Stoner, Isaac Stoner, Henry Stoner, Jr., Thomas Smith, (see Samuel Summers under "T"), Wm. Tate, David Tate, Hugh Tate, Samuel Tunmire, John Thompson.

P. 799: James Templeton, Isaac Thompson, Wm. Thompson, John Tumbleston, Joseph Tanner, Peter Tunmire, Thomas Tigart, Wm. Tummans, Samuel Tummans, Jacob Tips, George Tucker, Sr., Moses Thompson, Peter Thompson, Wm. Tucker, John Tigart, Samuel Summers (see Isbel Thompson under "J").

P. 800: Arthur Travers, Sarah Thrasher, Samuel Tate, John Templeton, James Thompson, Nicholas Trosper, Elijah Trosper, John Tounsend, John Tarter, John Tramble, Archibald, Templeton, Moses Templeton, John Templeton, John Taylor, Moses Terry, Jonathan Tipton.

P. 801: Joseph Thomas, Thomas Triplet, John Tucker, Wm. Timmons, Wm. Thornton, Moses Teague, Wm. Teague, Amos Tribble, John Teague, Edward Teague, Stephen Underwood, Wm. Umphreys, Wm. Ussery, Sally Usbun, Sherwood Vaughn, Isaac Vanhorn, James Unphreys.

P. 802: Joshua Vaughn, Jesse Vanderpool, Wm. Walton, John Williams, Elisha Williams, John Webb, George Walton, Wm. Webb, Thomas Winkle, Conrod Winkle, Jr.,)Winkler), Wm. White, Benjamin Walker, Tilmon Walton, Andrew Wood, Abraham Wiggings, John Wins.

P. 803: Wm. Walker, Robert Wesley, Wm. Wiseman, Benjamin White, Frances Winchester, Phelix Wild, Abraham Winkler, Thomas Willcher, Jolly West, Ruben Walker, Peter Wise, Moses Wilkinson, Jesse Wilson, Christopher Winscot, Thomas White, Drury Williams, Deep Wallis (Waters ?).

P. 804: Charles Wilcher, Heanry Weaver, Conrod Winkler, Wm Webb, Jr. Charles Wakefield, Sr., Charles Wakefield, Jr., Robert Wilson, Hyram Williams, Wm. Wilmouth, General Wilson, Edward Wilson, James Wood, Henry Wood, Jacob Winkler, Sr., Mathias Winkler, Joseph Wilson.

P. 805: John Wakefield, Thomas WakefieldHenry Walton, Alexander Wakefield, Jewell Watkins, John Waggley, Thomas Watkins, Robert Wilson, Wm. Wilson, Allice Wilkins, Thomas Williams, Lewill Watkins, Joseph Wilson,

Wm. Wiseman, Abirilla Wikers, (fem), James Wood (Woods ?), Alexander Wise.

P. 806: John Wilson, Martin Wiseman, Joseph Wilson, Michael Wilson, Isaac Winhorn, Joshua Winford, Rebacca Woods, Elizabeth Williams, John Wilson, George Watts, Wm. Winn, Joseph Winkler, Conrod Winkler, John Wilson, Thomas Winkler, Lawrence Winkler (see James C. Webb, under "C").

P. 807: Thomas Winkler, Jr. Charles Walker, John Woolbrook, Isaac West, James Walker, James White, Wm. Watkins, John Welch, Dorset Woods, John Williams, Wm. Walton, Sr., James Wilson, Azariah Woodward, Ezekiel Wiggins, Ruben White, Wm. Ward (see Wrights under "R").

P. 808: Peter Yount, Rachel Young, Strob Young (Strawbridge Young), Joshua Young, Thomas Young, Moses Young, Joseph Young, Jacob Young, James Young, Benjamin Yearly.

P. 806: Also, inhabitants of Morganton: David Tate, Wm. Tate, Wm. Walton, John Williams, Elijah Williams, John Spear, Bennet Smith, Joseph Spencer, James McIntyre, John Jones, John Hicks, Robert Capehart, Thomas Bushell.

Note: Names in the 1800 Census will not be found in the main index, since these are mainly in alphabetical order.

Microfilm Cmf 1

108

TAX RECORDS

1794 - Pre-1800's

1784. Capt. Simerel's Co. (acreage, polls)

Name not legible, overage, 400 a., Name not legible, o, 1,.
Name notlegible.o.,1; Name not legible, 50, 1; Name not legible., 2 , o:
Name not legible, 236, 1; Fredrick Gryder, 450, 2; John Fincannon,
100, 2; Thomas ?Prowell, 500, 2; John Townson , 620, 3; Mark Ammons,
(?), 1; ...asa Sharp, overage 55, 1; Nickles Day, 50; Joseph Greenway,
300; John Allin, 275; Richard Ramsey, 75; Thomas Green, overage 200;
William H(art)ley, 150;Peter Thompson, 250; ...annath M..insey; Robert
Natherlin , 60; James Pots, David McElray,James House, Andre Haslet, Elisha
Hammons, 150; ...euel Smith, 200, 1; Henry Holsclaw, 50, 1; Christean
Absher, 280, 2; James Madley, 1; Willis Hicks , 150, 1; John Blair,
Colbert Blair, John Mc...eal, 100, 1; Fredrick ...saw, 350, 1; Henry
Hill, 300, 1; John Cox, 1; Johnanthan ..., 125, 1; William ..., 300,1;
John ....; Name not legible; John Bradford, 100,1; John Durham, 120,1;
William Stone, 1; James Day, 100, 1; John Coffey, 150, 1; Ephraim
Holt, 1; Laban Day, 100, 1; William Stoks, 50, 1; James Powell,
overage 480; Edward Day, underage, 100; John Hinds, 500,.2

....Coffey, 60; Elener Stoks, 1 ....;   .... Oneil, 100, 2;
.... Howell, 1; .... Grayson, 100, 1; ... ..bray, 1 ;.... Hartley,
300; ...d Owings 50, 1; .... Baird, 150, 1; William Tucker, 164, 1;
....h Medley, 1; ...h Murrah, 200, 1; ....ah Powell, 400, 2; ... James,
50,1; William ...mes, 50, 1; Ambry (?) Powell, 250, 1; Check Swaringen,
100, 1; Jospeh McCranany 1 , .; Joseph McCrany , 1, Abraham Sudreth,
20u, 2; Elias Powell, Sr., 500; George McCrary, 160, 1; Edward ...ig,
470, 1; John Paly, 300, 1; Alexander Gray, 100, 1; John Day, 310, 1;
Isaai Earthman, 300, 1; James Calyear, 400, 1; Josiah Mason, 1; John
Sumter, 1; James Critchlow(?), 1; Name Not legible: Solomon 270,1;
John Coffey, 750, 1; George H..., 740, 1; Mycara ...in, 200, 1;
William ...ter, Jr., 587,1; James Sam..., 1; George ...ey(Cathey?),1,;
Martin Colter, 2; Robert Fleming, 280, 1;   , Robert
Fleming, 280, 1.
                                    /U.
Adam Setzer 20; Jospeh Alexander, 300;Stephen/Alexander, 135;
Thomas Crage; Phillip ...yer; Thomas Winkler, 393; Adam Winkler, 130;
John ...; George Sigmon, 253; Thomas Dry; Phillip Martin; Gabriel
Jackson, 200; General Wilson; Chesley Dobs, 200; Joseph Grenway, Sr,
100; Willim ...uker, 200; Thomas Sumter; George Tu(cker, Sr., 100;
William Conway; William Conway; James Rob..., Jr., 150, 1; Albert
Corpening, 1850, 1.

Waightstill Avery, 2920 on E. side Appalachian Ridge; 10, 752 on
W. side Appalachian Ridge; 36½ acres lots in Charlotte, back lots; 2
lots in Salisbury, unimproved; 2 lots in Morganton; 12 male slaves; 9
female slaves; 1 free pole self; 1 stud horse. Total land 13,690 a.

1794. Company Unknown, but according to 1793 list is Capt. Austin's:

Stephen Medlock, 100, 1; Jacob Winkler, 1; Ephraim Winkler, 1; Lorance Winkler, 1; John Price, 100; David Price, 200, 1; William Dockrey, 50, 1; Isam Gipson, 1; Luranah Jones, 50, 1; James Pressley, 100; Mager Gibson, 55; John Medlock, 100, 1; Joseph Gipson, 50, 1; James Dockery(?), 1; George Dockery, 50, 1; Jacob Little, 1; James Flachow (?),1; William Rob..., 150, 1; Benjamin Austin, 650, 1; Phillip Austin, 200, 1; William Austin, 900, 1; Henary Reed, 550, 2; William Reed, 400, 2; James Reed 737, 1.

Abraham Hunsucher(Hunsucker), 200, 1; Peter Hunsucher(Hunsucker), 100; John Hunsuchher (Hunsucker), Sr.,88,1; George Tomson, 512, 1; John Barnes, 250,1; Edward Teague 614; Isac Grinstaff, 60, 1; John Hunsucker, Jr., 1; John Teague, 100, 1; Hugh Fox, Sr., 250, 1: Hugh Fox, Jr., 1; Robert Pain, 300, 1; George Pain, 124(?), 2; John Ford, 1; John White, 200, 1; James Pain, 1; Ames Tuttle(?), 1; Joshua Hedley, 1; William Shurrel, 1; Matthew Cox, 1; Jacob Winkler, 320; John Hedley, 1; Jacob Winkler, 320; John Hedley, 160;,1; Thomas Scott,300, 1; Elexander West, 200, 1; Samuel Lowry, 500;   ; James Lowry, 200,1.

John Smith, 150,1; Elisabeth Green, 600, 2; Alijah Green, 150,1; James Oxford, 260,1; Richard Brown, 450,1; William Brown, 150,1; Andrew Steel, 370, 3; Samuel Steel, 200, 1; John Falls, 1; Barnet Pain, 200, 3; James Harvey, 1; William Fulorton, 245; Adam Fulorton, 200, 1; Daley Walker, 150,1; Charles Walkor, 200, 1; Jesse Taler, 200,1; Charles Medlock, 200, 1; William Boyed, 300, 1; John Boyed,150, 1; Thomas Bradburn, 450, 2; John Bradburn, 1220, 1; Elisha Hedley, 100,1; Joshua Freeman, 60, 1; Martin Keller, 100,1; Jacob Keller, 100, 1; Nickle Keller, 100,1; Chri son Keller, 150,1.

Absolam Brown, 150,1; Absolam Penanton, 250,1; Jonas White, 148,1; Joshua White, 1; John Watters 157,1; John Eats, 1; Jesse Perkins, 1; Henary Baker, 100, 1; Joseph Jones(?), 50,1; Thomas R...d, 122; Neanvaire Barns, 100, 1; Samuel Austin, 600,1; Joseph Holsclaw, 100,1; Nathan Presley, 100,1.

1794. Capt. Thomas White's Company.

William Penland, 820,1; Samuel Alexander, 350,1; Benjamin Parks, 550, 3; Thomas Parks, 380, 3; Tittuss Fox, 300, 1; George ...osley; Thomas White, Jr., 550,2; Larkin Parks, 100, 1; John Jones,; Ezekiah Inman, 300,1; John Miller, 50,1; John Parks, 150,1; James Fox, 200; James Barns, 150, 2; Olive Branch, 50, 2; William Penley, 194(?); Name caught in Binding; Name caught in Binding; Reuben White, 100,2; John P...., 131, 1; John Wakefield, 240, 1; Thomas Wakefield, 200,2; Thomas White, 970, 2; John Erwin, 200, 2.; Thomas White, 970, 2; (cont'd) cont'd:

Thomas White's Co.: Felix Hill (?), 100, 1; Stephen Perey, 200, 1; John (Colwell)Brown, ,5; John Simpson, 150, 1; Joshua Penley, 200, 1; Nimrod Brewer, 1; William Lain, 1; James Harbeson, 1,; Christian Shifler, 1; Adam Lewis, 1; Benjamin Rose, 1; Paul Anthony, 200, 1; Phillip Shefler, 400; John Washam, 1; Isaac Phillips, 1; James Baxter, 1; Wiley Scott, 200, 1; Henary Inman, 1; .... Deck, 1; Anderson Branch, 1; Thomas Smith, 1; John Penley, 1; Jonathan Rose, 1; Henary ...(German), 1: Elijah Fox, 1; Robert Penland, 425, 1; Henery Wakefield, 350,3; (Several names caught in binding); Arter Erwin, 287, 4; David McDaniel, 100, 1; William Sherel, 500, 3; James Prichord, 325, 1; Abraham Wagerly; Thomas Wiseman, 1; John Baker, 273, 1; ...ity Sherel, 114, 2; William Penley, 100, 1; Alexander Harbison, 300,1; James Alexander, 550, 1; Moriah Scott, 200, 1; Nathan Fox 1; Henry Baker, 200, 3; Charles Baker, 489, 1; Name not legible, 500, 1; Paul Antony, 900, 1; John Mc.... 1.

1794. Capt. James Mackey's Co. (A few names legible.)

Michael Pierson, 400, 1; William Bailey, 563, 1; Thomas Pierson, 200, 0; Robert Pierson, o, 1; Isom Choat, 333, 1; George Derreberry, 100, 1; Andrew Dereberry, 100, 1; Henry Dereberry, 100, 1; Reuben Walker, 347, 1; John Pierson, 1240, 1; .... Hips, 150,1; William Robertson, 132, 1; John Hiatt, 640, 1; John Jewell, 300, 1; Robert Creswell, 200,1; John England, 50, 1; Elijah Browning, o, 1; .... Patton; Ephraim Ferrel; James Hartley, 0, 1; John Hartley, 0, 1; Bartlet Anderson, 0,1; Matthew Hip, 100, 1; James Templeton, 150, 2; .... Oneal, 200, 1; George Scott, 0,1; Abraham Plumley, 400, 1; Joseph Morgan, 1510, 1; Alexander Bailey, 491, 1; Solomon Good, 122,1; Christopher Pierson, (?), 0.

1795. Capt. Henry Highland's Company. (Acreage, polls.)

John Crays, 10, 1; Michael Houch, 100,1; Joseph James, 100, 1; Vezy Husbands, 50, 1; William Davis, 150,1; John Hughes, o, 1; Bennit Bradford, 50, 1; John Goodlo Smith, 150,1; Joseph McDowell, 1,000, 10; David McDaniel, 100, 1; Peter Yount, o, 1; Richard Davis, 0, 1; Cunrad Crider, 100, 1; Joseph Perkins, 0, 2; Jean Perkins, wid., 600, 4; David Barringer, 0, 0; Agent for Mary Cul....; William Crisp; William Readen; Albert Corpening, 1000; Cunrad Winkler, son of Thomas, 0, 1; Benjamin Coffey, 0, 1; Eli Little John, 24, 1; James Fare, underage, 169, 0; William Gibson, 200, 1; James Moodey; 150, 1; Christopher Amborn, 0, 1; Hugh McKay, 190,1.

Jonathan Fare, 200, 1; Ambrose Hand, 100, 1; Thomas Crage, 60,1; Samuel Crage, 62, 1; James Shearl, 200, 1; Jacob Baldwin, 15, 1; Adam ...., 20,1; Stevin, underage, 102, 1; John Brown, 260,0; Daniel B...inger, 900, 1; Thos. Willsher; Jacob Tips, 400, 1; William Fesmier, 100; ...bis Staleans; William Little; ...m Stalean;

.... Martin, 100; ....per, overage, 100; .... Harper, Jr.; ....
...fare; .... Crag; ...eas ant Cha....; Elisha C...., underage;
William Cra(g)...62; William Mc...ey, 180; Samuel Owings , 313;
Josiah Mason, 0, 1; John Franklin, Jr., 200,1; Jacob Forney, 900;
Phillip Giger, 304; Fertinent Flishman, 100; Abraham Fleming, 845, 6;
Joseph Ingland, 100, 1; Thomas Ingland, 137,1; Charles McDowell, 3500,
5; Peter Holt, Jr., 0, 1; David Crawford, 401; James Murphy, 557, 8;
Alexander Erwin, 338, 4; Brice Collins, 640, 5; John Brown, Jr.;
Robert Fleming, 280; Elizabeth McKinney, o, 2; Hagey McKiney, 300;
John Clark, 350, 1; Nancy Clark, 400, 1; James Stoks, 0,1; Andrew
Gossit, 0, 1; Jansey Conrod Winkler, 186, 1; Samuel Clark, 50, 1;
Peter Arney 0, 1; Abraham Gossit, 0,1; Thomas Brown, 100, 1;
Peter Anthony, 100, 1; John Franklin, 500, 0; Robert JohnstonMiller,
300, 1; John Franklin, 500, 0; Robert Johnston Miller300, o; Martin
Colter, 310, 0; John McGimpsey, 1250, 2; William Hidenland, Jr.,
100,1; Thomas Day, (?), 1; William Sumter, Sr., 500,; William Sumter,
Jr.; James Crage; John Hennesey; Name not legible; ... Winford;
Adam Cook, John Harper, Sr., 200; Johanah   Clark, 300; Joseph
Alexander; John Moody; Thomas Moody, Sr., 219; Thomas Harenson(?),
300, 1; G.... Cook, 172, 1; Sam Enney(Errey?), 322; John ....,323;
Phi... ...tin, 245;   Samuel ...ns, 150, 1; John ...on, 0, 1;
John E...., 185, 3; William .... 285, 1; Jaremiah Clark, 0, 1;
Benjamin Clark, 0,1; George Elliot, 0, 1; Mareday Harper, 0, 1;
Thomas Long, 250,1; Christy Dobs, 200 or 500, 1; William Erwin,
agent for T. Harris, 440; Allen Stoks, 300, 1; Thomas Winkler, 393, 0;
Abraham Winkler, 0, 1.

1795. Capt. Bradshaw's Company (Acreage & Polls)

        William Mashborn, 0,1; George Craford, 150, 1; Moses Templeton,
50, 1; John Wilemon (?), 0,1; Matthew Mashborn, 63, 1; John Jones,
825, 1; John Armstrong, 0,3; John Oaks, 75,1; James Smith, 50,1;
James Mashborn, Sr., 370; Jesse Stroud, 1221, 1; John Wallice, 50,1;
David Mashborn, Jr., 60,1; Elijah Mashborn, 0,1; John Plemon, 50,1;
John Templeton, 0,1; Lewis Mashborn, 0, 1; Jabob Martin, 50,1;
Obediah Brachaw, 100, 1; Richard Hailey, 327; Peter Stroud, Jr., 275,1;
Thomas Morris, 0,1; James Huse(?), 175,1; Joseph Kerby, 100, 0;
William Thompson, 423,2; Hodge Rabourn, 414, 2; Archibald Templeton,
(torn); William Morress, (torn); Isaac Alewaters, 270,2; Mark Hailey,
130,1; William Green, 275; Peter Stroud, Sr., 370; Elijah Green,
173,1; Benjamin Harris, 100,1; Joseph Noblet, 0,1; Thomas Williams,
75, 1; Adam Clem, 0,1; Samuel Davis, 200,1; William Sumors, 200,1;
James Umphress, 160,1; IsaiahBrachaw, 100,1; Robert Woody, 0,1;
Stephen Low, 100,1; Josiah Curley or Curby, 100,1; Joset(?) Smith,0,1;
Luke Hugin, 40,1; Thomas Plemon, 175,1; Drury Mashborn, 190,1;
Clemon Daves (Daives ?), 0,1; David Mashborn, Sr., 210,0; John Martin,
Sr., 210,0; John Martin, Sr., 300, 0; Phillip Goodbread, 255,0;
Peter Plemon, 175, 0; Joseph Goodbread, 206,1; James Mashborn, Jr.,165,1.

1795 Capt. John Hawkins Co., taken by Benjamin Adams. (Acreage/Polls)

John Wilson, 975, 7; William Kilton, 1172, 3; John Cason, 1990, 7;
Robert Trosper, 100, 1; Benjamin Corthern, 338, 2; James Neal, (torn),
2; John Hawkins, (torn), 2; Elijah Patton, (marked out); Daniel
Alexander, 100,1; Robert Turner, 0,1; John Reed, 301, 1; William
Alexander, 100, 1;   John Reed, 301, 1; William
Neal, 320, 3; Lewis McCartney, 400, 2; Samuel Atkins, 0, 1; Andrew
McClure, 0, 1; Ezekiel Wiggins, (torn), 1; Thos. McClure, (torn, 1;
Charles Brown, 0, 1; Ezekiel Patton, 687, 4; William Cathey, 387, 3;
James Glasgow (?), 50, 1; Meseck Burchfield, 250, 2; Robert Hambrick,
200, 1; Nicholas Trosper, 100, 2; Mills Higgins, 150, 1; Benjamin
Curtice, 0, 2; James McDowell, 300,4; J... Fortune (?), 0, 1;
...es Nealey, 300, 8.

1795 Capt. Thomas Lain's Co. (Incomplete)   (acreage and polls)

MartinDeavinport, 1025; John Browning, Sr.; William Wiseman,
460; Samuel Bright, 600; William Mays, 50; Benjamin White, 732;
John Baker, 272; George Crossnore, 300, 2; William Davis, 100; David
B...., 500; William ....; Thomas ....; Charles M...., 100; John
Go...,100, 3; Name not legible; William ...., 100; Moses Y...., 100;
William ....; James ...., 53; James ...., 130; Joseph Wilson, 200;
Abel Simpkins, 125; John McKinney, 600; Henry King; John Mullins;
John Rose; Lazarus Tilly, 100; Solomon Knight; Johnathan Knight, 300;
Swinfield Hill; Martin Browning, Jr.; Thomas Wiseman; Martin Wiseman;
James Mackey, 537; Joseph Mackey, 640; Thomas Mackey, 610; Robert
...well; Isum Shoat, 333; Name not legible; William Cosby, Jr.; John
Creswell, 100; Martin ...., 100; John ....; Anders Deryberry, 100;
GeorgeDeryberry, 100; Name not Legible, 640; John Hailey, 240; John
....; William ....; Robert ....; George ....; Michael Kellor, 344;
John Kellor215; .... Oneal, 330; Name not legible, 322.

1795 Capt. Connely's Co. (Acreage Only)

William Bracher, 300; Abraham Harshaw, 550; John Spencer, 150;
John Gibbs, 200; James Moore, 500; Clizby Cobb, 1020; Joseph Bo...,200;
Thomas Hughs, 225; Stephen Ballew, 212; Robert Me..., 200; John
Phipps, 3981; John Murrah, 150; John Shell, 800; Crate Wagon (?);
Wm. Paine, 500; Wm. Clarck(?), 100; Gilbart Bowan (Bowman), 700; Jacob
Deribure, 200, Seth Brach, 250; Jacob Settlemear, 550; John Barnhart,
400; Josiah Bracher, 150; Thomas ....ng; John Ballard; John Griffy,
200; Joshua Penly,300; Edward Bowman, 300; Groves Bowman; Sherred
Bowman, 50; Conrod Winkler; Jacob Masters; John Connelly, 550; William
Ballew, 100; Barlow Baker, 100; James Connelly, 189; William Penly,
100; George Ballew, 90; Volentine Crider, 100; JamesGorman; William
Thornton; Benjamin C....; Christopher W....; Thomas Man...., 150;
Wm. Connelly, Jr., 100; Michal Grinestaff; Christen Shell, 150; George
Houk, 200; ... .; Jon... ...on, 200; Henery ...ters(Masters ?),
200; William Crye, 200; Daniel Smith, 120; Michael Hart(?), 120;
Peter Houke, 115;

Thomas Winkler, 50;   Jacob Yount, 386;   Joseph Winkler, 200;   John
Berry, 254½;   James Berry, 122;   Wm. Fun Cannen, 260;   Hircem(?)
Williams, 200;   Thomas Watkins;   Uel Watkins;   Thornton Pendergrass;
Wm. Connelly, Sr., 119;   John Crider, 200;   Martin Crider, 150.

1795, Capt. Austin's Co.   (Acreage & Polls)

     John Medlock, 100;   Jesse Reed, 100, 1;   Luke White, 300, 1;
William Fox, 150;   John Barnes, 300;   Abraham Hose, 200;   William
Robarts 150, 1;   Henry Hose, 200, 1;   William Archaw(?), 300, 2;
James Guinn, 100, 1;   James Spradling, 300;   Andrew Free;   James Flachar(?);
Larkin Carley, 100, 1;   Thomas Bradburn, 450, 2;   John Bradburn, 800;
Samuel Austin, 600;   ... Perkins, 100, 1; Henary Baker, 70, 1;
...eph Jones, 0, 1;   Thomas Reed, 60, 0;   ...air Barnes,150, 1;
Samuel Austin, Jr., 500,1;   Joseph Holsclaw, 100, 1;   Stephen Medlock,
100, 1;   Jacob Winkler, 0, 1;   Efram Winkler, 0, 1; esley,100;
.... Gipson, 50, 0;   James Dockery, 0, 1;   James Dockery, 100, 1;
Nathan Presley, 100, 1;   David Price, 100, 0;   Name not legible;   William
Reed, 400, 2;   George ...lan, 275, 1;   Elijah Adams, 310, 1;   Isaac
Chapman, 0, 1;   Samuel Oxford, 200, 1;   Joseph Gipson, 50, 1;   Samuel
Lowery, 300, 0;   John Smith, 150, 1;   Elesebeth Green, 60 (or 600 ?), 2;
Elijah Green, 150,1;   James Oxford, 260,1;   Richard Brown, 250,1;
William Brown, 150, 1;   Andrew Steel, 400, 3;   Samuel Steel, 200, 1;
Barnet Payne, 200, 3;   William Fullerton, 225;   Adam Fullerton, 200;
Charles Walker, 2..(?);   Jesse Toler, 250, 1;   Charles Medlock, 160, 1;
William Boyed, 300, 1; John Boyed, 150, 1;   Elisha Hedley, 100, 1;
Martin Keller, 150, 1;   Jacob Keller, 100, 1;   Nicholas Keller, 0, 1;
Christon Keller, 150, 1;   Absalom Brown, 150, 1;   Absalom Penanton, 250, 1;
Jonas White, 148, 1;   Joshua White;   John Weators(Weathers ?);   Benjamin
Austin, 850, 1;   ...m Austin, 900, 2;   ...p Austin, 350, 1;   Henary
Reed, 450,2;   Abraham Hunsuckar, 0, 1;   Peter Hunsuckar, 100, 1;
...ge Tomson, 350,1;   Jahu Barnes, 250,1;   ...d Teague, 340,0;   ... Teague,
200;   .... Tinery(?), 250, 1;   .... Payn, 334, 2;   John Ford, 0, 1;
...hm White, 200, 1;   ...nes Payn, 0, 2;   Amos Tuttle, 100, 1;   Joshua
Handley, 100, 1;   ...., 450(?), 1;   ...thow Cox, 0, 1;   Jacob
Winkler, Sr., 320, 0;   John Hedley, 190, 1;   ...obart Payn, 300, 1;
Thomas Scot, 300, 1;   ...ander ...., 200, 1.

1795, Company Unknown.   (A laminated page, faded, torn, probably Capt.
Morrison's Co.)   (Acreage & Polls)

     .... Billew, 200, 1;   John(?) Seller, Jr., 100, 1;   (Caleb) Barr,
550,1;   ... Moore, 319 3/4, 3;   (John(?) Penland, 555,1;   .... Clasby,
Sen., 600;   .... Gomery, 121, 6;   (Wm.(?) Patton, 150, 1;   .... Grags,
400, 1;   .... Cowan, 700, 1;   .... Probet, 150, 2;   .... Hicks, 100;
.... Pruatt, 350, 1;   William Moore, 220, 1;   David Hamack(?), 0, 1;
Daniel Rutherford, 142, 2;   Catrin Ward, 0, 1;   Nathan Burchfield, 250,1;

John Starling(?), 75, 1; James ...., Sr., 222, 1; John ...., 361, 0;
Ja... Hines, 0, 1; Eli... Patton(?), 300, 1; John Reed, 125, 0;
Hezekiah Hyatt, 203, 1; Edward Sutherland, 150, 1; Greenberry Wilson,
450, 3; Jno. Hall, Jr. 0,1; David McRath, 1340, and int. 300;
Charles ...ley, 300, 1; James Dyers, 400, 1; John McLadains, 200, 2;

1796, Capt. Sumrall's Co. (Incomplete) (Acreage)

Abraham Suddearth, 200; Thomas Stroud, 530; David Elrey;
A(mbrey?) Powell,; Elias Powell, Jr.; John Grider; William James, 50;
William Sumter, 487; Thomas Sumter, 125; Thomas Powell, 150; Benjamin
Powell; George McCrairy, 160; Kenneth McKiney, 146; James Day, 100;
James Pots, 600; James Crichlow, 100; Elija Powell, 200; Peter Engely,
100, John Townsend, 620; Solomon Smith, 370; Samuel Owings, 275;
Robert Netherly, 662; Simon Ramsey, 75; Albert Corpening, 1800;
Benjamin Coffey, 275; Wm. Sumter, Sr., 500; Adam Setzer, 200; George
Cook, 160; Michael Cook, 150; Samuel Love, 100; William Mooney, ·Sr.,
130; Adam Cook, 378; John Harper, Sr., 200; Benjamin Williams, 250;
Stephen Underdown, 115; Martin Coulter, 200; Michael Allen, 200; Marke
Ammons(?); John Boid, 150; James Buckner, 45; John Hays, (?), Jr.;
John Cox; Frederick Highsaw, 350; Barnet Huffman, 200; John McDaniel,
100; John Fincannon, 100; General Wilson, 172; Richard Ramsey, 75;
Fredrick Grider, 500; Abner Smalley, 344; George Hadley, 542; James
Moreley; Christian Abshear, 280; Peter Thomson, 250; Thomas James, 50;
Moses Thomson; Henry Sumter, 100.

1796, Capt. Austin's Co. (Acreage & Polls)

Benjamin Austin, 850, 1; William Austin, 350, 1; Phillip
Austin, 350, 1; Henary Reed, 450, 2; James Reed, 737, 1; Peter Hunsucker,
100, 1; George Tomson, 350, 0; Jahu Barns, 250, 1; Edward Teague,
340, 0; John Teague, 200, 1; Hugh Fox, 250, 0; Georg Payn, 334, 1;
John Ford, 0, 1; John White, 300, 1; Amos Tufle, 100, 1; Joshua Hedley,
100, 1; William Shurrel, 450, 1; Matthew Cox, o, 1; Jacob Winkler, Sr.,
250, 0; John Hedley, 160, 1; Robert Payne, 300, 1; Thomas Scot, 300, 1;
Elexander West, 200, 1; Samuel Lowry, 300, 0; James Lowry, 200, 1;
James Oxford, 260, 1; Richard Brown, 450, 1; William Crow(?), 150, 1;
Samuel Steel, 239, 1; Andrew Steel, 400, 3; Barnet Payn, 200, 2;
William Fullerton, 245, 0; Adam Fullerton, 200, 1; Charles Walker, 200, 1;
Jese Blew, 0, 1; Charles Medlock, o, 1; John Boyed, 400, 1; Elisha
Hedley, 100, 1; Martin Keller, 150, 1; Jacob Keller, 100, 1; Nicolas
Keller, 0, 1; Christon Keller, 150, 1; Absolom Brown, 150, 1;
Absolom Penanton, 250, 1; Jonas White, 148, 1; Joshua White, 0, 1;
John Waters, 157, 1; Henery Baker, 70, 1; Thomas Reed, 60, 1; Nenavi
Barns, 150, 1; Samuel Austin, Jr., 300, 1; Samuel Austin, Sr., 600, 1;
Joseph Holsclaw, 100, 1; Stephen Medlock, 100, 1; Jacob Winkler, Jr.,
0, 1; Efram Winkler, 0, 1; Lorance Winkler, 100, 1; John Price, Jr.,100, 1;

David Price, 100;   James Presley, 150, o;   Major Gipson, 50, 1;   Nathan
Presley, 100, 1;   Daniel Payne, 200, 1;   Peter Hose, 0, 1; William
Reed, 400, 1;   Elijah Adams, 310, 1;   Samuel Oxford, 200, 1;   Joseph
Gipson 50, 1;   Jesse Reed 100, 1;   William Fox, 150, 1;   William
Archer, (?), 300; James Spradling, 300, 0;   Anderson Free(?), 0, 1:
James Fletcher, 0, 1;   William Robards, 350, 1;   Frances, Doset, 0, 1;
Thomas Winkler, 50, 1;   Thomas Forester, 150, 0;   Thomas Bradburn, 656, 1;
Pliker Siler, 100, 1;   Nathan Austin, 350, 1;   Elijah Austin, 300, 1;
George Allen, 175, 1;   John Brown, 150, 1;   Nicolas Medlock, 100, 1;
Rander Jones, 50, 0;   Solomon Adams, 0, 1;   John Medlock, 160, 0;
George Bruks, o, 1;   Catten Spers, 200, 0;   David Spradling, o, 1;
Isaac Gipson, 0,1; Aron Boles, 200, 0; John Boles, 100,0; John Childers, 0,1.

1796, Capt. Andrew Beard's Co.   (Acreage & Polls)

Charles Petree, 0, 1;   Thomas Winkler;   George Howke, 200, 1;
(Two names not legible);   Thomas Hughes, 225, 1;   James Moore, Sr.,470, 1;
James Moore, Jr. 0, 1;   Samuel Giles, 120, 0;   John Crider;   John
Spencer, Jr., 150, 1;   Wm. Clarck, 100, 0;   .... Bowman, 200;
.... Johnston, 300;   Stephen Bowman, 900, 1;   Stephen Ballew, 183, 1;
Thomas Martin, 150, 0;   John Berry, 254;   .... Ballew, 250, 1;   Wm.
Thornton, -, 1;   James Berry;   .... Clark, 195, 1; Name not legible;
Wm. Connelly, Sr., 117;   John Shell, 800, 1;   Andrew Beard, 64541, 13,
with 5,000 in trust from ... Constable, N. Y. John ...., 414,1;   Joseph
Berry, 200, 2;   .... Paine, 680, 1;   Robert Melson (or Nelson?), 200;
John Barnhart;   Jacob Dereberry, 200;   Henry Stoner, 172, 3;   John Gibbs;
Zaddock Smith;   Michal Hart, 122;   Christian Shell, 150,1;   Name not
legible;   Wm. Connell, Jr., or Sr.;   John Hunsacor, 0, 1;
DanielSmith, 120, 1;   Jacob Yount, 366,1;   Zechariah Ennis(?),
0, 1;   Wm. Bracher, 300, 1;   John Wilson, 200, 9;   Henery Masters, 200, 2;
Abraham Horshaw, 550, 1;   Daniel Polk, 150, 1;   John Bradburn, 650, 1;
John Barnhart, 400, 1;   John Connelly, 760, 4;   Charles(?) Cochran;   Wm.
....;   Isaac ....; Jacob Martin, 300, 1;   John McGallard, 271,1.

1796, Capt. Hawkin's Co.   (Acreage & Polls)

Benjamin Cockran, 338;   Banjamin Yardley, o, 2;   Nicolas Trosper,
100,2;   Richard Yardley;   Alexander Davidson for estate of John Forsythe,
deceased, 291, 1;   Andrew Strain(?);   Daniel Alexander, 100, 1;   Thos.
Wilson, 600, 3;   Meashack Burchfield, 250, 4;   Robert Turner, 0, 1;
Elijah Patton, 1106, 4;   Wm. Cathey, 219, 3;   Frances McClure, 275, 1;
William Neill, 320, 2;   Robert Neill, o, 1;   Samuel Neill, 0, 1;   Samuel
Stout, 0, 1;   Robert Hambrick, o. 1;   William Atkens, 0, 1;   John Jetton,
594, 2;   Charles Brown, 0, 1;   Jesse Fortune, 0, 1;   James Neily, 331, 9;
Gustin Gunter, 0, 1;   James Mcdowell, 0, 1; James Neill, 90, 2;
Andrew McClure, 0, 1;   Thomas McClure, 0, 1;   John Holland, 0, 1;   Lewis
McCartney, 400, 2;   John Carson, 2536, 10;   Executors of Jos. McDowell,
deceased, 1050, 5.

1796, Capt. Morrison's Co.   (Acreage & Polls)

Jno. Penland, 550, 1; Thomas Bell, 320,2; James Bell, 0, 1;
John McDowell, 940, 3; Deward Letherwood, 750, 1; John Dunkin, 150,1;
Joseph Pyatt, 100, 1; Moses Wilkerson, 454, 4; Field Bradshaw, 336,3;
Robert Patton, 1636, 2; John Summers, 480, 1; (Hezekiah) Hyatt, 203;
Caleb Barr, 45, 1; John Andrews, 150, 1; Thomas Sellers, 222, 1;
John Polk, 96, 1; William Moore, 220, 1; Joseph Cowan, 536, 1;
Thomas Sellars, 50, 1; Robert Sellers, 100, 1; Elihu Hicks, 100, 1;
... Dysart, 300, 1; William Probit, 250, 2; Joseph Justice, Jr.,
50, 0; .... Moore; Jon. Hall, 1240, 1; Andrew Woods, 265, 1; William
McDowell, 447, 1; .... Patton, 300, 9; ...as Hemphill, 0, 1;
.... Hemphill, 300, 1; William Cosby, 600, -; Jesse Martain, 150, 1;
Daniel Andrews, Sr., 190, 1; Joshua Hall, 600, 1; .... Hodge, 560;
Name Not Legible; John Rutherford, 500, 4; J... Miclekelrath, 100, 1;
Daniel Andrews, Jr., 140, 1; William Patton, 150,1; .... Pruet, 350,1;
.... Pruet, 0, 1; .... & Hugh Tate, 450, 2; .... Dosse, 250, 1;
Thomas Roberts, 709, 2; Name Not Legible, 100, 1; William Dupree, 0,1;
.... Starling, 150,0; John Templeton,0, 1; William Morrison, Sr.,
600; John McLadoins(?), 200; Michel Binkley, 400, 1; William Gragg,
400; John Sellers, 100; Peter Rust, 350, 2.

1796, Capt. Moore's Co.   (Acreage not legible in most instances.)

John Webb; George Hays; Ambrose Coffey; Joseph Coffey; William
Webb; Jesse Moore, Sr.; Reuben Coffey, Sr.; William Umphries; John
Moore, Sr.; William Lee; William Scott; Thomas Hays; Milley Sercey;
Mary Coffee; William Gragg; ... Church; Daniel Moore; John Majors;
John Church; William Loving, Sr.; William James; George Hickmon;
Robert Church; Gabriel Loving; Joseph Rector; Thomas White; Deep
Waters; Samuel Neely; Samuel Turmire ; James House; John Goble;
Conrad Rader; Reuben Fletcher; Reuben Eastes; John Hight; Read ....;
Jonathan Boone; John Moore; James Crittenden Webb; John Loving;
Michael Gilbert; Len Eastes; Henry ....; George Carter; Thomas
Sherrill; George Holeway; Lewis Coffee; William White; In Trust for
Allen Martin, for Hambleton McLachey, for Selathial Weeks, for Dr.
Slighter Bouchell; Jno. Allen; George Scott; Isaac Emans; Gabriel
Jackson; Nathan Smith; Edward James; George Dowell; Charles Collet;
John Mitchell; Mainyard Gilliam; Abel Crisp; Rice Medaris; James
Wilson; John Green; Michael Wilson; William M....; Charles Wakefield;
Thomas Coldman.

1796, Capt. Henry Highland's Co.   (A Fragment)

Jonathan Fare; Thomas Moody, Sr.; Jacob Tip; John Franklin, Sr;
Abraham Stallions; Ambrose Hoard; Laurence Arney; Cunrod Winkler;
Thomas Moody(?); William Day; Reuben Stallions; Christopher Amburn;

John Franklin; Abraham Fleming; Samuel Harris; William Davis; Thomas
Day, Sr.; John Brown, Sr.; Eli Little John; Joseph England; John
Moody; John Cross; .... England; John Graves; Alexander Erwin;
Samuel Tumens(?); Peter Holt; William Patterson; John McGimpsey;
Joesph McDowell; Phillip Gyer; Thomas Winkler & Son, Abraham; Joseph
Alexander; David McDaniel; Daniel Bullener; Michael Houch(100,));
Peter Spoonhour; Charles McDowell, & in care of Miller Heirs.

1796, Capt. John Fox's Co.   (Incomplete) (Acreage & Polls)

William Penland, 860, 1; James Alexander, 600, 1; Alexander
Harbison,470, 1; James Fox, 200, 0; Noble Alexander, 470, 1; Samuel
Alexander Alexander, 120, 1; Titus Fox, 300, 1; John Jones, 250, 0;
Moses Frankling, 100, 1; Thomas Wakefield, 200, 1; James Fortner, 100, 1;
Benjamin Hase, 100, 1; Isaac Phillips, 0, 4; Olive Branch, 500, 1;
Anderson Branch, (?), 1; Benjamin Parks, 500, 1; Charles P....,
300, 1; Reuben (White ?)51, 1; Thomas White; Thomas Parks, 0, 2;
.... Parks; John (Duh ?), 0,1; (Henry) Inman, 0, 1; Samuel Gray.

1796, Capt. Benjamin Brittain's Co.   (Incomplete)   (Acreage)

Robert Morris, 199,48; William Tate, 42,232; William Cathcart,
182,960; James Kad(?), 100; William Jones, 415; Samuel Brown; John
Martin; David Ramsey; Nichlas Burns; .... Southerland; William
Southerland; Conrad Hiltebrand; John Kell; Zacharias Downs, Sr.;
William Morrow; Shadrack Sanders; Thomas Kell, Jr.; Thomas Kell, Sr.;
Joseph England, Sr.; Isaac Thomson; Fellis Wild; Samuel Brittain;
John Stillwell; Henry Hill, 290; Adam Smith, 300; Richard Gibbs, 100;
James Ropper, 50; David Bear, 213; John Hughes, 820.

1796, Capt. Hamphill's Co.   (Incomplete)

William Porter, Sr., 150, 0; Joseph Chaffin, 50, 0; ....
Mendenhal,100, 1; William ...., Jr., 100; Henery Noble, 100, 1;
Robt. Logan, 0,1; .... Freeman, 109, 1; John M...., 100,1; ....
Chaffin, 100, 1; Abner Chaffin, 75, 1; Joseph Chaffin, 150, 1; ....
Dement, 120, 1; Thomas Hemphill, 900, 5; Rabern Hodge, Sr., 200, 1;

.... Brevard, 200, 0; .... Smith, 25, 1; John Mann, 0, 1; John Petillo,
Sr., 100, 2; Samuel Hollonsworth, 228, 1; William England, Sr., 150;
Edward Yelkson(?), 186, 1; William England, Jr., 75, 1; William
Davis, 0, 1; Robert Hodge, Jr.; .... Devil(German for Teufel), 100;
John Bayars(?), 0, 1; Thomas Little, 100; James Clark, 100, 1;
Michael Southers, 92, 2; John Stone, 0, 1; Millinton Pittillo, 0, 1;
Archebel Slone, 0, 1; William Walton; John Pettillo, Jr., 160, 1;
Joseph Wilson(?); Robert Carither, 203.

1796, Capt. Highland's Co. (A Fragment)

Jonathan Fare; Thomas Moody, Senior; Jacob Tips; John Franklin;
Abram Stallions; Ambrose Hoard; Lawrence Arney;
Cunrod Winkler; Thomas Moody; William Day; Reuben Stallions.

1796, Capt. John Fox's Co. (One Page, Incomplete)

William Sherrall, 494, 2; Daniel Fox, 100; Bartlett Henson, Jr.;
Thomas Osbon; Henry Vinzen; John ....; John Panter, 135; John
Wakefield, 240; Joshua Penland, 200; William Barns, Jr.; Stephen
Penly, 100; James Parks; Isom Panly; Nathan Fox; Robert Penland, 425;
Charles Wakefield, 200; Benjamin Moore, 400, 1.

1796, Capt. Lain's Co., on east side of ridge. (Incomplete)

William Ainsworth, 520; John Ledford,, Sr., 250; Daniel Brown,
549; Benjamin Hensley, 200; Joshua Young; Charles Happer, 200; Henry
Gillespie, 280; .... Gillespie; John Chandler.

1796, Company Unknown (Incomplete) (Probably Capt. Bradshaw)

.... Plemon, 125, 0; O... Bradshaw; William Morriss; Moses
Templeton; Joseph Noblet; George Crafford; .... Woody; Clem Davis;
John Plimon; Adam Clem; Benjamkin Harris, 233; Thomas Smith; Archibald
Templeton; James Burn.

1797, Capt. John Fox's Co. (Acreage & Polls)

Noble Alexander, 410,0; Titus Fox, 500, 0; Daniel Fox,100, 0;
Joshua Pendley, 200, 0; James Fox, 200; Olive Branch, 50, 0; Henry
Inman, 300, 0; Charles Wakefield, 200, 0; Adam Lewis 100, 0; Thomas
Wakefield, 200, 0; Benjamin Moore, 400, -; Samuel Alexander, 120, 0;
Isaac Emmens, 363,1; William Pendley, 100, 1; Phillip Shifler, 450;
James Barns, 300, 1; George Reed, 100, 1; William Deavenport, 75, 1;
Name not Legible; Phillip Anthony, 617, 1; Samuel Parks, 360, 3;
George Parks, 237, 2; William Murphy, 0, 1; John Scott,200, 1; Bartlett
Henson, 290,2; Jacob Beck, 540, 1; Paul Anthony, 200, 1; Thomas(?)
Prichard, 320, 1; Joseph Folkner, 100, 1; John Pendley, 50, 1;
John Porter, 135, 1; Benjamin Rose, 100, 1; Thomas Parks, 412, 3;
HenaryBaker, 200, 4; Jonathan Rose, 100, 1; John ...iller(?), 50 or
500, 1; John ...irier; Wiley ....; Nathan Fox, 0,1; Elijah Fox, 0,1;
James Parks, 0, 1; Samuel Branch, 0, 1; Larkin Parks, 0, 1; Thomas
Wortham, 0, 1; Anderson Branch, 0, 1; Lewis Powel, o, 1; John Trammel,
o0,1; Lewis Powel, 0, 1; John Trammel, 0, 1; James Penland, 9, 1;

Ezekiel Inman, 9, 1; William Barns, 0, 1; Cris Shifler, 0, 1;
Randel Devenport, 0, 1; John Beck, 0, 1; Jacob or Isaih ...;
Isaac Phillips; Isaac Pendley, 0, 1; Abner Hindley, 450, 1; Jacob
Anthony, 350,2; Fredrick Rider, 315, 2; James Baker, 200, 1; Nancy
Pendley, 100; William Penland, 850, 1; Jas. Alexander, 600, 1;(A)..
..arbinson, 470, 3; John Wagerly, 350; Robert Penland, 425, 1; Abraham
Wagerly, 0, 1; William Lain, 0, 1; John Erwin, 360; John Wakefield,
240, 1; George Cross, 0; Rob't. Watson 50 or 500.

1797, Capt. Hemphill's Co.   (Acreage & Polls)

Thomas Littel, 100, 3; James Edmiston, 677, 2; Wm. Walton, Sr.,
115, 3; Richard Fortuan, 150, 3; Benjimin Allison, Jr., 40, 1;
M...tan Bangimva Allison, 100, 1; Bangmin Allison, Sr., 248; Bangmin
Bird, 162, 3; Alexander Kalley(?), 100, 1; John Man, 100, 1; Robert
Hodge, Jr.(?),200, 1; Joseph Jackson, 0, 1; Jerale Keallar(?), 100, 1;
Name not Legible; J... Logan, 100, 1; John Piltilow, Sr. 400, 2;
John Maffit, 107, 1; Jarit Smith, 50, 1; Abraham Holingsworth, 0, 1;
John Holingsworth, 0, 1; Samuel Holingsworth, 226; Zebulon Bravard,
200, 0; Am... Brown, 0, 1; John Pittelow, Jr., 160, 1; Hezakeah
Allison, 0, 1; Wm. England, Jr., 75, 1; Robert Curithers, Esq., 202,11;
MaryDemment, 120, 0; A...s Jackson, 0, 1; W... Davis, 100, 1;
T.... Davis 0, 1; Benjamin Burgoin, Esq., 325 3/4, 4; Capt. Thos.
Hemphill, 940, 5; Thos. Allison, 525, 1; Cornaials Raddare, 150, 0;
John Erwin, 150, 1; Charles Standlay, 115, 1;Jossiah Brandon, 100, 1;
Henery Allison, 50,1; John Jackson, 115, 1; John Noblite, 91, 1;
Millingeton Pittilow, 0, 1; Possey Allison, 97, 1; Samuel or Daniel
Eldridge, 175, 1; Wm. Givans, 260, 1; .... Parke, 100, 1; Wm. Porter,
Jr., 100, 1; Wm. Porter, Sr., 200, 0; Jos. Chaffin, 0, 1; Abner
Chaffin,75, 1; Thos, Bird, 628, 1; Robert McFee, 150, 1; Robert
Hodge, Jr., 100, 1; John Younge, 0, 1; John Burgoin, 100, 1; Wm.
Engling, Sr., 150, 0; Jos. Scolds; Samuel Scolds; Amis Chaffin, 105, 1;
John Jons Jocciey(?); Edward Jackson, 186, 1; Robert Logan, 0, 1;
Archabel Sloan, 0, 0; Thoms. McEntire, 510, 2; Elas Chaffin, 100, 1;
Patrick Sloan, 223, 1; H... Hambrick for his son, 200, 1; Elias Chaffin,
 1; Wm. Wood, 0, 1; Peter Freeman, 0, 1; Thos. ...o, 0, 1.

1797, Capt, Andrew Baird's Co.   (Acreage & Polls)

George Howk, 200, 1; John Connelly, 190, 0; Elizabeth Johnston,
300, 0; John Gibs, 200, 0; Samuel Gibbs(?), 350, 0; Stephan Ballew,
183, 0; James Moore, Jr., 470, 1; Gilbart Bowman, 800, 0; Andrew
Beard, 48,425(?), 1; John Bradburn, 616, 1; William Clark, 100, 0;
Thomas Martin, 950, 1; Five Names Not Legible; Thomas King, 221(?), 1;
John Spence(?), Sr., 76, 0; John Spence(?), Jr., 150, 1; ... Angelly,
100, 1; John Griffith, 200, 1; William Ballew, 100, 1; Thos. Chester, 100;
John Crider, 200; Michal Hart, 122; Joseph Winkler, 200; Daniel Smith, 120;

Thomas Church; Jacob Yonnt; 380(?); Thomas Smith, 100; John Wilson,
152(?); John Berry, 254: James Berry, 122; Christèn Shells, 150;
John Hunsuc_{or} ; Tobias Peterson, 40; Jacob Deribury,200, 1; Henry Hase,
200, 1; Jacob Masters, 160, 1;William Richmond,0,1;Seth Bracher, 200, 1;
Grover Bowman, 317, 1; Benjamin Clarck, 195, 1; Henry Masters, 100, 1;
.... (Wm.?) Paine, 680, 1; Jno. Connelly, 750; Name Not Legible;
Abraham Hershow; Wm. Bracher; .... McGallord; George Ballow; Joshua
Ballew; John Phips; Zedock Smith; Jacob Settlemier; Isaac Martin;
Seth Bracher; Daniel Polke; Widow Shell; Wm. Crye; Ben. Cobb;
Matthew Deene; Abraham Gorst or Gosst; Wm. Spencee; Wm. Crouse; Stofel
Cline; Joshua Perkins; Jno. Martin; Wm. Constable; Margret Wagoner;
Beverly Clarck; Wm. Carley; .... McGee; Reuben Lemons(?); Conrod
Winkler; Robert Nelson (or?) Melson.

1797, Joseph Dobson's Co. (Acreage)

    Elijah Paten, 987, 4; John Ensley, 0; Charles Brown, 0, 1;
James I...1, 90, 2; Benjamin Earley, 0, 2; James McDowell, 0, 1;
Elijah Trosper, 0, 1; Abraham Wiggins, 0, 1; Ezekiel Wiggins, 50, 0;
Miles Higgens, 150, 1; Mashack Burchfield, 250, 3; Samuel Neil,
0, 1; John McClure, 0, 1; Elexander McClure, 0, 1; Dan Ellexander,
100, 1; William Stephen, 0, 1; William Welch, 0, 1; James Glass, 50,1;
William Ussery, 200, 1; Aron Brite, 0, 1; Solomon Standsberry, 200;
Robert Morroson(?), 0, 1; Robert Turner; John Carter or Curtis, 0, 1;
Thomas C...y; Benjamin Curtis, 0, 2; Andrew McClure, 0, 1; Thomas
Curtis; David Curtis, 0, 1; Samuel Stout, 50,1; Samuel Adkins, 0, 1;
John ...son, 0, 1; Nicholis Prosper or Trosper, 0, 1; Robert Prosper
or Trosper, 50, 1; Mical Dun, 0, 1; Andrew Strain, 0, 1; Lewis McCartney,
400, 2; Benjamine Hide, 0, 1; William Hide, 0, 1; Abraham Plumley,
50, 1; Simon Hyett, 0, 1; Robert Gilmore, 0, 1; Samuel Gimison, 0, 1;
Richard Yearly; Christian Isom, 250, 1; William Ledford, 0, 1; Henry
Smith, 0, 1; Francis McClure, 275, 1; William Celton, 800,5; John
Carson, Esq., 2536, 10; Joseph Carson, 0, 1; John Mackey, 100 or 600,
1; John Gitton, 100, 4; John Dockerty, 0, 1; Francis Erwin(?), 0, 1;
Benjamin Hensley, 150, 2; Joshua Hardin , 0, 1; Joseph Dobson, 2576,1.

1797, Capt. Highland's Co.   (Acreage & Poles)

    Willaim Lawrence(?), 285, 1; Abraham Fleming, 825, 2; Christopher
Amburn, - , 1; John Franklin, 2.., 1; (William ?) Fismire, 100, 2;
Samuel .....; ...Annah E....; Elizabeth Mckinney(?); John Tribble(?);
.... Erwin; ...for Samuel Harris, -400, 00; Willaim Davis, 144, 1;
Thomas Day, Sr., 181, 1; John Brown, Sr., 260, --; Eli Little John;
Edmond Bair, 400, --; Joseph England, 100, 1; John Moody, 155, 1;
John Cross, 100, 1; .... England; John Groves; John Hughes(?);
Jacob ....; Alexander Erwin; Samuel Tumens, 150, 1; Peter Holt, --,1;
Willaim Patterson; John McGimpsey, 182, 2; J ,...kens(Akens ?);
Joseph McDowell(?), 1206(?), 8; Phillip Gyer, 340, 1; William ....,

...bson (Gibson ?), 200, 1; Thomas Winkler & Son Abram, 393, 1;
Joseph Alexander, 517, 1; D(avid) McDannel, 150, 1; Capt. Henry
Highland, -, 1; Daniel Bullener, 960, 1; Michael Houck, 100, 1;
Peter Spoonhour (Spainhour ?), 162, 1; Joseph Welch(?); Charles
McDowell, 4019(?), -; In Care for Miller Heirs, 300, 0; Two more
names illegible;.

<u>1798, Capt. England's Co.</u> (One half page, torn, both sides)
                          (Acreage & Polls)

        John Perkins, 1156; Robert Johnston Miller, 300; Jacob Farney,
902, 3; John Erwin, 185, 3; Joseph Perkins, 300, 4; Phillip Giger,
340, 1; John Hennasey, 400, 1; David Crawford, 400, 2; James Murphy,
300, 9; Bennet Bradford, 100, 1; Henry Baker, 100, 1; David
McDaniel, (?), 1; John M. Wilson; Samuel Clark, 150; George Martin;
Jacob Baldwin, 250, 1; Moses Franklin, 100, 1; John Brown, Sr., 0, 1;
Michael (Houk) 100; ...horn, Sherl, 306, 1; Alexander Erwin, 336, 6;
Samuel Tummon(?), 100, 1; Henry Hiland, 550, 6; John Grove, 300, 1;
Jacob Grimes, 100, 1; Johannah Clark, wid.; Charles McDowell, 4830, 5;
Joseph McDowell; Vezy Husband, 270, 1; William Hunt, 394, 2; William
Erwin, 1227,8; In partnership with Ford & Grenlee, 26½; Thomas
Winkler, 393; Jonathan Boon, 464, 2; Cunrad Rader, 150, 1; Gabriel
Jackson, 200, 1; Abraham ....; Abraham Winkler, 0, 1; Cunrad Winkler,
0,1; Peter Durmier, 0, 1; James Crage, 152, 1; Thomas Crage, 62, 1;
Samuel Crage, 62, 1; William Crage, 62, 1; Henry Crage, (torn);
Plasent Crage, 62, 1; Elisha Crage, 62, 1; John Moody, 200, 1; John
Moody, Sr., 76; Abraham Stalians, 400, 1; Reuben Stallians, 100, 1;
Thomas Day, Sr., 93,1; David Chester, 122, 1; John Franklin, Sr.,
446; John Harper, Sr., 100, 1; Thomas Largen, 290; Elijah Largen,
0, 1; Thomas Moody, Jr., 111, 1; Fendel Catherlin, 100, 100, 1;
Michael Cook, 250, 1; Adam Cook, 490, 1; William Gibson, 200, 1;
William Little john, 0, 1; Eli Little john, 250, 1; Laurence,Erney,
322, 0; Farthenant, 150, 1; Daniel Polk, 450, 3; Peter Spoon, 100,1;
William Laurance, 285, 1; Thomas England, 140, 1; William Harper,
160, 1; John Harper, Sr., 140, 1; William Day, 49, 1; William F...,
100, 1; Thomas Day, Jr., 49, 1; Thomas Sherl, 100, 1; Jacob Tips,
400, 1; Richard Shelton, 0, 1; Abraham Fleming, 790, 6; John Kincade,
640, 4; John Brown, Sr., 301, 0; Joshua Brown; Thomas Welker(?);
John Robeson(?), 0, 1; William England, 0, 1; Perkins,0, 1;
William Webb(?), 214, 1; Samuel ...., 72, 1; Thomas ...., 100, 1;
Edmund Faire(?), 400, 1; Robert Fleming, 350, 1; William Penly, 100,1;
John Clark, 250, 1; Nancy Clark, widow, 300, 2; Beniamen Clark, 0, 1;
John Lintz, 320, 1; James Rose(?), 300; John Tuc..., 300, 1.
Alexander McDowell, 350,1; Jaremiah Clark, 0,1.

<u>1798, Company Unknown.</u> (Probably Capt. Lain's) (One double page, torn)
                          (Only following names legible.)

        John Reid; David Reid; Charles Baley; Nathan Burchfield;

Joseph Thompson; Richard Medlock; Elisha Harden; Charles Baker;
NathanielArmstrong; John Green; Aron Burlonson; Thomas Burlonson;
George Robertson; Edward Robertson; Arthur Buckhanon; William
McKiney; John Mckiney; Benjamin Hansley; William Baley; David
Burchfield; Jesse Perkins; Joseph Jones; William Wiseman, Sr.,;
William Wiseman, Jr.,; James Wiseman; James Carson; Samuel Knight;
Samuel Spencer; Richard Jacks; William Dobbs; William Davis;
Thomas Wiseman; Benja. White;.

1798, Capt. John Fox Co(Poor condition. Only the following names are
                        legible.)

      James Canlay; John Jones; James Ramsey; Elizabeth McKinney;
Nathan Fox; ... Booth ... Harbison; Noah Fox; Allen Fox; William
Alexander; William McDaniel; Joshua Penly; Bartlet Henson, Jr.,;
Fredric Rider; Marthew Harbison   ; ... Sheffler; Phillip Shefler;
Randel Devenport; Paul Anthony, Jr.,; William Devenport; Benjamin
More; William Pendley; James Barns; George Reed; Stephen Pearcy;
.... Parks; Bartlet Henson, Sr.,; ... Alexander; Robert Penland;
.... Baker; Alexander Harbison; Nancy Pendley; James Folkner;
Thomas Parks; Rueben Odell (?); Jacob Beck, Sr.; Jacob Anthony, Sr.;
John Erwin; Isaac Pendley; .... Beck; Hezekiah Inman; .... Beck, Jr,;
Samuel Alexander; Thomas Wakefield; John Wakefield; John Patner;
Benjamin Rose; Jonathan Rose; John Barnes; Titus Fox; David Fox;
James Parks; Timothy ....; Archbabel Carnon; George Parks; Charles
Wakefield; Isaac Phillips; William Ray; Abner Ray; Abner Henley;
James Fox;AbrahamWagerly; William Harbison; Henery Avery; Noble
Alexander; Joseph Scott; .

1798, Company Unknown, probably Neill's:(One page, but not legible.)

1798, Capt. Joseph Dobson's Co., -(One page, but not legible.)

1798, Company Unknown. - (One page, but not legible.)

1798, Company Unknown. (Probably Robert Kirkpatrick's. (One page,
                         but not legible.)

1799, Company Unknown. (Probably Capt. Robert Kirkpatrick's.)
                        Acreage & Polls)
      Charles Coker, Sr., 300, 1; William Coker, 0, 1; Charles Coker,
0, 1; Jesse Moore, 550, 1; Jesse Moore, Jr., 100, 1; Daniel Moore,
100, 1; Reuben Coffey, Sr., 175, 1; John Coffey, 0, 1; Reuben
Coffey, 0, 1; James Coffey, 275, 1; Joseph Coker, 50, (?); James

123

Holland, 180, 1; William Lee, 200, 1; James ....; Name not legible;
.... H....; John Moore, Sr., 300; John Moore, Sadler, 50, 1;
Benjamin Adkins, 200, 1; Reuben Estes, 700, (?); John Loving, 500, 1;
Lewis Harris, 150, 1; Mainyard Gillum, 100, 1; Harriss Gillum; John
Harris, 0, 1; Laban Estes, 160, 1; Reuben Fletcher, 600, 1; William
Williams, 100, 1; John Church, 100, 1; Robert Church; Thomas Church;
Absolom Baker, 50; Robert B...rnt; Charles Weakfield, 225, 1;
Thomas Weakfield, 200; Benjamin Weakfield, 200; .... Ammons, 163;
Henry Baker, 200, 1; George Hickman, 0, 1; Rolings James, 200, 0;
George Scott, 150, 0; John Goble, 150; Samuel Turmire, 100; Joshua
Gilbert, 150; John Goldsmith; John Crisp; William Crisp; Thomas
Wilson; .... Wilson, overage, 400; William Wilson; William ....;
George ....; Jacob Snead; Thomas Powers, overage, 100; George
Hutchinson or Hutchings; Robert Kirkpatrick, 400; Hardy Mills; Rice
Medearist, 300; Dennis Framel, 50; Len Estes, 140; James Macmuran,
100; Waddey Thompson; Gabriel Loving, 140; Moses Stapp, 100, 1;
Nathan Smith, 0, 1; George Failler, Jr.; .... Miller; ....be Shupman;
.... Jackson; George ....; William Love; Joseph Prock; Name not
legible; Thomas Anderson; James Jackson; John Dowell, 50; George
Dowell, 120, 1' Jonath.. Boone, 300, 1; Jesse Boone, 625, 1; George
Hays, 90, 1; Thomas Hays, 50, 2; John Parr, 0, 1; William Edmunson,
100, 1; James Giddens, 50, 1; Joseph White, (Jr. ?), 300, 1;
Michell Gilbert, 100, 1; William ....; Name not legible; Samuel
Wesley; John Nealey; William Markes(?), 100, (?); Austin Moore,0,1;
John Holland, 0, 1; William Webb, 0, 1; James Webb, 0, 1; Deep
Watters, 50, 1; Phillip Church, 0, 1; William Davis, 0, 1; Peter
Turnmire, 0, 1; Alexander Weakfield, 0, 1; Daniel Richards n; Wiley
Scott, 200; James Moody, 150; James Sherrill, 200; William ..., Sr,
250; Joseph H....; Abraham ....; William White, 1166(?); Thomas
White, 125, 1; W. White, 500; and for John Megie, 200; Charles Collett,
underage, 166; Gabriel Jackson, black man, 200, 1; David McDaniel,
100, 1; Conrod Render, 150, 1.

No Date - Pre-1800, Capt. Lain's Co. on W. side of Blue Ridge.
                        (Partially Torn)

    John Browning; William Wiseman, 460; Joseph Jones, 30; Samuel
Bright; Chesley Dobbs; George Crossnore; David Baker; John Mullins,
Sr.; Moses Young; Nathaniel Armstrong; Richard Medlock; Thomas
Burleson; Joseph Buchanan; Thomas McKinney; John Gra(ham);
Averillah Vick; William Hill; Swinfield Hill; Joseph Standley;
William Ingram; J.... Perkins; .... Wadkins; .... Wadkins; E....
McKinney, 100; Simon Ramsey; James Wilson, 50; James Brown; Ambrose
Mullins; William Davis, 100; Lazarus Phillips, 100; ,,,, Greer, 100;
William Fullwood, 98; Deavenport Wiseman; William Wiseman, 100; Martin
Browning; William Dobbs; Alexander Cole, 200; Thomas Deavenport,
120; Nathan D...ton, 100; Benjamin White; William McKinney; William
De....

No. Date, Pre-1800: Capt. William Greenway's Co. (Acreage & Polls)
        (Booklet is in excellent state of preservation.)

        John McCrary, no land, 1; Benjamin Coffey, 125, 1; John Allen,
0,1; William Tucker, 375,1; James Medley, 50, 1; Henery Smith, 50,1;
 Ruben Bray, 0, 1; Stephen Mayfield, 100, 1; James Absher, 150, 1;
Fredrick Grider, 400, 1; William Peremon, 200, 1; Christian Absher,
150, 1; William James, o, 1; James Blare , 100, 1; Laben Day, 180
Or 110 ; Edward Day, 100, 1; James Crutchlo, 200, 0; James Day,
124, 1; Robert Harris, 0, 1; Samuel Smith, 200, 1; John Owing,
0, 1; Jeremiah Murrey, 214, 1; Peter Tomson, 250, 3; General Wilson,
264, 1; John Baley, 300, 0; John Cannon, 200, 1; Sam Low, 130, 0;
Richard Green, 140, 0; Richard Green, Jr., 0, 1; Thomas Prowel, 330,
2; James Walker, 230, 1; Benjamin Baley, 0, 1; Samuel McDaniel,
150, 2; John Day, 350, 0; Thomas Green, 0, 1; Joseph Gilbert, 0, 1;
Thomas McCrary, 70, 1; Colbort Blare, 218, 1; John Blare, 300, 1;
Moses Tomson, 0, 2; George Hartley, 864, 1; James Presley, 200, 0;
Elijah Gilbert, 100, 1; John Gilbert, 50, 1; Isaac Sherel, 160, 1;
William Smith, 50, 1; Susannah Simkin, 130, 0; John Smith, 0, 1;
Mikel Cook, 240, 1; Richard Herren, 0, 1; Gabriel Loving, 244, 1;
Thomas Norman, 0, 1; William Brown, 150, 1; James Pots, 600, 2;
James Lowry, 0, 1; John Grider, 200, 1; John Bradfird, 200, 0;
Frederick Grider, 0, 1; William Golbsay, 0, 1; Lewis Powell, 450, 1;
Henry Sumter, 225, 1; Thomas Sumter, 0, 1; William Repito, 290, 0;
David Repito, 100, 1; Andrew Highsaw, 0, 1; Samuel Highsaw, 0, 1;
John Clarke, 560, 1; Elias Powell, 200, 1; Benjamin Powell, 0, 1;
Robert Nathery, 1500, 3; William Nathery, 0, 1; Isaac Story, 200, 1;
William Baley, 0, 1; Joseph Long, 0, 1; Ruben Coffey, 490, 1;
William Greenway, 300, 1; Aron Williams, 200, 4; Peter Canon, 218,1;
Jacob Grider, 0, 1; Gabriel Smith, 210, 1; Allen Stoakes, 100, 1;
Aley Smith, 110, 1; James Collar, 300, 1; John Stoaks, 0, 1; John
Coffey, 100, 1; Frederick Highsaw, 350, 0; Benjamin Powell, 170, 2;
Joseph McCrary, 600, 0; Samuel Smith, 50, 1; John Bush, 100, 1;
George Tucker, 100, 0; Edward Long, 240, 0;   Elisha Dehart, 65, 1;
Thomas James, 100, 1; John Holt, 100, 1; Peter Holt, 360, 1; Elias
Powell, 150, 1; James Mullines, 100, 1; Samuel Hendrickson, 0, 1;
Jesse Lunsford, 0, 1; John Hendrickson, 0, 1; (Not Legible) Prock,
200, 1; Thomas Briant, 120, 1; Cresey Angley, 100, 0; William
Absher, 0, 1; Drewry Williams, 225, 6; Henry Killian, 50, 0;
William Powell, 100, 1; Conrod Elrod, 0, 1; Abraham Suddreth,700, 3;
William Ramsey, 100, 1; Peter Elrod, 200, 1; John Baird, 275, 1;
John Townson, 645, 3; Thomas Suddreth, 0, 2; John Paseley (Pressley ?),
200, 1; Elizabeth Vandypool, 0, 1; John Hyns (?), 100, 0; Richard
Ramsey, 73, 0; John Spenser, 140, 0; James Howell(?), 112, 0; Dyel
Simes, 0, 1; Joshua Gilbert, 118, 0; Abner Smalley, 325, 0; William
Freeman, 140, 0; Reuben Dehart, 0, 1; Nathan Dehart, 0, 1; Thomas
Green, 0, 1; John Green, 100, 1; Jesse Wilson, 375, 1; William
Holtsclaw, 100, 1; Alexander Gray, 400, 0; Nickles Day, 900, 1;
Colbert Blare, Sen.(?), 0, 1; Samuel Owing, 260, 0; James Stoaks, 100,1;

Christian Prock, 0, 1; John Tucker, 0, 1; William Haley, 250, 1;
Susy Hartley, 300, 0; Lewiston Sumpter,10, 1; A. Allen, 375, 0;
Alexander West, 200, 0; John Speck, 200, 1.

No Date. Pre-1800, Capt. Joseph Young's Co., West of the Blue Ridge.
                    (Acreage & Polls)
                (Poor condition, torn, many names illegible.)
     Martin Deavenport, 948, 2wh., 2 bl; John Browning, 400, 3;
William Wiseman, 560, 3; Thomas McKinney, 550, 1; John Gouge, 200,1;
Charles ...., 0, 1; Samuel ...., 0, 1; Several Names illegible;
Nathan Armstrong, 0, 1; David Birks, 0, 1; Richard Birks, 0, 1;
Richard Medlock, 0, 1; John Rese(?), 0, 1; Roland Birks, 50, 1;
John Taylor, 0, 1; Joseph Jones,130, 0; George Crossnore, 100, 1;
Samuel Bright, 300, 1; James Carson, 590, 1; David Baker, 670,1;
John Miller, 0, 1; William Davis, (?), 1; Daniel Holderfield;
William Mullins; .... Hughs; .... Taylor; .... Simpson; .... Brown;
.... Bright; .... Taylor; Matthew Jones; Alexander Cole.

No Date. Pre-1800. Capt. White's Co.   (Acreage & Polls:
     Martin Browning, 100, 1; Charles Browning, 0, 1; Geo.(Gen ?)
Hu White, 0, 1; Nicholas Browning, 190, 1; Jacob Carpenter, 170, 1;
John Browning, 450, 0; John Blalock, 100, 1; Charles Hopper, 500, 0;
Zachariah Hopper, 200, 1; Richard Blalock, 100, 1; Joseph Jones,
250, 0; Benjamin White, 880, 0; William Davis, 500, 0; Joarg
Bowen, 0, 1; William Wiseman, Sen., 500, 0; William White, 0, 1;
John Hopper, 0, 1; Joseph Wilson, 400, 1; Hillory Carioway,0, 1;
Adam Hopus, 0, 1; Moses Caroway; Samuel Wels, 0, 1; Abner Davenport,
100, 1; Martin Davenport, Sr., 1528, 0; William Phillips,
David Browning, 350, 1; David Retheford, 295, 1; William Vance,
0, 1; John Vance, 0, 1; Moses Worshburn, 130, 1; Thomas Davenport,
170, 1; Henery English, 150, 1; Daniel Cowell, 0, 1; Bargis
Williams, 200, 1; Edward Griffen, 0, 1; Elizabeth Waldrip, 0, 1;
Fethrick Link, 260, 1; William Waldep , 0, 1; David Cox, 240, 1;
Joshua Young, 350, 1; Aaron Harden, 0, 1; Thomas Yong, 480, 0, &
3 blacks; Abel Simpkins, 100, 1; Asa Martin, 0, 1; Lesebeth
Simpkens, 100, 1; Thomas Triplet, 150, 1; Forg Triplet, 100, 1;
Richard Roberts, 0, 1; John Chanley, 250, 1; Benjamin Hensley, Sr.,
200, 0 ; David Brown, 1050, 0; Joseph Roach, 100, 1; Charles
Mackheny, 0, 0; I Black; William Ainsworth, 820, 1; Samuel Brown,
326½, 1; Tomes or Flemes Carson, 200, 0; Edward Letherwood, 300, 1;
Tomas or James Davenport, 468, 0; William Cox, 500,1; Amos Henson,
150, 1; William Phillips, 250; Marting Davenport, o,1; Thomas Coles,230,1;
John Freeman, 0,1; William Triplet, 150,1.

No Date. Pre-1800. Capt. Dobson's Co.   (Acreage & Polls)
                (Poor, torn, faded.)
     James Vaughn, 304, 1; James McDowell, 607, 1; James England,
96, 0; Edward Williams, 50, 1; Shadrack Stillwell, 250, 0;

....al Sullivan, 500, 0; Not Legible, 213, 1; ....Newell, 0, 1;
.... Dunkan, 250, 1; Frank Winchester, 100, 1; William Shelton,
0, 1; Frank Winchester, 100, 1; William Shelton, 0, 1; Willis
Wiggans, 50, 0; Amos Hensley, 495, 1; Charles Bracon, 100, 0;
Peter Ledford, 300, 0; Benjamin Henderson, 0, 1; Merret Burgin,
610, 1; William Becknal, 0, 1; William Murphy, 9613(?); ...aydal
Wilson, 0, 1; John Sharrel, 0, 1; .... Jemison, 100, 1; ....
Jemison, 150, 1; .... Cooper , 0, 1; .... Floid, 0, 1; Thomas
Jones, 0, 1; James Pitman, 0, 1; Briant Gibs, 200, 1; William
Carter, 300,1; William Crowder, 150,1; George Correl, 0, 1,
John Gibs, 200, 0; Elijah Evans, 150; Robert Endsley, 0; John
Robeson, 0; William McKee, 150; Benjamin Garrish, 0, 1; Man Shote(?)
0, 1; William Laurance, 0, 1; Silas Murphy, 100,1; Eli Sharpe, 0, 1;
Jonathan Abbot, 0, 1; John Bitticks, 150, 1; Joshua Curtice, 388,0;
Robert Crowder, 400, 0; William Browning, 0, 1; John Hill, 50, 1;
Thomas Haney, 0, 1; David Bever, 75, 1; Benjamin Bever, 75, 1;
Alexander Dobson, 700, 1; Agnes Young, 414; Thomas Robeson, 0, 1;
Charles Hawkins, 100, 1; John Hawkins, 0, 1; William Morrow, 50; ·
Tilman Stilwell, 0, 1; Benjamin Green, preacher, land lying in Cove,
100; Levy Ledford, 0, 1; Frances Mathes, 0, 1; William King, 105,1;
John McDowell, 0, 1; Widow Wilson, 430 on Buck Creek, 0; .... Hawkins,
100, 1; Not Legible, 150, 1; Solomon Lackey, 0, 1; William Kids,
0,1; Levy Curtice, 0, 1; Archabald Gibs, 0, 1; William Laurance,
0,1; Benjamin Ballard, 100, 1; John M. Greenlee, 14950, 1; Jason
Carson, 566, 1; Antony Mathis, 0, 1; William Wages, 0, 1; Benjamin
Hensley, 0, 1; Levy Watts, 0, 1; William Endsley, 0, 1; Amos Forister,
0,1; Lewis Clark, 0, 1; Asa Mullins, 0, 1; John Findley, 0, 1;
Charles Findley, 600, 1; Charles Findley, Jr., 250, 1; John W.
Carson,150, 1; Howell Buggs, 0, 1; Thomas Curtice, 0, 1; John
Inmon, 0, 1; Samuel Inmon, 0, 1; John Powell,0, 1; Jacob Stillwel,
0, 1; Elijah Patton, 589, 0; William Kelton, E. Patton, Agent, 725;
John Kirkland, 0, 1; Richard Hutchins, 0, 1; Moses Brown, 0, ?;
Benjamin Hensley, 0, ?; Stogdal Wilson, o, 1; John Cobb, 50 on
Garding Buck, 0; Thos. L. McEntire, 210 - 156 on Clear Cr; 160 N.
Catawba, 60 on B. Creek, 50 on Muddy Cr, 1 store; Edward Good, 80;
William Waffef, 0, 1; Paton Harris, 0, 1; Col.John Carson, 500, ?.
John Dobson, 700, 1.

No Date, Pre-1800: Capt. Newland's Co. (Acreage & Polls)

    Thomas Winkler, 0, 1; Lewis Lowman, 250, 1; Conrod Winkler,
125, 0; Joseph Winkler, 200, 1; John Wilson, 300, 1; Thomas Hilton,
100, 1; Conrod Burns, 122, 1; Peter Houk, 100, 0; Adam Suttlemire,
200, 1; Jacob Horn, 180, 1; Thomas Smith, 100, 1; James Smith, 100,1;
James Smith, 100, 1; Henry Lints, 100, 1; David Frankum, 100, 0;
William Lorance, 250, 1; Mical Heart, 112, 0; Jacob Heart (Houk?),
50, 0;   John Sulls , 0, 1; Tunnis Hoglin, 50, 1; George Hileman,
450, 0; Elias Moyer, 0, 1; David Beael, 150, 1; Wm. Richman, 100,1;
Wm. Ballew, 100, 1; Wm. Connley, 170, 2; Stephen Ballew, 193, 1;

Samuel Giles, 350, 0;   Justice Beach, 200, 0;   John West, 0, 1;
Wm. Bradshaw, 400, 1;   John Connelley, 805, 0;   Jesse Bery, 0, 1;
Peter Been, 173, 1;   William Frankum, 40, 0;   Robert Grasey , 0, 1;
George Houk, 200, 0;   Thomas Martin, 350, 1;   Thomas King, 0, 1;
Shepherd Bowman, 900, 3;   David Montgomery, 150, 1;   ...mes Hardin,
0,1;   Wm. Morrow, 0, 1;   Thomas Largin, 300, 1;   John Givins, 150, 0;
James Campbell, 75, 1;   Robert Stephens, 0, 1;   Wm. McDaniel, 100, 1;
Seth Bradshaw, 200, 2;   Joseph Frankum, 0, 1;   Henry Tucker, 0, 1;
Wm. Humphres, 140, 0;   Robert McCall, 122, 0;   Samuel McCall, 0, 1;
John McCall, 0, 1;   James McCall, 0, 1;   John Shell, 200, 1;   Abraham
Husher (Harshaw ?), 650, 4; Josiah Bradshaw, 125, 1;   Peter Melson,
200, 1;   Jonathan Dawson, 0, 1;   James Gormon and George Pearce,
0,3;   Benjamin Clark, 195, 1;   Wm. Clark, 100, 0;   Thos. Chester,
50, 1;   Clement Dorset, 0, 1;   James Meloney, 0, 1;   Wm. Spenser, 300, 1;
John Spenser, 160, 1;   Daniel Smith, 120, 0;   John Bradburn, 50, 0;
Jeremiah Helton, 0, 1;   Peter Helton, 0, 1;   Wm. Crouse, 0, 1;   Zadock
Smith, 1266, (?);   John Smith, 0, 1;   Samuel Smith, 0, 1;   Henry Haas,
370, 1;   Wm. Word, 0, 1;   Valentine Grider, 50, 1;   Christian Shell,
250, 1;   Wm. Cortney, 0, 1;   Joseph Griffith, 0, 1;   Abraham Gosset,
0, 1;   Wm. Sammons, 0, 1;   Charles Shell, 0, 1;   Isaac Stoner, 100, 1;
Henry Stoner, 100, 1;   John Griffith, 300, 1;   Andrew Baird, 650, 7;
Partnership Lands, 32844: Jacob Suttlemire, 1300, 0;   Wm. Little, 0,
1; John Martin, 250, 1;   Benjamin Pugh, 0, 1;   James Frankum, 0, 1;
Jacob Martin, 300, 1;   James Moore, 470, 2;   Joseph Carnes, 0, 1;
Wm. Martin, Sr., 300, 1;   Wm. Martin, Jr., 200, 1;   Jessey Martin,
360, 1;   Isaac Martin, 100, 0;   Jacob Seger, 150, 0;   Isaac Griffith,
0,1;   Freddrick Raby, 50, 1;   Abner Payne, 286, 1;   Jacob Yunt, 386, 0;
Clisby Cobb, 2,000, 0;   Benjamin Cobb, 320, 2;   John Cobb, 470, 1;
Archibald Cobb, 320, 2;   Samuel Ekins, 408, 0;   John Ekins, 0, 1;
Joshua Ballew, 300, 1;   Wm. Ballew, 0, 1;   Hiram Ballew, 0, 1;   Wm.
Givens, 0, 1;   Obediah Givens, 0, 1;   Groves Bowman, 317, 2;   Gilbert
Bowman, 550, 0;   Henry Hallmon, 200, 0; Hiram Williams, 0, 1;

"Not Given In:" Paul Cockran; Wm. Sides; Wm. Tunmire; Thomas Payne;
JohnMcGalliard, "a tract sold by Ephriam Evens to John Bradburn lying
by Cobbs Coleing Ground that John Bradburn's mill is on sold to Moyer."

No Date,   Pre-1800: Summoned by James Carrel & Samuel Parkes.
(Acreage & Polls)

    David Culberson, 150, 0;   Henry Gerley, 200, 0;   Benjamin Wise,
100, 1;   Samuel Mackey, 300, 1;   Thomas Culberson, 100, 1;   William
Culberson, 200, 0;   James Asque, 100, 2;   Jossey Hyett, 202, 2;
Hugh Conley, 361, 0;   Thomas McTigart, 490, 2;   William Kerley,
50, 1;   Daniel Kerley, acreage unknown, 1;   Tilmon Walton, acreage
unknown, 0;   Jessey Smith, 80, 1;   John Miller, 150, 0;   Robert Gipson,
0, 1;   James Barns, Sr?, Jr?. 0, 1;   James Sparkes, 0, 1;   Peter Shaver,
0,1;   Elijah Fox, 0, 1;   David Wadkins, 0, 1;   Robert Wadkins, o, 1;

John Wadkins, 0, 1; Peter Shaver, 0, 1; William Brooks, 0, 1;
Lessey Hurt, 0, 1; Thomas Simmons, 0, 1; William Rust, 0, 1;
Charles Pearson, o, 1; Caleb Odle, 0, 1; Joseph McGimpsey,
"refused to give his taxable says he has land and the sessors
may find it if they could"; Thomas Carlton, 496, 0; Isaac
Phillips, 150, 1; William Penly, 200, 0; Thomas Wakefield, 366,
3; Mangram Jones, 72, 1; William Foolwood , 260,4; Samuel
Alexander, 192, 0; also, Agent for James, 150, 0; William Gibs,
240, 1; Benjamin Moor, 449, 5; Briant Conley, 100, 1; William
Wilson, 100, 1; Paul Anthony, 300, 0; William Pearcy, 200, 1;
John Pless,300, 1; Robert Penland, 530, 0; Joshua Pendley, 200, 0;
Jacob Hice, 0, 1; William Culberson, 300, 1; Jonathan Rose, 530, 1;
William Conley, 400, 4; Robert Wilson, 0, 1; Abraham Corpening,
960, 2; Isaac Penley, 0, 1; Abner Phillips, 0, 1; Joseph Phillips,
0, 1; Noble Alexander,606, 0; Joseph Scot, 250, 1; John Scot, 450,1;
Christopher Shufler, 690, 2; Joshua Penley, Jr., 0, 1; John Beck,
209, 1; Nicholas Beck, 380,1; George Redd, 100, 0; John Barrier,
250, 1; Thomas Scot, 200, 1; Joseph Beck, 290, 1; John Branch, ·
120, 1; John Michener, 0, 1; Henry Crump, 0, 1; Thomas Webb, 0, 1;
Jacob Hice, Jr., 100, 1; James Barns, Sr., 223, 0; John Wakefield,
100, 1; Stephen Pearson, 560, 2.

Wiley Jones, 0, 1; Thomas Parkes, 620, 2; Zachariah Boothe, 250, 1;
George Sigmon, 600, 0; William Ginks, 0, 1; Timothy Sisk, 180, 1;
Bartlet Henson, Jr., 200, 1; John Phillips, 200, 1; William Parks,
Sr., 195, 1; James Parks,, 185, 1; Benjamin Parks, 150, 1; George
Parks, 0, 1; George Parks, Jr., 47, 2; Ambrose Parks, 55, 1;
NathanielPearson, 125, 1; James Marlow, 250, 1; Ambrose Parks, agent
for heirs of Larkin Parkes, 145, 0; Jeremiah Shook, 50, 0; Samuel
Branch, 270, 1; James Fox, 230, 1; William Conley, 340, 1; James
Branch, 100, 3; John McGimpsey, 6935, 6; and, for heirs of Michael
Snider, 500, 0; MOses Harden, 0, 1; Peter Spainhower,200, 1; Anderson
Branch, 0, 1; James Owens, 0, 1; James Jackson, 0, 1; Bartlet
Henson, Sr., 330,8; Samuel Parkes, 400, 4; James Carrell, 670, 4;
Polly Pearcey, 175, 0; Stephen Pearcey, 355, 0; Ellis Margudes, 0,1;
Willis Carrell, 590,6; Conrod Hice, Sr., 203, 0; Conrod Hice, Jr.,
0,1; John Conley, 500, 2; Benjamin Thirston, 330, 3; George Hice,
370, 0; Joshua Fincher, 0, 1; Philip Anthony, 570, 1; Alexander
Erwin, Sr., 917, 5; Stephen Gipson, 200, 1; Alexander Erwin, Jr.,
80, 5; John Penly, 50, 0; Isaac Phillips,"agent for Robt. Watson,
deceased in this World,500; Peter Limbock, 375, 1; Leonard Hice, 0, 1;
Jonathan Fincher, 157, 1; James McDowel, 86, 1; Michael Petman, 0,1;
William Alexander, 500, 2; Perrian M. Daniel (or McDaniel ?), 0, 1;
Hardy Wiggins, 0, 1; Zachariah Langdon, 0, 1; William Winters, 0, 1;
Peter Rust 355, 3; John Fox, 285, 1; Lewis Powell, 250, 1; Henry
Penland, 100, 1; Stephen Branch, 60, 1; William McGimpsey, 400,0;
Nathan Smith, Jr., 0, 1; Joseph Perkins, 500, 6; Stephen Jackson,
0,1; William Jackson, 0, 1. George Parkes (or Parker), 0, 1;
John Perkins, 1015, 4.

No Date, Pre-1800: No Company Listed. (Probably Capt. Austin's Co.)
(Acreage & Polls)

John McKiney, 250, 1; Joseph Buckanan, 150, 1; Arthur Buckanan, 150, 1; John Green, 100, 1; David Baker, 2400, (?); Thomas McKinney, 500, 3; Thomas Baker, 0, 1; Shadrack Green, 150, 1; Samuel Pitmans, 143, 0; Thomas Huse, 270, 1; William Ingram, 150, 1; George Honsucker, 50, 1; Thomas Howell, 0, 1; Richard Stanley, 0, 1; William Bailey, 0, 1; Henry Stafford, 0, 1; James Chambers, 0, 1; James Burleson, 0, 1; William Baker, 0, 1; Aron Tomas, 150, 1; Aaron Burleson, 200, 1; John Hunsucker, 0, 1; John England, 100, 1; Jeremiah Sparks, 100, 1; Simon Burleson, 100, 0; Isaac Grindstaff, 100, 0; Jacob Boaman, 200, 1; David Banks, (?), 0, 1; George Lowdermilk.

No Date, Pre-1800: Capt. Austin's Co. (Not legible and only a few names can be read.)

.... Hedley; Allan Roberts; Matthew Cox; Jno. Bradburn; .... Keller; James Teague; .... Austin; George Dockery; John Dockery; Samuel Walker; .... Hedley.

No Date, Pre-1800: Capt. Hemphill's Co. (Not legible.)

No Date, Pre-1800: Capt. Morrison's Co. (A few names are legible.)

Hezekiah Hyatt; William Morrison; Francis Patton; William Patton; John Sumners; Joshua Hall; Joseph Johnston; Elijah Hall; John Hall; William Moore; Robert Shermon; Henry Justice; Elihugh Hicks; John Dunkin; Edward Leatherwood; John Andrews, Sr.; John Andrews; Richard Davis; Andrew Woods; Thomas Morrison; James Hemphill.

No Date, Pre-1800: Company Unknown. (A fragment with very few names.)

John Chandler; John Wilson; Joshua Young; Moses Young; Anson Baley; Daniel Holyfield; Johnston McKiney.

No Date, Pre-1800: Capt. Laughron's Co. (Acreage, mostly on Muddy Creek, Young's Fork & Beaver Dam.)

Hugh Harris, 294; Hugh Harris, Jr., 0; Drury Mashburn, 400; William Mashburn, 270; John Quin, 200; David Mashburn, 238; William Thomas, 360; Charles Herney, 136; Peter Apply, 63; John Mashburn, 175; John Morris,103; William Morris, Sr., 400; Samuel Johnson, 317; Joseph Goodbread, 206; Col. H. Raburn, 50; Isaac Bradley, 180;

William Morris, 200; Joseph Kerley, 300; James Hicks, 500; Coonrade
Canseler, 335; John England, 300; Samuel Davis, 200; Wm. Davis,
235; Mathew Mashburn, 337; John Brite, Sr., 577; James Mashburn,
499; Elisha Mashburn, 118; Hugh Loughron, 190; Mary Loughron, wid.,
100; Susanah Mashburn, 102; William Garrit, 0; John Welch, 37;
Thos. Patton, 0; James Black, 0; Daniel Black, 50; Matthew Black,
320; Daniel Hicks, 0; James Mashburn, 0; Samuel Reed, 0; William
Brite, 183; Alexander Baning, 125; Micajah Vaughn, 150; Titus
Pendergrass, 0; Nathaniel Bevans, 0; John Mitchel, 50; Benjamin
McDaniel, 50; John Green, 145; Mary Mashburn, 90; David Stroud,
108; Huldy Mashburn, 65; John Hardin, 0; William Patton, 160; John
Finger, 0; Phillip Flannigan, 0; William Green or Grier, Jr., 150;
John Glass, 150; James Jeany(?); James Nickles, 160; ....
Pendergrass, 0; David Mashburn, 0; Joseph Pitman, 784; William
Hardin, 90; Mary Morrison, 455; Joseph Garrit, 100; Elizabeth Smith,
100; Robt. Woody, 367; George Garding, 360; James Brite, 82;
Charnal Pendergrass, 0; Thos. Nelson, 100; Lanuel Patton, 50; William
Patton, 150; Peter Stroud, Sr., 332; Thos. Grinsland, 0; Obediah
Bracher, 0; ...tur Ledford, 100 on Nix Creek; ...al Brite, 0; Peter
Stroud, Jr., 455; William Stroud, 285; joining William Green, Sr.;
Joseph Tanner, 150; Samuel or Lamuel Jones, 540; Wm. McGee, 84;
Steurd McGee, 50; Elijah Moores, 140; George Teel (Deal ?), 297;
Samuel Johnson, Sr., 402; John Allen, 500; Matthew McCasling, 100.
John Harbin, 150.

No Date, Pre-1800: Capt. (Mont)fort's Co. (Poor Condition)
(Ac reage)

Thomas Allison, 250 & 275; Richard Allison, 295; Thomas Allison,
Jr., 325; Bird Allison, 0; Henry Allison, 330; Moses Allison, 0;
Merit Burgin, 100; John Burnet, 0; Alney Burgin, 157 & 300, 100;
Richard Bird, 382, 845, 785; Jonathan Bird, 420; Harbert Bird, 0;
John Blalock, 0; Merrit Burgin, 420; and for Heirs of, 1555; John
Burgin, 100, 100,100, 50; Elizabeth Burgin, 0; Alney Burgin, Jr.(?),
0; Henry Barring, 325; Moses Curtice, Jr., 15, 80, 50, 150; Ursley
Curtice, 100; Thomas Crage, 200; Susannah Clark, 200; Robert Crage,
0; Thos. Curtice, 100; John Daughrety, 80; G. H. Davidson, 1400;
James Greenlee, 450, 750; David Greenlee, 2521, 200, 300, 150, 100,
50, 50; Jacob Gilliam, 100; Lavender Fortune, 377, also for John
Fortune, 187; Andrew Hemphill, 309; James Hemphill, 250; David Humphries,
207; Thos. Hemphill, 355; Mary Hemphill, 144; Thos. Hemphill, Jr.,
390; Andrew & James Hemphill, 340; James Jackson, 0; John Kelly,
350; Elijah & Elishea Kerley, 0; Rebecca Logan, 308; John Largent,
335; Thos. Lytle, 1525; Elender McCay, 673; also agent for John, 50;
Charles Mackey, also for A. Jordan, 211; John Mofit, 82½; Wm. McFee,
Jr., 0; John Maffet, Jr., 80; John Parlen(?), 0; Randle Paten, 0;
Burcn Ricketts, 200; John Ricketts, 200; Michael Reel, 345, 100, and
agent for John (Jr.?), 100; Wm. Smith, 200; Burton Smith, 0; Elizabeth
Welch, 100; Joseph & Robert Williams, 100; Levi York, 0.

No Date, Pre-1800: Company Unknown. (Probably Capt. Henry Highland Co.)
(One faded page, torn.)

Adam Cook; William Gibson; William Mooney; Thos. Winkler;
William Fismire; Robert Fleming; Jacob Boldwin; Abraham Stallions;
Reuben Stallions; .... Murphy; Alexander Erwin; Charles McDowell;
John Henry; .... Fears; .... Fears; Thos. Moody; Thos. Day; Lorence
Arney(?); Christy Dobson; .... Brown; .... Fears; .... Bulinger;
.... Anthony; .... Winkler; .... Perkins; .... Humphreys; Henry McKiney(?)
Adam Winkler; .... Setser.

No Date, Pre-1800: No Company Listed. (Dark & Faded)
(Acreage & Polls)

John McKinney, 250, 1; Joseph Buckanan, 150, 1; Arthur Buckanan,
150, 1; John Green, 100, 1; David Baker, 2400, - ; Thomas McKinney,
500, 3; Thomas Baker, no land, 1; Shadrack Green, 150, 1; Samuel
Pitmans, 143, 0; Thomas Huse, 270, 1; William Ingram, 100, 1; George
Honsucker, 50, 1; Thomas Howell, no land, 1; Richard Stanley, no land, 1;
William Bailey, no land, 1; Henry Stafford, no land, 1; James Chambers,
no land, 1; James Burleson, no land, 1; William Baker, no land, 1;
Aron Tomas, 150, 1; Aaron Burleson, 200, 1; John Hunsucker, no land, 1;
John England, 100, 1; Jeremiah Sparks, 100, 1; Simeon Burleson, 100,1;
Isaac Grindstaff, 100, 0; Jacob Boaman, 200, 1; George Lowdermilk, no
land, 1; David Banks, no land, 1

CR. 14.120-121

BILLS OF SALE 1792 - 1799

John Downing to James Downing, stock and household furnishings, Jan, 18, 1792: Wm. Gardner & Henry Oneil, Wit.

Jacob Tenneson to Christian Isom, stock, Apr. 3, 1793: Moses Webster, John Roge(?), Wit.

Phillip Stevens to Jeremiah Thomson, horse, Sept, 2, 1794: Erik Enloe, Henry McKinney, Wit.

William and Elizabeth Hamilton to Joseph Hughey, Jan 5, 1794, " all and every of our clames of land which said Elizabeth Hamilton is entitled ...of the land of her former husband, Sam. Hughey, Esq., dec'd." James L. Harbison, John Williams, Wm. Penland, Wits.

Tilman·Walton to Wm. Walton, Jr., 3 negroes, Filliace, 20, Jacob, ·15, Daniel, 5, Dec 26, 1798. Thomas Walton, Jonathan Franklin, Wits.

William Bradshaw, planter, to Field Bradshaw, a negro boy slave 1½ years old, Zekil. 1798. Ack.

Elizabeth Burchfield to Wm. England, Sept 25, 1798, a horse. Robert Carithers, Reuben Dement, Wits.

John Renschawof Burke to John Pierson, Sr., Oct 6, 1798, 50 a, in Co. bounded by John Burcheses & Wm. Robinson's, to Mt. on Waiters of Hunting Cr., being plantation John Renschew leaves upon it now. John H. Stevelie, Wit.

John James of Brunswick Co., N. C., to Thos. McEntire, Negro Sam, 20, very black, Sept. 18, 1798. Robert Logan, John Young, Wits.

Jno. White of Burke to James McEntire, Jan 25, 1799, 2 feather beds & furn, pewter plates, flax wheel, etc. John Mays Wm. McEntire, Wits.

C.R. 14.099. Mics. Papers, Bills Sale, Prom. Notes, 1782-1800.

March, 1792: Wm. Davidson, Sen.; Jno. Alexander; Benjamin
Hawkins; Jas. Murphy; Wm. White, Esq.' Jos. McDowell; Wm. Morrison,
Esq.; Alexander Erwin, C. C.; Thos. Hemphill; Chas. McDowell; Jno.
Carson; Jacob Forney; Henry McKenny; Wm. Penland, Esq.; Jno.
Connely, Esq.; James Alexander; Alexander Harbeson; James Greenlee,
Esq.; Jos. McDowell, Sr.; Andrew Woods; Jno. Rutherford.

Jan., 1793: Benjamin Davidson; Robt. Hodge, Sr.; Thomas Little;
Benjamin Ellison; Jas. Edmisten; Richd. Framey; Abraham Suddereth
Jno. Blair; Jno. Coffey; Jos. Hollon; Joseph Pruet; Thos. White, Jr.;
Geo. Penland; Alexander Harbison; Samuel Alexander; Jno. Penland;
Willm. Boyd; Dayly Walker; Jas. Moor; Jas. Lock; Patrick Oneal, Jr.;
Alen Fox, Thos. Wiseman; Martin Devinport; Joshua Young; George
Cathey; Henry Wood; Cap. John Shell; Gabriel Lovin; Jesse Boon;
Leonhard Lionser; Allen Baily; John Stillwell, Phillip Britton;
John Wilson; Reuben White, Jr.; Samuel Holanswirth; Alex. Long;
Hugh Tate; ThomasPeirson; Thomas Alleson; William Cosbey, Jr.;
James Taylor; James Carson; Martain Devenport; David McCracken;
Thomas Young; Daniel Moore; Daniel Brown; William Edmondson; Jessee
Boon; John Hinds; John Day; John Coffey;, Jr; John McDaniel;
Thomas Scott; John Hedley; Alexander West; William Paine; Fredrick
Grider; Samuel Smith; Edward Long; George Pain; Phillip Anthony;
Alexander Harbison; Eli Little John; James Baker; James Homer Sherrell;
William Sherrell; William Scott of the Globe; John Fox; Paul Antony,
Jr.; Henry Sumpter; Elijah Patton,C.Cr;Richard Brown; Hugh Fox, Jr.;
William Roberts; "summoned J. Bradburn, Esq., in behalf of Michal
Grindstaff vs Wm. Murphy"; "On motion of Reuben Wood, Esq., Atty."
orderedthat Allen Fox, Esq., send up papers in providings in the case
of James Penland vs Simon Hoyett.

Jury appointed to view "...R,land for Iron Works": Alex. Erwin,
C.C. to the Sher."; Thos. McEntire, who deputized Hugh Conley to execute
the order Jan 31, 1792; John Connelly; Wm. Connely; Abner Smalley;
Jno. Barnhart; Jacob Derebery; Jno. Spencer, Sr.; Wm. Sherral; Thos.
Scott; Fredrick Cryder; Jno. Cryder; Jno. Shell; Jas. Moore, Sr.;
Hugh Connelly; Michael Grindstaff; Samuel Smith; Jno. McDonald;
Hugh Fox.

July, 1793: George Penland; Alexander Harbison; Samuel Alexander;
James Kerley; Alen Fox; Reuben White; John Erwin, Jr.; Benjamin
White; Frederick Shull; Jno. Penland; Wm. Green; Wm. Morris; Thos.
Williams; Thos. Allison; Benjamin Wallace; George Davidson; George
Cathey; Mashack Burchfield; Thos. Young; Francis Patton; Robert
Patton, Sr.; Thos. Knite; James Carson; Isaac Cocks; John Kell;
Wm. Kelle; Robert Kelle; Michael Pierson; Samuel Mackey; James
Montgomery ; Edwrd. Leatherwood; Daniel England; Isaac Morton;

John Petillo; Wm. James; Andrew Mitchell; John Polk; Jas. Morgan, summoned as Constable; David Culbarson₁ Rd. Morrow, summoned by Thos. McEntire.

Octo., 1793: Hodg Reburn; Robt. Hodge, Sr.; Geo. Davidson; Meshick Burchfield; Wm. Gardner; Jno. Hall, Sr.; Wm. McDowell; Abraham Horshaw; James Moore, Sr.; and Jr; Mical Hart; Wm. Baldwin; Jno. Fips; Jos. Baker; Jno. Heas; Jno ...awmen; Elis Powell; Wlis Powell; Martin Cowlter; Jacob Tips; Thos. Welsher; Jos. Alexander; Robert Fleming; Edmund Fairs; Josiah Bratshar; John Franklin, Jr.; Geo. Holloway; Daniel Moore; Howell Adams; Wm. Davis, Sr.; Alex. Balay ; James McMeckey; Jos. Scott; Wm. Kelton; Eli Little; Henry Mckinney. On Reverse: Joseph Young, J.P.

Jan, 1794: John Bailey; James Potts; John Blare; John Coffee, Jr; Jessey Moore, Jr.; Will Edmeston; James Webb, Jr.; Will Gragg; - James Hemphill; Robt. Sellars, Jr.; Will McDowell; Geo. Hodge; Wm. Gardner; Isaac Atwaters; Jessy Stroud; Robt. Curruthers; Hugh Fox, Jr.; John Boyd; Richd. Brown; John Steal; Joseph Hawkens; Reuben Walker; John Hall; Thomas England; Zacherias Downs, Jr.; James Thompson; John Penland; Patrick Oneal, Jr.; Wm. Bailey; Jacob Forney; Jacob Anthony, Jr.; Abraham Fleming; Geo. Penland; John Erwin, Jr.; Alexander Wakefield; James Homer Sherrell.

Oct, 1794: Isiah Bradshaw; Wm. Green; John Stillwell; Wm. Kelle; Christian Borthell(?); Elijah Patton, Cain Creek; Fredrick Shull; Robert Patton, Sr.; Robt. Balew; Peter Rust; David Rust; John Simpson; Michael Pierson; Joshua Hall; Reuben White; Benjamin White; Thos. Wakefield; Alexander Wakefield; John Duckworth; John Pettet; James Mackey, Cap.; Thos. Kell; Charles Hopper; John Disard; Andrew Wood; Wm. Scott; Thomas White, Cap.; Charles Baker; George Hays; James Pots; Samuel McDaniels; Solomon Smith; John Blaire; William Reed; Barnet Pain; Christian Keller; George Davidson .

July, 1795: (Appointed at April, 1795, term) Jacob Keller; Richard Brown,C.C.; William Givens; George Daveson; Mager James Neely; William Kellor; John Reed; John Pogue, Moody Creek; Joshua Young; Strubridge Young; Isaac Cocker; Robert Hodgs; Hennery Baker; John Fox; David Glasby Cove; Wm. Scott, Globe; Wm. Edmonson; Thos. Hayse; John Dowell; Leonard Eastes; Wm. Dever, Jr.; Hennery Sumpter; John Day; Elisha Hammons; William Connlly, Jr.; John Crider; George Hartley; John Morrall(?); Wm. Cry; Solomon Good; Hennery Miller; Absolem Penetant; Daniell Payne; Robert Payne; Joseph Cathier; John Franklin, Jr.; Phillip Austin; Wm. Reed.

1st June at Bullinger's Mill, 19th at Moll's Company, 20th at Capt.
Mackey, at Austen's the 3rd Saturday, at Moors the 4th day of July, next at
Capt. White, the 21th of June 1795.

Wm. Penland vs Clark, with interest for the time James Greenlee judge-
ment July term, vs Clark 1792.

March, 1797: Wm. White, Jas. Younge, David Baker, Wm. Devenport,
Brice Collins, Robart Henrey, Arthur Erwin, Jas. Greenlee, John H. Steveley,
Thos. McEntire, John Connlley, John Hughes.

Sept. 1798: Robert Kell (or Keel) Andrew Beard, Thomas Devenport, John
McGempsey, Abner Henly, Jonathan Boon, Joseph Dobson, David Craford, Petter
Moll, Albert Colpney, James Nail, Benjamin Austin(on reverse) "set Charles
McDowell's name in place of Cobs in supe vs. Flanninim, Exec. by Thos. McEntire.

Jan. 1799:   Jas. Gilbert, Jas. Webb, Lewis Harriss, George Hays, Wm.
Cry, Wm. Connelly, Jr., Phillip Austin, John White, Samuel Nail, Elijah Patten,
B. Smith, Leonard Estis, John Armstrong, Francis Patton, Wm. Thompson, Robt.
Young, Strawbridge Young, Danl. England, Wm. Duckworth, Jonathan Duckworth,
Wm. Laurence, Jno. Moody, Thos. Case, Vezy Husband, Jno. Harper, Edmd. Fare,
Thos. Largin, Ab. Hartshaw, Hugh Fox. Wm. Roberts, James Oxford, Thos. Foster,
Jr., John Erwin, Thos. Little, James Clark, John Boyd, James Carson, John
Moullins, Sr., Jno. Presly, John Duckworth. (A notation "moving to Sandey"
could apply to either Jno. Presly or Jno. Moullins.)

April, 1799: (appointed at January term.) Thos. Parks, Jos. Purkins,
Bruce Collins, William Penley, Philip Antony, John Wakefield, Hezekiah Inmond,
Bartlet Henson, Sr., Jesse Moore, Sr., Abrum Fleming, Charles McDowell, John
Townson, Elias Powell, Jr. Wm. Ginnings, Wm. Cnucklowy not found, Abraham
Sudderth , Wm. Pereman, Fredrick Grider, Edward Jackson, Patrick Sloan, Reuber
Coffey, Wm. Porter, Jr., Samuel Park, Thomas Rogert (or Tigert), JacobYount,
Phillip Britin, Peter Rust, Ezekiah Hyet, Michel Kelbon, John Pearson, John
Brown, James Boss (?), Shadrick Stilwell, Nicols Burns, Henery Avory, Phillip
Britton, John Person, Sr., Michael Kelborn, James Greenlee. Harbison, S.L.,
Joseph Dobson, J. H. Stevelie, John Hughes, Daniel Moore.

March, 1799: Phillip Austin, Benjamin Burgin, Alex,,Erwin, Thomas
Hemphill, Alexander Harbison, Thos. Coleman, Len Estes, John Connelly, Conrod
Hildebrand, John Erwin, Jr., William White, William Devinport.

July, 1799: John Moore, Cap., John Church, John Martin, Jr., John
Griffith, Andrew Beard, Cap., John Spencer, Jr., Jacob Derry Berry , Thos.
Payne, Jr., Hennery Stoner, Sr., Jacob Tips, Robert Fleming, Daneal Polk,
Steven Underdown, Elijah Patten, Samuel Macay, William Niel, William Kelton
(Cumberland), Major James Neeley, Thomas Hickton, Joseph Hawkins, Samuel Britt
Phillip Brittain, John Greenlee, Jr., Benjamin Brittain, John Pendaland,John
Rutherfordton, Drury Williams, Alex. Gray, Benjamin Powell, Sr., Benjamin
Bird, Thomas Hemphill, Richd. Fortune, John Logan, Lewis Coffey, Jesse Moor,
Jr., Reuben White. J. Erwin, C.C.

{(Jurors CR14.104 - 1792-1800))

JUSTICES OF THE PEACE 1777 - 1800

Benjamin Adams, 1794; John Alexander, 1783,1784; James Alexander, 1789;
James Blair, 1777,1778, 1783; Hugh Brevard, 1779, 1794; John Bradburn,
1785, 1787, 1789; James Brittain, 1787-1790; George Brown, 1787, 1788;
Benjamin Burgin, 1796; Francis Cunningham, 1778, 1780, 1781, 1785; John
Carson, 1788-1789; Thomas Campbell, 1785; John Connelly, 1780,1790;
Albert Corpening, 1792, 1793, 1796; Robert Carrithers,1794, 1796; M.
Coulter, 1796; Alexander Cole, 1800; James Davidson, 1783-1785; John
Davidson, 1789; John Davenport, 1784; William Davenport, 1800; James
Greenlee,1779, 1784-1788; Samuel Greenlee, 1783; John Hardin, 1779,
1782-1785; Samuel Hughey, 1787-1790; Phillip Hoodenpyle, 1792; Robert
Holmes, 1786; Shadrack Inman, 1784; James Jones, 1786; ... Kirkpatrick,
1785, 1787; James Little, 1789; Peter Moll, 1779, 1782-1783; ... McDowell,
1778, 1782-1783, 1785, 1787; Alexander McGinty, 1789; Ephraim McLean, 1778;
James Macay, 1785;   Robert Montgomery, 1788-1790; John Moore, 1788-1789;
William Morrison, 1778, 1786; William Moore, 1782, 1784; James Murphy,
1782; William Murphy, 1796; Joshua Murphy, 1796; Robert Nelson, 1789;
William Penland, 1783-1789; Abraham Scott, 1778; Joseph Steele, 1782-
1783; William Sumpter, 1782, 1787; Samuel Spencer, 1783; Matthew Sharpe,
1778, 1780; Robert Woods, 1788;   Andrew Woods, 1778-1779; William White,
1782-1790; Charles Wakefield, 1788-1789, 1795; Joseph White, 1785, 1789;
William Wofford, 1786-1790; Joseph Young, 1800; John Bird, 1785.

(Arranged from Miscellaneous Court Papers.)

JUSTICES OF THE PEACE AND
MILITIA OFFICERS
1782 - 1806

Raleigh, 1795:

Hodge Reburn, James Mackey, Conrod Hildebrand (not qualified), Peter
Thompson (not qualified), Thos. Coleman, a Rev. off., Reed Hite, resigned;
John Penland, not act., David Crawford (Moffet a way), p. assessor; Andrew
Baird, resigned; Wm. Dervenport, removed; Wm. Walton, not acted;   New
Ones: Waightstill Avery, Wm. Crye, moved away, Annanias Allen, Drury
Williams, resigned, Wm. Tate, resigned, Jno. Rutherford, not attend,
Alexander Glass, resigned, Joseph Hawkins, Peter Mull, dead, Joseph
McDowell, dead, Joseph White, removed, Peter Thomson, not qualified, William
Wofford, removed, David Vance, removed, Robert Montgomery, Senr., removed,
James Britton, removed,   Samuel Huey, dead, John Carson, James Alexander,
removed, Will Whitson, removed, Will. Davidson, Jr., removed, Henry
Reed, not qualified.

137

Fayette, 1788:

Benjamin Burgin, resigned; Benjamin Adams, removed; James Murphy, re-appointed; Phillip Hoodenpyle, removed; John Hines, not qualified; Albert Corpenny.

New Bern, 1791:

Jno. McDowell, Jr.; Robert Craig, resigned; Jno. Henry Stevely; Joseph Young, resigned.

1792:

Arthur Erwin, not qualified; Jos. Reed, not act.; David Baker, not qualified; Alex. Cole.

1793:

Joseph McDowell, dead; Wm. Irwin; John Hall, dead, d. 1811 (added in); Peter Thompson, not qualified; Henry Reed; James Coffee, dead; Robert Caruthers, resigned; Benjamin Adams, resigned; Allen Fox, resigned. Benjamin Austin, reappointed.

Nov. 1795:

James Meeley, not qualified; Martin Colter, removed; William Davenport, removed; Charles Baker, not qualified; David Ramsey, removed; Thos. Beaushell, not qualified; Wm. Walton, not qualified.

Raleigh, 1796:

Grover Bowman; Brice Collins, not qualified; William Pain, not qual-ified; John Blair, resigned; John Coffee, dead; Daniel Moore; Benjamin Parks; Joseph Dobson; James Naile, not qualified; John Hawkins, not qual-ified; David Baker; John Hughes, dead; Thomas McIntire, not qualified; James Buchannon; Paul Anthony, Jr.; Isaac Thompson; Robert Kill, runaway.

1798:

Bennet Smith, removed; Phillip Austin; John Burgan; Amos Chaffin, resigned; Sols. Smith; Leonard Estes, resigned; Wm. White; Jno. Bradburn.

1804:

John Grover; Aaron Brittain; Greenaway; Patterson.

1805:

John Buchanen; Alexander Erwin, Sr.; Daniel Brown.

1806:

Cunrad Bost; Robert Carswell; Thomas Coleman; John Greenlee;
James Morgan.

Field Officers:

Joseph McDowell, Col.; Robert Holmes, Lt. Col.; Joseph McDowell
(P.G.); First Major; Joseph White, Sec. Major.

Tarboro, 1787:

Joseph McDowell, Lt. Col.; Joseph White, First Major; David Vance,
Sec. Major.

1792:

Henry McHenry, Sec. Major.

1793:

John Carson, 1 Major; John McDowell, 2 Major.

Nov. 1795:

John Carson, Lt. Col., Com.; John McDowell, 1st Major; John McGimsey,

2nd Major.   (Also, see under J.P., Thomas Coleman, a Rev. Ofc. 1795.)

G.O. 147, pp. 21-24.

Members of General Assembly

From Burke County 1778-1800

1778. Charles McDowell, Senator; Members of House of Commons, Ephriam NcClain and Jas. Wilson.

1779. Ephriam McClain, Senator; Members of House of Commons, Thos. Wilson, Wm. Morrison.

1780. Ephriam McClain, Senator; Members of House of Commons, Hugh Brevard, Jos. McDowell.

1781. Andrew Woods, Senator; Member of House of Commons, Hugh Brevard, Jos. McDowell.

1782. Charles McDowell, Senator; Members of House of Commons, Waightstill Avery, Jos. McDowell.

1783. Same as above.

1784. Charles McDowell, Senator; Members of House of Commons, Waightstill Avery, J. McDowell.

1785. Same as above.

1786. Charles McDowell, Senator; Members of House of Commons, J. McDowell, David Vance.

1787. Charles McDowell, Senator; Members of House of Commons, J. McDowell, Jos. McDowell, Jr.

1788. Same as above.

1791. Jos. McDowell, Senator; Members of House of Commons, J. McDowell, Jr. David Vance.

1792. Jos. McDowell, Senator; Members of House of Commons, John McDowell, Jos. McDowell, Jr.

1793. Jos. McDowell, Senator; Members of House of Commons, Waightstill Avery Alex. Erwin.

1794. Jos. McDowell, Senator; Members of House of Commons, Alex. Erwin, John McDowell.

1795. Jos. McDowell, Senator; Members of House of Commons, Alex. Erwin, Conrad Helderbrand.

1796. W. Avery, Senator; Members of House of Commons: Wm. White, Alexander Erwin.

1797. James Murphy, Senator; Members of House of Commons: A. Erwin, Conrad Helderbrand.

1800. Andrew Beard, Senator; Members of House of Commons: Wm. Devenport, Wm. Walton.

==================

Colonial and State Records of N. C. for Members of Assembly in Burke County.

    Vol. 12, pp 102, 125,265,286,568, 655, 836.
    Vol. 13, pp. 735, 784, 944.
    Vol. 16, pp. 1, 50
    Vol.17, pp. 264, 269, 794, 877, 884, 919.
    Vol. 18, pp. 1, 11, 226, 238.
    Vol. 19, pp. 1, 60, 129, 233, 400, 416, 511, 717, 760.
    Vol. 20, pp. 1, 4, 119, 127, 301, 475.
    Vol. 21, pp. 1, 193, 244, 729, 871.
    Vol. 22, pp. 1, 12,36, in Convention.

SOME MILITARY RECORDS OF REVOLUTIONARY WAR

July Term, 1796: Samuel Gyles ordered exempt from poll tax. Petition: "I being a Citizen now ... appeal for relief (due to) a wound I received in the Armey..."

(CR. 14.103 Misc. Papers)

July 26, 1821: Tilman Walton ... in Court ... age about 61, enlisted as Pvt. under Capt. James Franklin in Va. Cont. Establishment 3 yrs, ab. Nov. 26, 1776 in 10 Va. Reg. under Col. Edward Stevens...and Capt. Clough Shelton in his Co. as an orderly Sgt. in 6th Va. Reg. by Col. John Green; served 2 yrs. until Cornwallis' capture. In Brandywine, Germantown, Monmouth; enlisted at Amherst, Va. 3 yrs, dschgd. Dec. 6, 1779 Morristown, N. J. No income, has featherbed, working tools, is carpenter and millwright, is old, infirm and has old, infirm wife 51 years old, 2 sons not free, one about 15, the other 12.

(CR 14.103 Misc. Papers)

William Temple Coles, Maj., certifies that John Bowman "balleted in" as soldier in Capt. Taylor's Co., Burke Co. David Conyers to serve in his room (court duty).

(CR. 14.103 Misc. Papers)

Petition of Thomas Case, Burke Co. ... wounded by Cherokee Indians ... rendered him incapable of gaining support by sweat of his brow. Signed: Charles McDowell, Wm. Moore, John Harden, Alex. Erwin, Joseph Mc-Dowell, W. White, Wm. Stuart.

(Leg. Papers, Box 25, May 1779)

Pension Abstract S 7661 Rev. Pens. Va. Service, N.C. Agency: Daniel Sullivan res. of Burke Co., 70 yrs. or about, applied Jan 29, 1833. Pvt. in Militia 16 or 17 yrs, Guilford Battle ... & about Moravian town, Stokes Co. Born Mar. 2, 1763 Pittsylvania Co., Va. bound out, lived in Henry Co., to Burke about 1833. Rd. Bird, Minister, Burke Co. knew him 20 years....

John Bowman, Sher. of Burke Co., fell in the service of his country at Battle of Ramsower's in June 1780.

(State Recs N.C., Clark, XXIV, Chap. LXII, p 633/4

John Robinson, Continental soldier. C.1779)

(L.P. 1778-1779, Folder 30)

Col. Joseph McDowell; Lt. Col. Robert Holmes; Maj. Joseph White; Maj. David Vance; Maj. Henry McHeney; Maj. John Carson; Maj. John McDowell;   Maj. John Carson; Maj. John McGimsey.

(GO 147 - 21/4)

Deposition of John Carson re: Dr. Robert Wilson and his older brother, Jason Wilson...1818.

(N. C. Military Papers, Rev. War, Folder 58)

1800 Deposition to Andrew Beard that he, Wm. Richmond, is only brother of John Richmond, dec'd., who died in service, and of Temperance and John McDaniel, 640 a. issued 1800.

(N.C. Military Papers, Rev. War, Folder 143)

1802 Morganton Letter of W. W. Erwin to John Craven, P. Atty: Phillip Brittain of Co. to Wm. W. Erwin.

(N.C. Military Papers, Rev. War, Folder 169)

1802 P. Atty: David Chester, soldier to Abner Henley.

(N.C. Military Papers, Rev. War, Folder 171)

Duplicate Land Warrants Committee Report: Gen. Joseph McDowell purch. 640 a from Wm. Tucker heirs and in 1785 placed in office of Martin Armstrong land on Harpeth R. join. Henry Hiland, and in 1791 sent warrant to Armstrong office by Wm. Stewart of Davidson Co (Tenn.) who was killed by Indians after returning home.

(N.C. Military Papers, Rev. War, Folder 305)

(See Vol. II, 156-160 for others.)

See the following from Burke County in:

N. C. Troops In Continental Line and N. C. Pension Roll, 23rd Congress.
(Dept Archives and History, book on shelf.)

PENSIONS 1818-1822

Burke County, p. 26:

Pvt. Robert Crosson (Cresson)(d. Jan 5, 1822),age 94
Pvt. Andrew Cresson, age 83
Pvt. Charles Jenkins, age 88
Pvt. Job Pendergrass, age 71 (d. Dec. 1831)
Pvt. William Ridley, age 84
Pvt. Tilman Walton, age 74

Burke County, p. 61   PENSIONS 1831

Pvt. Samuel Alexander, age 78
Pvt. John Arwood, age 72
Pvt. Benjamin Austin, age 74
Corp. David Baker, age 85
Pvt. Sherwood Bowman,age 76
Pvt. Stephen Ballen (Ballew), age 72
Pvt. William Crawley, age 75
Pvt. Jonathan Curtes, age 87 (d. Jan 22, 1834)
Sgt. George Clontz, age 74
Pvt. Conrad Crump, age 81
Pvt. William Culberson, Sr., age 94
Pvt. Samuel Davis, age 81
Pvt. John Duckworth, age 76
Pvt. Joseph Dobson, age 78
Pvt. William Freeman, age 76
Pvt. John Fox, Sr., age 70
Pvt John Green, age 72
Pvt. Solomon Good, age 74.
Pvt. William Gragg, age 76
Pvt. Charles Haney, age 86

Burke County, p. 62:   Pvt. George Hodge, age 74
Pvt. David Hays, age 74
Pvt. Adam Hoppis, age 80
Pvt. Leonard Hise, age 78
Pvt. Robert Kincaid, age 70
Pvt. James Kincaid, age 80
Pvt. David Montgomery, age 79
Pvt. Daniel Moore, Sen., age 69
Pvt. William Morris, Sn., age 84
Pvt. Lewis Powell, age 75
Pvt. George Poplin, age 81

145

```
                         Pvt. John Presnell, age 83
                         Pvt. Samuel Reed, age 79
                         Pvt. George Silver, age 83
                         Pvt. Daniel Sullivan, age 71
                         Pvt. Aaron Stacy, age 74
                         Pvt. Joseph Starnes, age 78
                         Pvt. George Sigman, age 78
                         Pvt. Thomas Smith, age 70
                         Pvt. Benjamin Spence(r), age 73
                         Pvt. John Stewart, age 72
                         Pvt. John  Swink, age x
                         Pvt. Isaac Thompson, age 79
                         Pvt. Jacob Tips, age 86
                         Pvt. Samuel Turner,age 72
                         Pvt. Lawrence Unger, age 78
                         Pvt. Reuben Walker, age 74
                         Pvt. Henry Woods, age 81

Burke County, p. 63:     Pvt. John Cason (Carson), age 82
                         Pvt. Sedgewick Springs, age 79
                         Pvt. Stephen Williams, age 71
```

See the following from A Census of Pensioners For Revolutionary or Military
Services with their names, ages and places of residence, as returned by the
Marshalls of the several Districts under The Act For Taking the Census (6th)
Washington, 1841.   (Dept of Archives and History, book on Shelf.)

Burke County, p. 137:   (As of June 1, 1840, resided with:

```
                         Birch Allison, 78, self
                         Daniel Sullivan, 80, E. D. Sullivan
                         John Arrowwood, Sr., 78, self
                         Adam Hoppis, 86, Self
                         George Hodge, 80, self
                         John Duckworth, 83, John Duckworth, Jr.
                         Sherwood Bowman, Sr., 81, Self
                         Lewis Powell, 78, Self
                         Nicholas Fry, 97, John Berry
                         Benjamin Spencer, 80, Self
                         John Swink, 88, Self
                         Stephen Ballew, 77, Self
                         Daniel Moore, Sr., 76, Self
                         Samuel Alexander, 80, Self
                         Benjamin Austin, 81, Self
                         David Hayes, 92, Self
```

INDEX TO WILLS

1784 - 1900

As stated in Volume II, p. 174, only seven wills are preserved to 1809, due to the destruction of the records in April, 1865, by command of Gen. Gillam of the U. S. Army (Northern) when major records were burned on the courthouse lawn in Morganton.

Will Book I, 1793-1905: Ave - Joh...(Cr 14.123): earliest abstracted in Volume II, pp. 174-175: George Dale, 1805; James Devine, 1794; John Durham, 1802; John Englin (England), 1795; William Fullerton, 1798. (see complete list following.)

Will Book II, 1793-1905: Ker - Win (CR 14.124: None abstracted in Volume II as all of much later dates. (See complete list following.)

Miscellaneous Records (Folder), 1787-1900: (CR 14.928.3): Abstracted in Volume II, p. 175: Mary Probst, 1809; James Morrison, 1790. (See complete list under Miscellaneous Wills, 1790-1880 following.)

This Volume III will give indicies of all wills up to 1900 and Xerox copies may be obtained from the Department of Archives and History under file numbers as were abstracted. Sometimes the file numbers are changed.

Will Book I: Ave - John..., 1793-1905 (CR 14.123, p 53 ff:
        Waightstill Avery, p. 1, 1823; W. W. Avery, p. 6, 1864; Wm. Bradshaw, p. 9, 1864; Oliver (Olive) Branch, p. 10, c1879; Wm. L. Brittain, p.12, 1863; Wm. Coffee (Coffey), p. 13, c1839; John Connelly, p.14, 1868; George Dale, p.21, 1805; James Day, p.22, 1827; Nicholas Day, p.23, 1815; James Devine, p.24, 1794; Mary Dunkin, p.25, 1833; John Durham, p.26, 1803; Adam Durmire, p.23, 1825; Samuel Dysart, p.28, 1805; Wm. Dysart, p.29, 1837; Sarah Edmiston, p.30, 1835; Daniel England, p. 31, 1819; John England, p.32, 1795; Thomas England, p.33, 1821; Wm. England, p.34, 1832; Alexander Erwin, p.35, 1829; Arthur Erwin, p.36, 1821; James Erwin, p.37, c1842; Matilda Erwin, p.38, 1843; Ulysses R. Erwin, p.40, 1835; Wm. A. Erwin, p.41, c1846; Wm. W. Erwin, p.43, 1837; Mary Louise Espy, p.45, 1836; Delphi Estes, p.46, 1818; Laban Estes, p.47, 1817; Reuben Estes, p.48, 1811; Joseph Fair, p.49, 1818; Charles Finley, p.50, 1829; Elizabeth Elmira Fleming, p.51, 1842; James Fleming, p. 52, 1831; Robert Fleming, p.53, 1823; Jacob Forney, p.54, 1841; Peter Bergner Forney, p.55, 1867; Lavender Fortune, p.56, 1839; George Foster, p.57, 1817; Hugh Fox, p.58, 1828; John Franklin, Sr., p.59, 1819; John Franklin, p.60, 1837; Wm. Fullerton, p.61, 1798 ; Jacob Har;haw, p.67, 1868; S. S. Horshaw, of Union Co., Ga., p.76, 1876; Abraham Hoyle, p.79, 1867; D. H. Johnson, p.80, 1865, Wm. Fullwood, p. 62, c1850.

Will Book II, Ker - Win, 1793-1905 (CR14.124): Aaron Kerley, p.1, 1875;
Milton W. Kincaid, p.4, 1867; Wm. W. Kincaid, p.7, c1864; Jacob Lael,
p.9, 1872; Marcus R. London, p.12, 1871; A. J. McGimsey, p.15, 1869;
Anna M. McKesson, p.22, c1865; George W. Mathews, p.24, c1863; Henry M.
Oneil, p.25, c1857; Carter Orders, p.26, 1866; Mary Patton, p.27, c1860;
Catharine Ramsey, p.29, 1869; Martha Rector, p.32, c1841; Nancy Runnells
(Reynolds ?), p.33, 1869; Jacob Seagle, p.39, 1868; Rebecca Scott, p.43,
1866; Wm. C. Tate, p.44, 1869; Hugh Taylor, p.51, 1882; John Vanhorn,
p.58, c1842; Martha Walton, p.59, 1868; John Lewis Warlick, p.73, c1865;
Temperance Winters,p.75, 1869.

Combination of Will Books I & II:

I.   John Lewis Warlick, p.1, 1865; Wm. W. Kincaid, p.2, c1864; W. L. Brittain
p.3, c1863; George W. Mathews, p.4, c1863; Mary Patton, p.5, c1860; Henry
M. Oneil, p.10, c1857; Wm. Bradshaw, p.11, c1864; Anna M. McKesson, p.14,
c1865; Carter Orders, p.16, 1866; Rebecca Scott, p.17, 1866; D. H. Johnson,
p.19, 1867; Peter Bergner Forney, p.20, 1867; John Kincaid, p.21, 1863;
Absolom Hoyle, p.23, 1867; Thomas Carlton, p.24, 1867; John Sudderth, p.26,
1865; John Conley, p.44, 1868; Jacob Seagle, p.48, 1868; Martha Walton,
p.50, 1868; Frank McElrath, p.53, 1873.

II.   John Conley, p.1, 1868; Jacob Seagle, p.5, 1868; Martha Walton, p.6,
1868; Jacob Harshaw, p.10, 1868; Dr. Wm. C. Tate, p.7, 1869; Temperance
Winters,p.21, 1869; Milton W. Kincaid, p.22, 1869; A. J. McGimsey, p.25,
1869; Isaac T. Avery, p.27, 1869; Jacob Settlemire, p.46, 1813; Martha
Rector, p.47, c1841; Catharine Ramsey, p.48, 1869; W. W. Avery, p.50, 1864;
John McElrath, p.52, 1870; Robert V. Patton, p.58, 1871; John H. Pearson,
p. 61, 1871; Edward Jones Erwin, p.63, 1871; Rachael Abernathy, p.66, 1871;
Marcus R. London, p.68, 1871; John Wilson, Sr., p.69, 1872; Christena
Heavener, p.73, 1872; John S.Park(e)s, p.75, 1873; John Kincaid, p.80,
1873; Babel Moore, p.82, 1874; James Anderson, p.86, 1874; John Caldwell,
p.90, 1857; Hugh Conley, p.98, 1875; Sophia Alexander, p.103, 1875; George
Corpening, p.108, 1856; Abel Hartsoe, p.114, 1875; David Wilson, p. 116, 1875;
Joseph D. Ferree, p.120, 1875; Isaac Conley, p. 122, 1876; Jacob Harshaw
Corpening, p. 124, 1875; Lucy Conley, p.127, 1877; John Moore, p.131, 1877;
James Hulton, p.135, 1877; Adolphus Smith, p.136, 1876; Peter Ep(p)ley,
p. 139, 1877; Sidney S. Harshaw, Union County, Ga., p.143, 1876; Wm. Alex-
ander, p.149, c1865; Alexander Hamilton Erwin, p.153, 1877; Phillip Warlick,
p.157, 1878; J. P. Beck, p.161, 1878; Clabourne Branch, p.165, 1878;
Joseph Buff, p.170, 1878; Chas. McDowell, p.186, 1859; Alexander Duckworth,
p.192, 1879; John Rutherford, p.195, 1880; Peter Denton, p.197, 1879;
Rachel W. Pearson, p. 200, 1880; Robert H. Alexander, p.202, 1880; Emanuel
Austin, p.205, 1880; William Bradshaw, Jr., p.209, 1881; Rachael Morrison,
p. 211, 1880; Sarah A. Happoldt(?), p.215, 1881; Julia M. Gaither, p. 219,
1882; James A. Duckworth, p. 225, 1882; Hugh Taylor, p.227, 1882; Joseph
G. Helton(?), p.230, 1882; William Icard, p.234, 1882; Wm. B. Patton, p.238,
1882; Nottingham Murphy of Phil., Penn, p.241, 1883; Louis Lowman, p.247,1883;

Joseph Simpson, Sr., p.251, 1883; Stephen Rose, p.255, 1883; Jane S. Pearson, p.259, 1883; Anderson Denton, p.262, 1883; John Collett(?), p.266, 1884; Jefferson Toney, p.269, 1884; Louisa Allatt, p.271, 1884; Joseph Benfield, p. 274, 1885; Edward Jones Largeant, p.277, 1884/5; Mary McElrath, p.281, 1884; Michael Huffman, p.285, 1885; Allen Conley, p.299, c1859; Catherine Rector, p.303, 1885; Wesley Smith, p.306, 1885; Nancy Conley, p.309, 1885; Andrew Eppley, p.313, 1885; Mary L. Pearson, p.316, 1886; Wm. P. Robinson, p.329, 1886; John Hudson, p.332, 1886; Elijah Page, p.336, 1886; Mary McRee, p.340, 1887; Christinia Brittain, p.343, 1887; Elijah Bradshaw, p. 345, 1887; Nancy Bailey Moore, p.355, 1887; Waightstill Avery, p.356, 1821; Donald Fraser, p.367, 1888; Michael Spainhour, p.371, 1889; George Hodge, p.374, 1889; Robert Burton Anderson, p. 376, 1889; Laura Seagle Avery, p.378, 1890; Caleb Shuping, p. 380, 1890; Wm. Buff, p.382, 1890; Ann E. Erwin, p. 387, 1890; Minerva R. Caldwell, p.398, 1890; Oliver (Olive ?) Branch, p.401, 1890; Sarah Mull, p.405, 1890; Thomas S. Alexander, p.411, 1890; Thomas A. Dorsey, Sr., p.415, 1890; John Smith, p.419, 1890; Anna D. Biscoe, p.421, 1890; Daniel D. Morgan, p.426, 1891; James M. Greenlee, p. 431, 1891; James R. Kincaid, p.434, 1891; Robert Morris of Phila., Penna, p.440, 1806; Mary Morris of Phila,. Penna, p.445, 1827; Maria Nixon of Phila., Penna, p.450, 1852; Hetty Nixon of Phila., Penna, p.457, 1856; J. F. Hoyle, p.463, 1891; Jacob Hart, p.466, 1891; Sarah Elvina Pearson, p.470, 1891; Wm. A. Perkins, p.474, 1891; J. R. Pearsall, p.477, 1891; S.C.W. Tate, p.480, 1892; W. R. York, p.483, 1892; W. W. Conley, p.486, 1892; Burgess Sidney Gaither, p.488, 1892; Marcus Avery, p.491, 1892; Thomas Conley, p.492, 1892; J. W. Conley, p. 499, 1892; Harriet S. Pearson, p. 502, 1893; J. H. Howard, p.505, 1893; L. P. Warlick, p.508, 1893; Posey H. Beck, p.511, 1893; Daniel Burns, p.514, 1893; Josiah V. Blackwell, p.516, 1893; Jacob H. Hallyburton, p.520, 1894; Aaron Kerley, p.523, 1894; Joseph N. Edmunds, Charlotte, Co., Va., p. 524, 1894; Middleton Stilwell, p. 528, 1894; Sallie Brown, p.530, 1894; Cecelia M. Erwin, p.532, 1894; Robert Avery , p.534, 1894; Joseph A. Bayles (Boyles ?), p.536, 1894; Sarah Wise, p. 538, 1894; Elizabeth Robinson, p.540, 1894; John Penley Dellinger, p.542, 1894; Newberry Pruit, p.544, 1898; Alfred Moore, p.551, 1895; Stephen W. Winters, p.557, 1896; Daniel P. Johnson, p.565, 1896; Jacob L. Carpenter, p.569, 1896.

Will Book III, 1897-1900:

Bartlett A. Berry, Sr., p.3, 1897; Joshua C. McCurry, p.13, 1897; Adelaide L. Avery, p.19, 1897; M. Corinne Avery, p.26, 1897; Calvin Houke, p.33, 1897; John Pitts, p.37, 1898; Allison Wagner, p.42, 1898; John F. Epley, p.46, 1898; Sophronia Rutherford, p.49, 1898; N. P. Beck, p.53, 1899; A. W. Wilson, p.56, 1898; Robert Patterson of Phila., Penna., p.58, 1899; Sylvanus Deal, p.78, 1899; Lear Moore & Eliz. Moore, p.82, 1899; Wm. Martin, p.84, 1899; W. E. Brittain, p.87, 1899; Abel K. Hurt, p.91, 1899; Samuel Simpson, p. 94, 1899; W. M. Winters, p.97, 1899; John Saulman, p.100, 1900; Wm. F. Camp, p.102, 1900; Leah H. Bumgarner, p.104, 1900; Harriet RebaccaDellinger, p.106, 1900; Bartlett A. Berry, p.108, 1900; John Rutherford, p.110, 1900; Eliza Scott , p.112, 1900; Susan Forney P. Michaux, p.114, 1900; J. W. Berry, p.120,1900; Francis M. Gibbs, p.122, 1900; Jane Robins, Wid. of Christopher of Co. Kent, Eng., p.123, 1900.

MISCELLANEOUS WILLS 1790-1880 (CR14.103):

James Morrison, c1790; Mary Probat, c1809; Ann Donahue of Wilkes Co., c1822; Amos Henslee, 1828; Rebacca Jopling of Nelson Co., Va., 1852; Daniel Jones, 1832; Wm. L. McRee, c1855; W. W. Avery, c1864; George W. Saulman, c1890; Richmond Phillips(n.d.); Christopher Robins of Kent Co., Eng, 1887; Christen Bortals, 1843; Jesse Moore, 1826; Rachel Morrison, 1880.

From Guide to Private Collections in the North Carolina State Archives, prepared by Beth Crabtree, 1964:

Wm. Sudreth, Sr., 1784 (See his will abstract in Volume II,p.174.)

ABSTRACT OF WILL OF WILLIAM NEILL, BURKE COUNTY., TO TENNESSEE

A complete copy typed of a handwritten will sent by Helen Broadbent, 892 Osmond Lane, Provo, Utah, 84001, stated that a copy was made by a son and taken into Tennessee, in possession of E. Neill Raymond, 44 Laurel Drive, N.E., Atlanta, Ga. 30342. She also sent a copy to the Department of Archives and History, in Raleigh, N. C.

An abstract:

William Neill, of County of Burke and State of North Carolina...wife Sarah have by her choice bed, 2 cows, 1 horse and saddle...her wearing apparel and half of household furniture.

... my ...(?)Jane ... 5sh ... son-in-law John Webster 5 sh...son-in-law Jacob Haws 5sh ... son-in-law James Neill 5sh...my (?)...shillings... Son Andrew Neill...10lbs money ... son-in-law John Plumley 5 lbs ... son Gilbreth ...negro wench Sine ... ½ household furniture... plantation divided bet. 3 sons Samuel, Robert and Gilbrith.. residue personal est ... to sundry legatees as above ment. The sundry sums willed ... 3 sons, Samuel, Robert and Gilbrett, Exrs.

June 21, 1797

                                        William Neill(Seal)

John Carron

Catherine Arthurs

True copy taken...orig. in my office, April 28, 1800.

Attest, J. E.

MISCELLANEOUS ESTATES 1790-1810

Adm. Bond 1799 of Ceanna (her mark) Amburn, Christoph Amburn, dec'd, with Jacob Forney and (not legible).

Adm. Bond of Geo. Eslinger and Michael Haffner, undated, with Martin Cline and Jno. Coopeny. (Dec'd not named.)

Adm. Bond of Jno. Montgomery with Wm. Fariss and Jonathan Kemp. No date and dec'd not named.)

Adm. Bond of Catherine Yo ung (signed Katherine), with William Patton, undated, dec'd not named.

Adm. Bond of Adam Derryberry and Jno. Hips, undated and dec'd not named.

Geo. Cathey and William Davidson's Bond for Margaret Davidson, wid., undated and dec'd not named.

Adm. Bond of Jean Saveryuneror, John Sigmon and (name not legible), undated and dec'd not named.

Adm. Bond of Thomas Fisher (sig.) with John Fisher, undated, dec'd. not named.

Hoard, Am., 1801. Sale of Estate by Peggy Hoard and Wm. Sherrill.

(Unarranged at End of letter "Z" in Estates Papers.)

(Marriages occurred prior to dates mentioned.)

Austin, Benjamin and Mary (Wid. of Isaac Bradburn, d 1781.)
Ballew, John and Mary, 1785
Beltis, John and Nancy, 1784.
Campbell, Robert and Margaret, 1780.
Cline, John and Barbary, 1779.
Cooper, John and Jean, 1780.
Forgy, Samuel and Margaret, 1784.
Hamilton, William and Elizabeth, 1794, (Jan. 5) at which time she released
    her claims to land of former husband, Sam.Hughey, Esq., dec'd.
Harbison, William and Nancy, 1786.
Harshaw, Abraham amd Anne, 1784.
Houston, Archibald and Rosa, 1788.
Hughes, John and Ann, 1786.
Hughes, John and Keziah, 1786.
Little, Abraham and Mary, 1778.
Long, John to Ann Beaty, 17 Dec. 1783 (Linclon Co., M. B. and Burke Co. Ests.
    of father John.)
Lowman, Lewis and Margaret, 1788.
Moorland, William and Sarah, 1784.
Murray,William, dec'd., wid., Elizabeth, 1784.
McDowell, Charles M.Mary Bowman, wid. of John Bowman (dec'd. June 1780),
    Mary, dau. of William Tate, dec'd. 1780.
McKee, William and Mary, 1788.
Neill, William and Sarah, 1797.
Nelson, David and Mary, 1788.
Nicholson, James and Sarah, 1783.
Parks, Benjamin and Agnes, 1778.
Rees, Abraham and Nancy, 1786.
Robeson, David m. Jean McKinney, 1777, dau of James,
Shelton, Palentine had a wife (?), 1779.
Smith, John and Catherine, 1788.
Spencer, John and Mary, 1778.
Stewart, James and Sarah, 1787.
Stevens, Philip and Mary, 1790.
Thompson, David and Elizabeth, 1786.
Ussery, Will and Juda (Judith), 1778.
Whitacar, James and Mary, 1785.
White, William and Sophia - before 1773.
White, Reueben (dec'd. in S. C. by 1777) wife a dau. of Erasmus Allen.
Winters, George and Catherine, 1783.
Witt, David and Sarah, 1779.
Young, Joshua and Rachel, 1780.

(From Miscellaneous Court Papers, Civil and Criminal Cases, 1778-1790.)

Marriage Bonds of Tryon and Lincoln Counties, North Carolina. Curtis Bynum, 1929, pp. 82, 34, 119, 112, 99, respectively:

Connelly, William, of Burke Co., to Rebacca Sherrill 7 Nov 1793; Lincoln Co, Surety: Jacob Sherrill of Burke Co.

Spencer, Joshua of Burke Co. to Sally Robinson, wid., 24 Jan 1819: Sureties: Doctor Spencer and Ganaway Spencer; Wit. Mic Cline.

Settlemire, Jacob of Burke Co. to Hannah Phillips, 3 Jan 1821: surety: Isaac Ash; wit: Mic Cline.

Powell, Phillip of Burke Co. to Elizabeth Hermon, 26 Apr. 1821; Surety: Michael Hermon; wit: Mic Cline.

From Pensions:

Grider, Jacob, m. 13 Apr 1789, Elizabeth Repatoe, Burke Co.(W-3980)

Grider, John, Sr., m. 1781, Isabel Blair, Burke Co. (W-358)

Grider, Valentine, m. Feb 1816, Nancy Fugate, Burke Co. (W-11082)

From Marriage Bonds (book) Burke County, 1810-1839, with original copies available.

Baker, Peter - Sarah Presnell, 1811; Nathan Presnal.
Beard, Findley- Cynthia Freeman, 1839.
Dorset, Solomon - Elizabeth Bradburn, May 1, 1819.
           - Elizabeth Crasmon, Dec 25, 1824.
Gipson, Edward - Kitty Weaver, 1810.
Gipson, Henry - Betsy Hollar, 1823.
Gipson, James - Rebecca Hogan, 1828.
Gipson, Robert - .... Smith, 1812.
Gipson, Samuel - Jane Black, 1818.
Gipson, Wm. - Lotty Tull, 1819.
Payne, Henry - Margaret Oxford, 1812.
Payne, Robert - Mary Baker, 1809.
Pool, Jesse, Jr. - Elizabeth Austin, 1827.
Pool, Wm. - Mary Austin, 1829.
Smith, Abraham - Elizabeth Bradford, 1812.
Swann, Aquila - Mary Chapman, 1839.
Teague, Edward - Drucilla Bently, 1821.
Turnmire, Adam - .... , 1815.

White, Jacob - Polly Dockery, 1827.
White, John - Saray P. Dumas, 1818.
White, Joshua - Mary Bowman, 1824.

(Other references to marriages will be found in Wills, Estates, Orphans ...
1792-1810...from Court Minutes in this Volume.)

WHERE TO LEARN MORE ABOUT SOME OF THE PIONEERS

In the Morganton Herald, beginning January 11, 1894, or in book
form, "Sketches of the Pioneers In Burke County History," by Col.
Thos. Geo. Walton, the following names and pages will be helpful
in book form:

page 3, The Walton Family
"   8, John Bowman, Wm. Tate, John McDowell
" 9-10,Waightstill Avery and Avery Family
"   13,Hon. Samuel P. Carson, Hon. Felix Walker, Gen. Israel Pick-
        ens.
"   14, Hemphills
"   16, John Duckworth
"   18, Ransom Herne
"   19, Robert Caldwell
"   21, The Perkins
"   23, Parson Robert Johnston Miller
"   24, David Corpening and wife Mary Perkins (of Jos.)
"   25, The Ballews and John Rutherford
"   29, Dr. Thomas Bouchelle
"   30, Daniel Forney
"   34, James Patton, Sr.
"   36, Hon. Pinckney Henderson
"   38, Christopher Bechtler
" 40-2, Old Sheriffs (Wm. Morrison, Peter Mull, Frank Morrison,
        Thomas McEntire from Ireland, Hugh Tate, Hodge Rabourne,
        Mark Brittain, Samuel McD. Tate, Wm. C. Butler, Col. Sam-
        uel Tate, John Boone, John H. Pearson (of Isaac) (dates
        1790-1836)
"   50, Old Time Preachers
"   53, Col. David Crockett
"   56, Dr. Joseph Dobson
"   67, The Bradshaws of Lovelady Ford (Wm. and Elijah, bros.)
"   65, The Corpenings; The Estes Family
"   64, The Connellys
"   63, Col. John Carson
"   59, Mark Brittain
"   59, Hon. James Graham
"   58, Conrad Hildebrand

(File No. GR 975.685 W 2415 at N. C. State Library, Raleigh, NC.)

156

Two valuable volumes are in this 1984 order form from Southern Historical Press, P. O. Box 738, Easley, S. C., Publisher: The Rev. Silas Emmett Lucas, Jr., one of my most valued clients for many of the pleasant years I spent at the Dept. of Archives and History in Raleigh as a professional genealogist. He has given me permission to include the following in this book:

SOUTHERN HISTORICAL PRESS
P.O. Box 738 • Easley, SC 29641-0738

White, Emmett R.
REVOLUTIONARY WAR SOLDIERS OF WESTERN NORTH CAROLINA: BURKE COUNTY, VOL. I. Pub. 1984. 330 pp., index. ISBN 0-89308-536-7

Price: NC 18 $38.50

The contributions of the Revolutionary War Soldiers of Western North Carolina during the conflict of 1775-1782 were immense. The rolling hills of the Carolina Piedmont were as much a battleground as those of Pennsylvania and New Jersey. Kings Mountain, Ramsour's Mill, Cowpens, the Indian Wars and many other conflicts all helped to change the course of American history. Unfortunately, from a historical standpoint, very little written data is available concerning the contributions of the Western North Carolina Militiamen. Many of the western counties, though their soldiers contributed greatly to the war effort, are historically "silent." This work is an effort to unravel and to present in a systematic way something about their lives and exploits.

The initial two volumes will be devoted to Burke County. Each soldier will be written up as to his Early Life (as much as could be made available), his Military Experiences, his Later Life, including marriages, children, occupations, etc. Also included will be his Land Transactions and Census Locations. Where available, burial sites will be given as well as pension awards.

Following completion of the Burke County editions, similar works will begin on the remaining western North Carolina counties. Early research is now in progress for Wilkes, Surry, Rowan, Mecklenburg, Lincoln, and Rutherford counties.

Some of the family names appearing in Volume I, Burke County, include the following: Samuel Alexander, Birch Allison, Philip Anthony, David Asher, Waightstill Avery, Alexander Bailey, Charles Baker, David Baker, John Baldwin, Joseph Ballew, Richard Ballew, Robert Ballew, William Beekman, Samuel Blair, Casper Bolick, John Bowman, Marshall Bowman, Sherwood Bowman, Josiah Brandon, Robert Brank, Jr., William Brittain, Philip Burns, John Carson, George Cathey, Ellis Chaffen, John Chapman, Mordecai Clarke, Micheal Cline, George Clontz, Benjamin Coffey, James Cowden, Richard Crabtree, Thoms Craig, William Robert Crawley, Conrad Crump, Jonathan Curtis, William Cuthbertson, Martin Davenport, John Davidson, William Davidson, Andrew Derreberry, Chesley Dobbs, John Dobson, Joseph Dobson, Jr., Joseph Dobson, Sr., M.D., Esau Dotson, George Dowell, John Duckworth, John Dysart, Isaac Earthman, Joseph England. Alexander Erwin, Sarah Robinson Erwin, Philip Evans, John Fincannon, Reuben Fletcher, John Forbis, John Fox, Sr., Titus Fox, John Franklin, William Freeman, Nicholas Frye, George Gabbert, Jacob Gabbert, John Gibbs, Solomon Good, William Gragg, Isaac Grant, Grave Greenlee, James Greenlee, Jacob Grider, John Grider, Martin Grider, Adam Grindstaff, Jacob Grindstaff, Micheal Grindstaff, William Gudger, William Hamby, Joseph Hancock, John Hardin, Edward Harris, David Hays, Thomas Hemphill, Leonard Hice, George Hodge, Adam Hoppis, Micheal Houck, Nicholas Houck, Abram Hunsucker, Churchwell Jackson, William James, Joseph Jones, James Kell, Robert Kell, Thomas Kennedy, James Kincaid,

John Kincaid, Sr., Robert Kincaid, Jacob Lawler, John Littlejohn, Samuel Lusk, Thomas Lytle, Charles McDowell, Joseph McDowell (QM), Margaret O'Neal McDowell, Ephraim McLean, David McPeters, Samuel Mackie, Richard Matlock, Daniel Moore, Jesse Moore, William Morrison, Andrew Nill, Patrick O'Neill, Walter O'Neill, Robert Patton, Samuel Patton, John Penly, George Poplin, James Potts, Lewis Powell, John Presnell, Joseph Pyatt, Adam Rainboult, Samuel Reed, John Rockett, Peter Rust, Adam Setzer, John Shell, Lewis Sherrill, Andrew Shook, Jacob Shook, George Silver, Daniel Smith (1), Daniel Smith (2), Capt., John Smith, Samuel Smith, Thomas Smith, William Smith, Benjamin Spencer, Aaron Stacey, Joseph Starnes, Thomas Sumter, John Swink, William Tabor, Leroy Taylor, Isaac Thompson, Conrad Tipps, Jacob Tipps, Samuel Turner, Lawrence Unger, David Vance, Henry Wakefield, Elijah Walker, George Walker, James Reuben Walker, Jesse Walker, Tilman Walton, William Walton, Jr., William Walton, Sr., Joseph White, Reuben White, James Wilson, James Wilson, II, John Wilfong, William Wofford, Belfield Wood.

Walton, Col. Thomas George
SKETCHES OF THE PIONEERS IN BURKE COUNTY HISTORY (N.C.). Orig. pub. 1894 and 1924. Repr. 1984. 96 pp., index, soft cover. ISBN 0-89308-538-3

Price: NC 17 $15.00

The articles comprising the first part of this book, pages 5 through 67, were written in 1894 and were published in the old Morganton Herald. They were reprinted in the Herald in 1924, beginning April 10, and were found in the papers of Elisa M. Pearson. Those articles found on pages 68 through 89 were copies from manuscripts of Col. Walton; these are now in the possession of his granddaughter, Mrs. Harry Boggs.

This book contains sketches of the following pioneers in Burke County history: Avery, Ballew, Bechtter, Bouchelle, Bowman, Bradshaw, Brittain, Caldwell, Carson, Collins, Connelly, Corpening, Dobson, Duckworth, Erwin, Estes, Forney, Graham, Greenlee, Hemphill, Henerson, Herne, Hildebrand (2), Lenoir, McDowell, McEntire, Miller, Morrison, Murphy, Newland, Patton, Perkin, Person, Picken, Rutherford, Stevelies, Tates, Walker, Walton.

OCCUPATIONS 1794-1809

Spinning wheel maker: John Penland 1794.

Bricklayer: Wm. Bradly 1795.

Weaver: James House 1799; Isaac Cox 1808.

Wagon-maker: Wm. Ryel 1809.

Shoemaker: Michael Brock 1801; Jonathin Hargis 1805; Joseph Dobson
    1804.

Tanner: David Tate 1805.

House Carpenter and Joiner: Paul Anthony 1803; John McGalliard 1805.

Blacksmith: Wm. Connelly 1807; John Litten 1806; Henry Baker 1804;
    John Grider 1802; Jonathan Summers 1803; Wm. Tacker 1801;
    Thomas McTagret 1802.

Wheelright and Chairmaker: Wm. Penland 1806.

Hatter: John McGuire 1806.

Tanner and currying of leather: Caleb Poor 1807.

Tailoring: John Erwin 1807.

Wheelright: Conrad Waggoner 1794.

Forge bloomer: James Gorman 1801.

Husbandry and farming: Samuel Brown 1797; John Townson 1801; Poovy
    Allison 1803; James Reed 1804; Wm. Tate 1807; Samuel Brown 1797.

Nailler: Robert Johnson 1808.

Court Minutes: Wills, Estates, Administrations, Orphans, 1792-1810;
pages 28-49.

SOME MISCELLANEOUS RECORDS

John Brazzal of Burke County found hanged in 1793. Jury found that he was not of right mind and hanged himself. (Leg. Papers 120).

Nancy Bruck (Brook?) of Burke County married William Bruck in 1799. He left her after four to five months and petitioned for a divorce in 1805. (Leg. Papers 213).

Michael Shufner, Jr. and wife Sarah (Smith) suit in Orange County by Tobias Smith who married her on Dec. 25, 1803. Isaac Teague, Burke County, mentuoned in 1812. (Leg. Papers 263)

Rev. Wm. P. Swanson married Emily Poole, daughter of Wm. Poole and was pastor of Ancient Baptist Church of Burke County in the section that became Alexander County in 1847. (See Pension of John Presnell, Sr., Jan. 10, 1834.)

Among later Burke County citizens named as Delegates of The Mecklenburg Declaration of May 20, 1775, with Resolutions in detail were John McKnitt Alexander (Clerk), Hezekiah Alexander, Waightstill Avery, and Col. Thomas Polk. (Colonial Records pp. 1263-1264)

The original Declaration of the above burned in 1800, along with a number of other papers of John McKnitt Alexander, the Convention Secretary. (The State, Mecklenburg County, Vol. 30, No. 24, p. 32, April 27, 1963.) On Dec. 7, 1956, headed as Charlotte, N. C., an announcement by Victor C. King, Compiler and Editor of his forthcoming Biographical Sketches of the 27 Signers was advertised by his printer.

Omitted in Vol. III, Miscellaneous Papers of Civil and Criminal Cases 1755-1790: File 1778:#1: Abr. Hosshew vs. Evan Hughes, July. (2) vs. Edward Mattock. File 1779: #2: Patrick Oneel vs. John Morrison, Oct; with John Cooper's Dec. 12 statement. Wm. Murry vs. Abraham Smally and James Martin, April. Tim. Ward vs. Joseph Dobson, Sr., April. File 1787: #1: John Hightower vs. Jos. McPeters, yeoman, April.

George Calvert Yount (May 4, 1794 Burke Co., N. C. - Oct. 5, 1865 Calif.) and parents, Jacob and Marillis (Killian) Yount, migrated to the Mississippi River section. At age 24 George moved to Mo., was a wealthy trapper when he removed to Napa Valley, Calif. to his ranch, Caymus Rancho. By 1850 he was one of the first wine-makers of that State, employing 100 friendly Indians. He was a member of the Masonic Order and has a very impressive monument at Yountville, a family-named town. (Sketch of the Life of George C. Yount, by Elizabeth Ann Watson; George Yount, The Kindly Host of Caymus Rancho, by Ellen Lamont Woods; Article in National Geographic Magazine (date unknown).

Baker, David, 7,8,9,16,21,
  22,26,124,126,130,132,
  136,138,145,157
  George, 1
  Henary, 110,114,115,119
  Henery, 115
  Hennery, 135
  Henry, 2,8,38,41,42,111,
  122,124,158,
  Henry Barlow, 9
  James, 16,22,120
  John, 111,113
  Jos., 135
  Mary, 154
  Peter, 154
  Thomas, 36,37,57,130,132
  William, 130
  John, 16,22,23
Balay, Alex., 135
Baldwin, Elisha, 52
  Jacob, 111, 122
  John, 53,157
  William, 1,21
  Wm., 1,135
Balew, Robert, Sr., 135
  Robt., 135
Baley, Benjamin, 125
  Charles, 122
  John, 125
  William, 123,125
Ballard, Benjamin, 127
  John, 113
Ballen, Stephen, 145
Ballew, ..., 116
  David, 39,44,45
  Family, 156,157
  George, 113
  Hiram, 128
  John, 153
  Joseph, 157
  Josh., 26
  Joshua, 121, 128
  Mary, 153
  Nancy, 44,45
  Richard, 157
  Robert, 157
  Stephen, 8,113,116,120
  127,145,146
  Vice, 45
  Vicy, 44,45
  William, 113,120
  Wilson, 45
  Wm., 127,128
Ballow, George, 121
Baning, Alexander, 131
Banks, David, 130,132
Barber, John, 14
  John, 14,53
Barnes, ...air, 114
  Edward, 17
  Jahu, 114
  John, 123
  Neanvaire, 110
Barnett, David, 18
Barnhart, Jno., 134
  John, 3,26,113,116
Barns, Brinsley, 22
  Jahu, 115
  James, 2,19,110,119,123
  James, Sr., 129
  John, 22,114
  Nenavi, 115
  William, 120
  William, Jr., 119
  James (Jr-Sr?), 128
Barr, Caleb, 8,38,114,117
  David, 53
  Samuel, 9
Barrier, John, 129
Barring, Henry, 131
Barringer, Daivd, 111
Bass, Johannes, 54
Bast (Bost), Johannes, 54

Bates, John, 50
Battle, John, 52
  Sarah, 52
Baxter, James, 111
Bayers, John, 118
Beach, Justice, 128
Beadle, David, 10
Beael, David, 127
Beal, Daniel, 15
Beale, Daniel, 14
Beall, Daniel, 11
  Fredk., 11
Bear, David, 118
Beard, Andrew, 4,7,8,120,
  136,142,144
  Andrew, Capt., 116
  Findley, 154
  John, 24
  Lewis, 8,9
Beare, John, 135
Beatty, William, 6,51
Beaty, Ann, 153
  John, 153
Beaushell, Thos., 138
Bechtler, Christopher, 156
Bechtter, Family, 157
Beck...., 123
  ...., Jr., 123
  Daniel, 9
  J.P., 148
  Jacob, 7,9,52,53,119
  Jacob, Sr., 123
  John, 120, 129
  Joseph, 129
  N.P., 149
  Nickolas, 129
  Posey, 149
Beckinstaff, Thos.?, 36
Becknal, William, 127
Becky, Elizabeth, 48
  Jacob, 48
  John, 48
Bedford, Jones, 26
Beek, David, 15
  Jacob, 15
Beekman, C.W., Surv. 30,32
  William, 157
Been, Peter, 128
Belew, Robert, 8
Bell, J., 4
  James, 117
  Thomas, 12, 117
  Thos., Const., 11
Bellew, Eliz., 26
  Geo., 25
  Hugh, 26
  James, 26
  Joseph, 25
  Joshua, 25
  Robert, 23,26
  Robt., 24,26
  Stephen, 26
Bellewe, J...., 8
Beltis, John, 153
  Mary, 153
Beneson, George, 53
Benfield, Joseph, 149
Bennett, ...es, 57
Bently, Drucilla, 154
Bergin, Benjamin, 13
Berrey, John, 8
  Lot, 8
  William, 8
Berry, Bartlett A., 149
  Bartlett A., Sr., 149
  Enoch, 22
  J.W., 149
  James, 114,116,121
  Jas., 26
  John, 114,116,121,146
Bery, Jesse, 128
Bevans, Nathaniel, 131
Bever, Benjamin, 127

Bever, David, 127
Bibb, Henry, 51,53
Billew, ..., 114
  Robert, 12
Binkley, Michel, 117
Bird, Bangmin, 120
  Benj., 27
  Benjamin, 5,25,136
  Harbert, 131
  John, 137
  Jonathan, 131
  Rd., Rev., 143
  Richard, 131
  Thomas, 8,25,120
  Thos., 27
Birks, David, 126
  Richard, 126
  Roland, 126
Biscoe, Anna D., 149
Bitticks, John, 127
Black, ..., 1
  Daniel, 131
  Geo., 52
  George, 53
  James, 37, 131
  Jane, 154
  Matthew, 131
  Thomas, 1
  William, 37
Blackwell, Fanny, 48
  Hamilton, 48
  James, 48
  John, 48
  John, H., 48
  Josiah V. 149
  Nancy, 48
Blair, Colbert, 42
  Isabel, 154
  James, 9,53,137
  Jno., 134
  John, 9,13,109,138
  Samuel, 157
Blairs, John, 135
Blalock, John, 126, 131
  Richard, 126
Blankenship, Lodwick, 7
Blanton, George, 50
  Jno., 50
  John, 6,13,17,19,50,52,
Blare, Colbert, 125
  Colbert, Senr., 125
  James, 125
  John, 125
Blasingham, James, 53
Blew, Jesse, 115
Bo..., Joseph, 113
Boaman, Jacob, 130,132
Bohanes, ..., 55
Boid, John, 115
Boldwin, Jacob, 132
Boles, Aaron, 116
  John, 116
Bolick, Casper, 157
Bolinger, Jacob, 1
Bolingir, Henry, 1
Bollinger, Henry, 3
Boon, Jesse, 134
  Jonathan, 46,122,136
Boone, Jesse, 124
  John, 156
  Jonath., 124
  Jonathan, 117
Booth, ..., 123
Boothe, Zachariah, 129
Borthell, Christian, 135
Bortlas, Christian, 150
Boss, James, 136
Bost, Conrad, 139
  Johannes, 54
  William, 30,54
  Wm., 54
Botts, Matthew, 47
  Seth, 47

Vanderpool, Elizabeth, 125
Vick, Averillah, 124
Y........, Moses, 113

More families of:
Miller, Morrison, Murphy
  157

Bennett, ...es, 36
McGinty, Alexander, 15,137
Murphy, William, 127,137
Pain, George, 21,110,134
Sudderth, John, 148
Sumpter, Hennery, 135

  Brown, etc., continued,
  Brown, ..., 126,132
  Abby, 48
  Absolam, 110,114,115
  Ailey, 40
  Am...., 120
  Charles, 113,116,121
  Daniel, 21,26,48,119
  134,139
  David, 126
  Elisha, 48
  George, 48,50,137
  James, 124
  Jno., 7
  John, 7,8,9,12,40,41,43,
  46,47,48,54,111,112,116,
  136
  John, Colwell, 111
  John, Sr., 118,121,122
  Joseph, 4,18
  Joshua, 122
  Moses, 127
  R.O., J.P., 53
  Richard, 7,8,25,110,114,
  115
  Richard, C.C., 135
  Richd., 135
  Sallie, 149
  Saml., 26
  Samuel, 13,48,118,126,
  158
  Sarah, 54
  Thomas, 18,43,46,112
  William, 110,114,125
  Wm., 53
Browning, Charles, 126
  David, 126
  Elijah, 45,111
  John, 14,124,126
  John, Jr., 9
  John, Sr., 9,10,113
  Martin, 113,124,126
  Nicholas, 126
  Rachel, 45
  Thos., 45
  William, 127
Bruck, Nancy, 159
  William, 159
Bruks, George, 116
Bryan, Lewis, 51
  Nathan, 51
Bryley, W., 51
Buchanan, Arthur, 9
  James, 138
  Joseph, 124
Buchanen, John, 139
Buckanan, Arthur, 130,132
  Joseph, 130

www.ingramcontent.com/pod-product-compliance
Lightning Source LLC
Chambersburg PA
CBHW021906020426
42334CB00013B/507